SWEET SEASONS

Also by Dom Forker

The Men of Autumn
The Ultimate Baseball Quiz Book
Almost Everything You Ever Wanted to Know About Baseball
The Ultimate Yankee Baseball Quiz Book
Baseball Brainteasers

SWEET SEASONS

Recollections
of the 1955-64
New York Yankees

by
Dom Forker

Taylor Publishing Company
Dallas, Texas

Copyright © 1990 by Dom Forker

All rights reserved.

Published by Taylor Publishing Company
        1550 West Mockingbird Lane
        Dallas, Texas 75235

Photographs courtesy of the New York Yankees.

Designed by Deborah J. Jackson-Jones

Library of Congress Cataloging-in-Publication Data

Forker, Dom.
    Sweet seasons: recollections of the 1955-64 New York Yankees/by
Dom Forker.
        p. cm.
    ISBN 0-87833-705-9: $18.95
    1. New York Yankees (Baseball team) — History. I. Title.
GV875.N4F68 1990
796.357'64'097471 — dc20   89-77765
                                                            CIP

Printed in the United States of America

10 9 8 7 6 5 4 3 2 1

To the Bayonne Celtics,
with whom I shared many a cheer and a beer
during these sweet seasons

CONTENTS

Sixteen pages of photographs follow page 116

ACKNOWLEDGMENTS

It took me three years and four summers to write *The Men of Autumn*. It took me just eight weeks to write *Sweet Seasons* — but they were the toughest eight weeks of my life.

There were many who helped to keep me from failing: Jeff Idleson, the assistant director of media relations at Yankee Stadium, who gave me access to former Yankee players' addresses and phone numbers as well as Yankee photo files; Jim Dunnigan, Jeff's assistant, who followed up courteously; the New York Yankees in general; Phil Linz, who introduced me to several former players; Jim Donovan, my editor, whose vision of this work sustained my own; my wife, Nancy, and my sons Tim, Geoff, and Ted, whose patience and cooperation enabled me to dispatch potentially disruptive phone interviews; and the personalities in this book, who have allowed me to offer you their stories.

To all of you, many thanks!

INTRODUCTION

The Yankees have had eighteen managers in the last eighteen years, during which they have won four pennants and two World Series. The Yankees of 1955-64 had three managers in ten years, during which they won nine pennants and four world championships. The latter time span is featured in *Sweet Seasons,* a sequel to *The Men of Autumn,* which focused on the 1949-53 world championship clubs. During those two eras the Yankees won fourteen pennants and nine world championships in sixteen years.

Casey Stengel is a central character in both books. *The Men of Autumn* showed how he took over the dynasty of Joe McCarthy, who had guided the Yankees to eight pennants and seven world titles in sixteen years, and improved upon "Marse Joe's" record. Casey won ten pennants and seven World Series in twelve years. The basic difference in their styles was that McCarthy used a set lineup while Stengel used the two-platoon system.

In *Sweet Seasons,* the managers change, but the contrasts remain. Stengel continued the two-platoon from 1955-60, but Ralph Houk reverted to the set lineup in 1961-63. Yogi Berra maintained that system in 1964.

Casey had little confidence in younger players, and strongly preferred veterans. He was also chary of praising players in public, preferring criticism to compliments. He believed that players like Hank Bauer, Gene Woodling, Gil McDougald, and Andy Carey played better when they were angry — and he was right. But players like Bobby Richardson and Clete Boyer needed a pat on the back to build up their confidence; and Casey didn't reach them. The Old Man was an expert, though, at delegating authority. He built a great coaching staff — Bill Dickey, Frank Crosetti, and Jim Turner — and he gave them authority. But Casey did not communicate well.

Ralph Houk, on the other hand, communicated with all of his players. Many told me that they always knew where they stood with him, and they played harder because of it. Ralph reverted to a set lineup, but before he did, he made a host of changes in Casey's lineup. He built up Richardson's confidence at second base, inserted Boyer at third base, made Elston

Howard his full-time catcher, went to a four-man rotation, and hired four great coaches: Crosetti, Johnny Sain, Wally Moses, and Jim Hegan.

Yogi Berra didn't get the time he needed to distinguish his managerial style. But there is an interesting parallel between Yogi and Casey. Two different empires — Casey's, and Ralph's and Yogi's combined — crashed because of decisions involving Whitey Ford.

Casey elected not to start Whitey in Game One of the 1960 World Series. Whitey, who was held back until Game Three, pitched two shutouts, the Yankees lost the World Series in seven games, and Casey was fired.

Yogi was afraid that history might repeat itself. In the 1964 World Series he started Whitey in Game One. But the suspicion here and elsewhere is that Ford had a sore arm before the Series, and aggravated it during that opening game. If Yogi had started Jim Bouton, the Yankees might have won the 1964 World Series, and Yogi might have guided the Yankees' fortunes for many years. As it was, Johnny Keane replaced Yogi as manager, and the Yankees plummeted to seventy-seven wins and fifth place.

Most of the players I interviewed for *Sweet Seasons* told me that Casey, Ralph, and Yogi were very good managers. Their styles differed, but in the long run, is the man the style or the style the man?

At the last Old Timers' Day, I met many of these former Yankee greats before the traditional three-inning game. And I walked the hallowed halls of the Stadium, where I talked with my boyhood hero, Joe DiMaggio. The days of Yankee glory seemed only yesterday. Then I watched the regular game from the press box, and the spectacle was not the same.

Al Downing has told me that the farm system was in trouble as far back as 1961, when he was rushed to the major leagues too soon. The Yankees needed a left-handed pitcher, and there were no others in the system. The next big left-handed winner, in addition to Downing, was Fritz Peterson, who won twenty games in 1970. Many of the players told me that the Yankees made a mistake in getting rid of Johnny Sain as their pitching coach, and Wally Moses as their hitting coach, after the 1963 season. They also thought that making Ford the pitching coach and Berra the manager in 1964 were titular moves. Ford was still in the ranks; Berra was coming up through the ranks.

But basically the team got old together, and it wasn't recharged by young blood as it had been in the past. Co-owners Dan Topping and Del Webb probably knew that they were going to sell the club, so they stopped putting money into the club's future. Then CBS bought them out and ruined the farm system completely. CBS wasn't concerned about things like farm systems, which couldn't be seen. CBS' neglect of the farm system eroded the Yankees' legacy.

During their dynasty years, the Yankees encouraged evolution from position to position. That changed after 1964. How much? Well, first base went from Joe Collins to Bill Skowron to Joe Pepitone to Mickey Mantle, when he was hanging on. At second base Horace Clarke succeeded Bobby Richardson, who followed Gerry Coleman. At shortstop Phil Rizzuto, Gil McDougald, and Tony Kubek gave way to Ruben Amaro. And at third base Charley Smith came after Boyer, who took over for Gil McDougald. Behind the plate Jake Gibbs was the successor to Ellie Howard and Yogi Berra. In right field Steve Whitaker replaced Roger Maris, who had replaced Hank Bauer. In center field Bill Robinson ultimately stepped into a position that had been manned by Mickey Mantle and Joe DiMaggio. Left field was a notable exception. For years the Yankees looked for someone to take Gene Woodling's place. They finally found him and Roy White gave the Yankees many fine years.

Houk took the reins again in 1966. Some of the players in this book were desperately hoping for a miracle at that time. But, according to Steve Hamilton, the magic was gone. It stayed away for eleven years, returned briefly from 1976-78, and now has been gone for eleven more years. Since 1978, the Yankees' only pennant win was during the strike-abbreviated season of 1981.

"Peaks and valleys," said Bob Sheppard, the public-address announcer at Yankee Stadium since 1951. "When I first came here, I thought it was the Yankees' divine right to win. They won pennants in twelve of my first fourteen years in the Bronx. But if you do anything long enough, I guess, things will balance out."

As I paradoxically end this book by writing the introduction, I am thinking about the decline of the Yankees. I have just read a quote by Don Mattingly in the Newark *Star-Ledger*. "We have hit rock bottom," he said. The bottom that he referred to was a 19-5 rout by the Oakland A's on August 30, 1989. The A's nineteen runs matched the all-time high against the Yankees at Yankee Stadium, a feat accomplished twice previously, by the Blue Jays in 1977 and the Tigers in 1925. The fourteen-run margin was the most lopsided loss in a season of lopsided losses. The Yankees' .433 winning percentage had the Bombers on a pace for their worst record since 1913. Bucky Dent's record since replacing Dallas Green had slid to 2-11 while the Yankees' losing streak had stretched to six games. And during that losing streak the Yankees were outscored 52-20.

Where are the Berras and Richardsons, the Skowrons and Howards, and the Mantles and Marises and Fords? Hopefully they're in the Yankees' future. But to recapture the Yankees' bloom, right now, we'll have to turn to the past — to a decade of *Sweet Seasons*.

Bobby Richardson

One March afternoon in 1989 I was in Lynchburg, Virginia, to see the opening of my son Geoff's baseball season with Lynchburg College. Bobby Richardson is the head baseball coach at Liberty University in Lynchburg, so I visited the Liberty baseball field to make contact with him. He and his son-in-law, John, were sitting in the box seats behind the dugout when I arrived. As it turned out, he had an afternoon game with Clarkson College (helmed by Mike Caldwell, the former Milwaukee Brewer pitcher) of Georgia.

"You know, your boy had some pretty good games against me last year," he said. "In two games he hit four home runs against us, all over the center-field fence, but in retrospect, it seems like he hit a home run every time he came to the plate."

Then he looked affectionately toward his son-in-law and told me of some of John's prodigious home runs when he played for Bobby at Coastal Carolina.

After Richardson retired from the Yankees in 1966, he was named to President Nixon's Council on Physical Fitness. He was also named the head baseball coach at the University of South Carolina. One year he and his team went to the Final Four and were beaten in the final two games by the University of Texas. In 1976, he unsuccessfully ran for Congress. Then he worked as a public-relations representative for Columbia Bible College until, in 1984, he became both the head baseball coach and the athletic director at Coastal Carolina College. In 1986 his team won the Big South Conference title.

For the past three years he has been the head baseball coach at Liberty University, where Al Worthington, the former major-league pitcher, is the athletic director and Jerry Falwell is the president.

1

He and his wife of thirty-three years, Betsy, live in Lynchburg and have five children, three sons and two daughters.

Would I be interested in managing a major-league team or running for public office again? My answer is no to both. I wouldn't be interested in managing a major-league team for the same reason I gave up playing at the age of thirty-one. The traveling. It takes you away from home too much and separates you from your family.

When I ran for political office the first time, it was an unusual thing. In 1969 Richard Nixon became the president. I was a good friend of his, and I was on the President's Council for Physical Fitness. In 1974 Mr. Nixon called me and asked me to run for Congress in South Carolina. I said no because the University of Miami had beaten us by only one game that year, and they went on to the College World Series. I had two All-Americans on my team; both of them were only juniors. Well, they came to me and said, "Coach, we feel that *we* can go to the World Series next year." And we did. We finished the season 51-6 but lost to Texas in the final two games. The next year, Gerald Ford was in the White House. He called me and asked me to run for Congress. We were on the phone for about an hour. It's pretty hard to say no when your leader is telling you that you should run for your President, your party, and your people. So I ran in 1976 on the Republican ticket, and lost by less than three thousand votes. I had worked out a leave of absence for the University of South Carolina coaching job, but I wanted to show everyone that I was serious about running, so I resigned. After that I was out of coaching for six years. During that time I served as a public-relations representative for Columbia Bible College. Then when the athletic director's and baseball coach's positions became available at Coastal Carolina in Myrtle Beach, I applied for the jobs and got them. I arrived there in 1984, and in 1986 we won the Big South Conference.

I didn't come to Liberty University to replace Al Worthington. Worthington had resigned from the baseball coach's job to accept the athletic director's position. But they had Al Dark lined up to take his place as the baseball coach. At the last moment, though, Dark took a job as the farm director for the Chicago White Sox. That's when I came into the picture. Jerry Falwell and I had dinner at a restaurant three years ago. During the evening, he said, "Worthington's retired as the baseball coach to work full-time as my athletic director. I want you to be my coach. The job's yours."

Jerry and I have been friends for twenty-five years. He had been after me for ten to twelve years to come to Liberty University. This time I said yes. We never even talked salary. I think I just started getting paid. I was excited about the possibilities of working at a small Christian college that is Division I, has good facilities, and plays a sixty-game schedule.

Baseball is still fun to me. But the fun now is not in watching major-league games or in playing on Old Timers' Days. My fun now is pitching to future major leaguers while they're getting their education. I love seeing them mold together as a team and as men.

You try to be a positive influence in their lives. Two men influenced me early in my life. One was my dad. He wanted me to play baseball, he constantly encouraged me to play the game, and he afforded me all the opportunities. The other was Conley Alexander. He was my junior high school coach, and he had a tremendous influence on me, not only in high school but when I got into pro ball, too.

In my first year in professional ball, I got off to a bad start. My dad came down and visited me. He and members of the organization encouraged me to report to Orlean, New York, where I would play against other seventeen-year-olds. I did, and I had an exceptional year there. Casey Stengel invited me to the Rookie Camp the next year. I had been a Phillies "Whiz Kids" fan when I was young. But when I was surrounded by Mickey and Whitey and Yogi and Hank and Gil and Gene, I knew that the Yankees were something special. At the age of nineteen, when I joined the parent club, I knew that my relationship with the Yankees was going to be *very* special. But there was nothing special about my first two seasons with the Yankees. In 1955 I got only twenty-six at bats and in 1956 I got even less — seven. I wasn't with the Yankees during those World Series. In fact, during the 1955 World Series I was at home in South Carolina, dove hunting. But the Yankees awarded me a one-third share. You can bet that made an impression on me. I never forgot that.

In 1957 I was in and out of the lineup. Billy got traded after the Copacabana incident, and I won the job for a while. But eventually I lost it to Gerry Coleman, who played there through the World Series. Gerry was a wonderful guy. Remember, I came up as a shortstop and was moved to second base. So I was Gerry's competitor. But that didn't matter to him. Every day he came out early and showed me the little things, which in the long run became the big things. He was a master of the double play. He could pivot so flawlessly and get rid of the ball so quickly. He was one smooth second baseman. I owe a lot to Gerry Coleman.

Coleman retired after the 1957 season, and it seemed as though the job was mine. But we had so many infielders in those days, and I wound up with only 182 at bats. Gil McDougald ended up at second base, and Jerry Lumpe was there, too. Andy Carey was at third. I think Casey was always concerned about my hitting, and he preferred to go with veterans over young players. I didn't like it then. I understand it more now. At Liberty University I go with young players now and then, but if they don't produce within a week's time, I tend to rely on the veteran players, too.

But at the time it was discouraging. So I went to management and said, "If I'm not going to play, I would appreciate a trade to another club so that I can get the opportunity somewhere." They told me to be patient, that my time was coming. Then in early 1959 they traded Jerry to Kansas City, and I played my first full season. I got 469 at bats and I batted .301. In fact, I was the only Yankee to bat .300 that year. Going into the last game of the season, I was batting .299. Casey wanted me to hit .300. He told me, "I want you to hit .300. If you get a hit your first time up, I'm going to take you out." Well, Billy O'Dell was pitching for Baltimore, and he was one of my best friends. When I stepped into the batter's box, the catcher said to me, "I'll tell you which pitch is going to be right down the middle." Umpire Ed Hurley told me that any close play was a base hit. Brooks Robinson played deep at third base so that I could drop a bunt down or beat out an infield hit. Well, Albie Pearson was out in right field, and he was one of my good friends, too. But I lined a drive to right field and he made a diving catch. So much for friendship. The next two times up, though, I got base hits and lifted my average to .301. Then Casey took me out.

The only psychology Casey ever used on me was talking about me. When I first came up, he would say nice things about me in the press. That made me feel good. You know, he was a master at public relations, and he had the press on his side. Quite often, though, he would needle you in the press. He also liked to talk loud enough so that you could overhear him. He would say, "He can't do this and he can't do that." You know, trying to get you mad. With me, he succeeded.

Casey could demoralize a young player. Quite often he would pinch hit for you in the first inning. He did that to Clete Boyer in the 1960 World Series. He did it to Gil McDougald, too. And he also did it to me. Do you know that after I set the World Series record with twelve runs batted in, in 1960, he pinch hit for me? Those things would make you mad.

I don't remember too much about the 1960 season. I know my batting average dropped almost fifty points. And I know I had a good World Series. (*He had eleven hits, one off the record at that time, and batted .367. One of his hits was a grand-slam home run, the seventh in World Series history. Two of his hits were triples. They came in one game. That tied a Fall Classic record. Overall he had a slugging percentage of .667.)* You know, I played in thirty consecutive World Series games. That's a record, too. But it also gave me a distinct advantage. If you play in that many games, you're bound to do something right.

My recollections of the Series? Well, there are four of them. In Game Three I set a record when I drove home six runs in one game. Four of them came on one swing. I hit a grand slam. But there's a story behind the story. We were winning 2-0 in the first inning when I came to the plate with the bases loaded. Casey gave me the squeeze sign, which is not a good play in that situation. But he wanted to get one more run. Anyway, I fouled the bunt attempt off. He gave me the squeeze sign again. Once more I fouled it off. Then Frankie Crosetti, who was coaching at third base, said, "Hit it to right, Bobby." They were showing a lot of confidence in me, right? But their primary concern was to stay out of the double play. Well, the next pitch I hit into the left-field seats, and that's how I got my grand slam.

Second, I drove home a record twelve runs in the Series, and Casey pinch hit for me. That was a little unusual, too.

Third, until this very day I don't understand why Casey didn't start Whitey Ford in the first game of the Series. I'm not taking anything away from Art Ditmar. He was a good pitcher and he had an outstanding year. But Whitey was the "Chairman of the Board." He was our bread-and-butter pitcher. They said they didn't want to pitch him on the road. Well, I'm not big on statistics, but I think if you check the records, you'll find that Whitey won just as many games on the road as he did at home. You just told me that his career ERA was 2.75, and that's the lowest for a left-handed pitcher with three thousand or more innings, and his World Series ERA was 2.71. That's consistency, and that's what Whitey Ford was all about.

Well, going into Game Six, we were down three games to two, and we had to pitch Whitey at Forbes Field in Pittsburgh. He responded with a 12-0 shutout victory. In Game Three, at Yankee Stadium, he had shut the Pirates out, 10-0. If Whitey Ford had pitched the opener of the 1960 World Series, it wouldn't have gone seven games, and the Yankees would have won.

The fourth thing that stands out in my mind is that I was the winner of the Most Valuable Player Award. I'm the only member of the losing team to have won it. After Bill Mazeroski hit that sudden-death home run, the Yankee locker-room was like a tomb. Ed Fitzgerald, who was the sports editor of *Sport* Magazine at the time, chose the MVP winner. He walked into the locker-room and told me that I had won the award. It didn't mean too much to me at the time. Of course, I appreciated the Corvette that went along with it. And later, when my hometown of Sumter, South Carolina, gave me a parade, and everyone turned out for it, well, I appreciated that, too. And yes, I certainly appreciate it now.

Ralph Houk meant a lot to me. He was probably the biggest influence on my professional career. I played for him at Denver for two years. Right from the start he gave me confidence. He told me I was his starting second baseman. That gave me the confidence I needed. With the Yankees, he continued to reinforce my self-esteem. In my mind he was an exceptional manager. I'm happy that I had the opportunity to play for him.

Ralph broke in as a major-league manager with the 1961 Yankees. That team had everything. It was an extraordinary club. Whitey Ford won twenty-five games. He lost only four. Roger Maris, of course, hit sixty-one home runs to break Babe Ruth's record. Mickey Mantle was hitting very well but was sidelined by a hip injury with two weeks to go. He ended up with fifty-four home runs. Four other players on that team hit twenty or more. Bill Skowron hit twenty-eight and Yogi Berra hit twenty-two. Both Elston Howard and Johnny Blanchard hit twenty-one.

Mickey Mantle was special. I batted .391 in the 1961 World Series, and I got a record-tying nine hits in a five-game Series. But when I think of that Series, I think of Mickey Mantle. He had an abscessed hip but he tried to play. He always did. We saw that blood oozing through his bandages, and we said to ourselves, *If he can play with his handicap, we can certainly play healthy.* He was an inspiration.

I led the league in at bats from 1962 to 1964. In 1962 my 692 at bats set a record for the most official plate appearances by a right-handed batter in one season. But I'm not especially proud of that record. I never walked more than thirty-seven times in one season, and I never struck out more than thirty-nine times in one year. You know that I wasn't swinging at bad pitches. And at 5'9" I wasn't an easy strike zone. Yet opposing pitchers didn't have any trouble throwing strikes to me. Why? Because Mantle, Maris, and Berra followed me in the lineup. They didn't want me to walk. They wanted me to hit my way on base.

My best season was 1962. I batted .302, I got 209 hits, I hit eight homers, and I drove home fifty-nine runs. All of those were personal highs for me. You'd like to bottle a season like that. Well, I think the difference was Wally Moses, our hitting coach. I don't really believe in batting instructors. But he was the best I ever saw. He encouraged me constantly, he taught me the finer points of hitting, and he built up my confidence. I agree with Johnny Sain: Ralph Houk, Jim Hegan, Wally Moses, Frank Crosetti, and Sain were the most complete coaching staff I've ever seen. Why they ever let some of those guys go, I'll never know.

At any rate, in 1962 I was voted the runner-up to Mickey Mantle as the league's MVP. UPI and AP contacted me and told me that Mantle had said that I should have won it. That was quite an honor. But the bottom line was, when Mantle played, we won. When he didn't, we lost.

We've been talking about good World Series that I had. Well, I had bad World Series, too. In 1962 and 1963. I think I batted .148 and .214. *(He did.)* Jack Sanford of the 1962 San Francisco Giants was a very good pitcher. And Sandy Koufax of the 1963 Los Angeles Dodgers was just awesome. But you have to expect to face good pitching in the World Series. It's pitching that gets you to the World Series. I know we faced some great ones. The 1957-58 Braves had Lew Burdette and Warren Spahn, the 1960 Pirates had Vernon Law and Bob Friend, the 1962 Giants had Sanford and Juan Marichal, the 1963 Dodgers had Koufax and Don Drysdale, and the 1964 Cardinals had Bob Gibson and Ray Sadecki. But the Yankees were used to facing good pitching. Everywhere we went, we faced the other team's top three pitchers. You could probably add thirty points to all of our averages if we played for any team other than the Yankees.

I've read that I was out of position on the play with Willie McCovey, that I was holding Willie Mays close at second. He was the potential winning run. But that's simply not true. I was right where I was supposed to be. I remember that Ralph Houk came out to the mound and asked Ralph Terry if he wanted to put McCovey on first base and pitch to Orlando Cepeda with the bases loaded. But Terry said no, he wanted to pitch to McCovey. I went back to my regular position. I do remember that just before Ralph's pitch to Willie, the second-base umpire said to me, "Heh, Rich, after the game can I have your hat for my ten-year-old son?" When Willie first hit the ball, it looked like a game-winning single. But the ball had overspin on it, and it came down to me. I just lifted my glove shoulder high and caught it. Willie hit the ball really well. But it was a simple play for me.

The play that preceded Willie's line drive was an interesting one. Remember, we were winning 1-0 at the time. Matty Alou was on first base with two outs. Willie Mays, who was the batter, hit a line drive to right-center field. It looked like it was going to go to the wall for the game-tying hit. But Roger Maris made a great cut-off and relay throw to me. The third-base coach held up Alou. If Alou had been thrown out at the plate, the coach would have taken the bat out of Willie's hands. I made a perfect throw to Elston Howard, but the ball touched an uneven spot on the infield grass and bounced high. Would Alou have scored if he had tried? Well, he might have slid in under Ellie's tag. But we'll never know.

Our "last hurrah" was 1964. Mine and the Yankees. During the regular season I batted .267, but I had my third good World Series at the plate. Overall, I batted .406 with thirteen hits, which was a World Series record until Lou Brock of the 1968 Cardinals tied it. In fact, I've been told seven of those thirteen hits came against Bob Gibson. But the thing about the 1964 World Series that stands out in my mind is a bad play I made. It was in Game Four and we were up 3-0 at the time. A double-play ball was hit to me near second, and I bobbled it. Phil Linz, who was playing short in place of Tony Kubek, who was injured, wasn't accustomed to playing with me. Anyway, he came across the bag on the inside, and he got clobbered by the runner when I gave him a bad toss. Ken Boyer hit a grand-slam home run, and the Cardinals wound up winning, 4-3. But we would have been out of the inning if I had made a routine play. I still think we would have won the World Series, though, if Tony Kubek had been at shortstop.

Looking back, I'd have to say that 1964 was the pivotal year in the rise and fall of the Yankee dynasty. After the 1963 season, Ralph Houk, who had led the Yankees to three consecutive pennants, moved upstairs and became the general manager. It was a tough spot for Yogi. One day he was our friend. The next day he was our boss. But I thought Yogi did a great job. He showed a lot of growth in the position. He handled the pitching staff really well, and he led a stretch drive that nipped the White Sox and Al Lopez at the wire. I think the decision to release him was made early in the season. But if I had made one play, we would have won the World Series. Would they have released him then?

Look at the overall job he did. He guided the team to ninety-nine wins during the regular season. And he didn't have a solid pitching staff. By contrast, Casey never won more than ninety-nine games in any of his pennant-winning seasons. And he had Allie Reynolds, Vic Raschi, Eddie Lopat, and Whitey Ford in his starting rotation. In the 1964 World Series Whitey pitched the first game with a bad arm. He didn't pitch again. If we had had a healthy Ford and a healthy Kubek, there's no doubt in my mind that we would have defeated the Cardinals in the 1964 World Series.

Returning to New York on the plane after the Series, Yogi was sitting next to me and my wife, Betsy. He said, "I've got a meeting with the owners tomorrow morning. Do you think I should ask for a two-year contract?"

Betsy laughed and said, "Heck, if Bobby had made that double play, you could ask for a three-year contract."

Of course, he didn't get the contract. I think that was the biggest mistake the Yankees ever made. First, it wasn't right. Yogi did a great job under adverse circumstances. Second, it was a public-relations blunder. Look at all the fans that switched their allegiance to the Mets after Yogi got fired. Most people don't know who the Yankee second baseman was during the late 1960s. Sure, *you* know that it was Horace Clarke. But how many other people know it?

No, I wasn't surprised by the decline of the Yankees in the mid- and late-1960s. I didn't think the collapse would be so total, though I had seen it happen to other good teams. I knew the Yankee success story couldn't go on forever. And there were signs that it wouldn't. Subtle signs. They started with attitude. Remember that I told you the Yankees awarded me a one-third World Series share in 1955, even though I played in a small number of games. That was a class act and it made a deep impression on me. You've told me about Johnny Mize and Johnny Sain coming over from the National League for September stretch runs and receiving full World Series shares. That was the Yankees I remember. Class. We even gave the bat boy a full share. Then in the early 1960s younger players, like the Boutons, the Pepitones, and the Linzes came up, and they'd say, "Full share for the bat boy? Heck, give him five hundred dollars. That's enough." Or they'd say, "He played only fifty games. Let's give him a quarter share."

Anyway, I retired after the 1966 season at the age of thirty-one. That might seem pretty young to you. But actually I wanted to retire after the 1964 season, when I was twenty-nine. By that time I had been in the major leagues for ten years, and I was tired of the traveling. Also, my children were growing up without me. I wanted them to have a father. But Tony Kubek had a back problem, and the organization didn't want to lose the middle of their infield at the same time, so they asked me to stay for one more year. After the 1965 season Tony was forced to retire, and they asked me to stay one more year and break Bobby Murcer in at shortstop. Remember, Bobby came up as a shortstop, but he was drafted into the service, and when he came back, they moved him to center field. Out of loyalty to the organization I stayed on for those extra two years. But I didn't want to.

At the time I wanted to get out of baseball. But obviously I didn't want to stay out of the game. I've coached at three different colleges: South Carolina from 1970-76, Coastal Carolina from 1984-86, and Liberty University from 1987 to the present. I like it.

I also like to go back to Old Timers' Day games. I'm going to three this year. It's a good chance to see some of the old players. Like Moose Skowron, who spoke at our sports banquet last spring. It's especially nice now, since they allow you to bring your wife along. It gives you the chance to take a little vacation, a break away from home, together. And they pay you one thousand dollars to make the appearance. That's nice, too. However, you might be surprised to hear me say that I'm not going back to any more Yankee Old Timers' Day games. I don't want to make a big thing out of this, but three or four of us have agreed not to go back there anymore. It's got nothing to do with George Steinbrenner. It's got everything to do with pride and tradition. The manager and the coaching staff are all ex-Phillies, and the players don't have any pride in the uniform. You said that Phil Rizzuto told you that if the players had more pride in the uniform, maybe they'd win a few pennants and World Series. I totally agree with the Scooter.

It's not the same anymore. The Yankees of my day won nine pennants in ten years. There was a lot of camaraderie and continuity and consistency on those clubs. George Weiss was an extraordinary general manager. Casey Stengel and Ralph Houk were outstanding managers. They had excellent coaching staffs, too. Casey had Bill Dickey, Jim Turner, and Frankie Crosetti. We've already talked about Ralph's great staff. We had solid pitching staffs, good defense, good hitters, and the long ball. We could do the little things, the important things, too: we could bunt, hit behind the runner, and take the extra base. We didn't give anything away and we capitalized on whatever we were given. In short, we were a team, a team of winners. And there were many reasons why we were successful: we believed in ourselves, we believed in our teammates, we believed in our uniform, and we believed in Yankee tradition.

Consequently we could rise to the occasion. Take Mickey Mantle in 1963, for example. Early in the season he broke his ankle in Baltimore, which had a wire fence in the outfield. He went back to the fence, jumped, and caught his ankle in the wire's end. His body was going one way and his ankle was going another. Well, he was out of the lineup for about two months. Finally we're playing the Orioles before about sixty thousand people at Yankee Stadium. Mickey had been taking batting practice, but he wasn't game-ready, so he was sitting at the end of the bench, not expecting to play. It was a high-scoring game, and we came down to our final out needing a run to tie the game. Ralph went walking up and down the bench, looking for a pinch hitter. He finally looked at Mickey and, I guess, the temptation was too much for him. He said, "Mickey, grab a bat, you're hitting." Mickey couldn't believe it but he went to the bat rack, and what followed was one of the most incredible scenes I've ever seen on a ball field. Some of the fans could see into the dugout, and when they saw Mickey grab a bat, they passed the word. Within a few seconds everyone in the park knew that Mantle was hitting, and when he walked out of the dugout, he was greeted with the most thunderous ovation I've ever heard. I was in the on-deck circle at the time. Mickey was very moved. He said to me, "I hope that I can at least hit a single for them." Then he stepped into the batter's box, but he couldn't hit because the crowd wouldn't stop cheering. He had to step out a couple of times before they quieted down. Finally he got into the box and, batting right-handed, he hit a game-tying home run into the left-field seats, just out of the reach of Jackie Brandt. Now remember, the home run only tied the game. We won in extra innings, 10-9, I believe. But that thunderous ovation rose again and didn't die down for ten minutes. Mickey was a true folk hero and the fans loved him. It was absolutely one of the most extraordinary performances and one of the most incredible sights I've ever seen.

Whitey Ford

Whitey Ford was the "Chairman of the Board." Elston Howard gave him that name in the early 1960s. Overall, he won 236 games and lost 106 for an all-time-high winning percentage of .690 (for pitchers with two hundred or more wins). He hurled forty-five shutouts, the most of any Yankee pitcher. He won ten World Series games, more than any other pitcher. And he did everything with consistency: in sixteen major-league seasons he compiled an ERA of 2.75, the best for any left-handed pitcher with three thousand or more innings pitched. In twenty-two games and 146 innings in World Series play, he had an ERA of 2.71.

Ford pitched three shutouts in World Series play, good for second place on the all-time list. He could easily have had two more, if Gene Woodling had caught a fly ball in 1950 and if Gerry Coleman had charged a ground ball in 1957. But in 1961 he did break Babe Ruth's record of twenty-nine and two-thirds consecutive scoreless innings. "Ruth had a bad year in 1961," Ford deadpans. "Roger Maris broke his home run record, and I broke his World Series record." Ford ended up with thirty-two and two-thirds innings of consecutive scoreless ball.

After his retirement in 1967, he became the Yankees' first-base coach for one year in 1968, but he didn't feel comfortable in the position, so he resigned. From 1969 to 1973 he made a series of bad investments, so in 1974, when owner George Steinbrenner offered him a position as pitching coach with the Yankees, he accepted it, and remained there until 1975, when he suffered a circulatory problem.

Since that time he has been an unofficial employee of the Yankees, helping out in spring training and in public speaking engagements. Also during that *time, his number (16) has been retired, and he has been inducted into the Baseball Hall of Fame.*

He lives with his wife of thirty-eight years, Joan, in Lake Success, New York. They have two sons and a daughter.

I had a rude awakening to the major leagues. It was in July of 1950, and we were playing the Red Sox at Fenway Park. They had that awesome lineup: Dom DiMaggio, Johnny Pesky, Ted Williams, Vern Stephens, Walt Dropo, Bobby Doerr, Billy Goodman, and Birdie Tebbetts. The first pitch I threw was a single, the second was a single, and the third was a double. I was pitching in relief of Tommy Byrne, and it didn't look as if it would be long before Casey started looking for more relief. Tommy Henrich came over from first base and said, "Heh, Eddie, Earle Combs, the first-base coach, is calling every pitch." Earle Combs was the center fielder for the Yankees' "Murderers' Row" team of 1927. He was a .325 lifetime hitter. It's no wonder, the way he could pick up pitches.

The next day Eddie Lopat and Jim Turner took me on the side and had me work from the stretch. They picked up what I was doing wrong right away. When I threw a fastball, I laid the inside of my wrist flat against my stomach. When I threw a curve, I laid the side of my wrist against my stomach. Combs picked it up right away. When I started to throw a fastball, he would holler to the hitter, "Be ready." When I started to throw a curveball, he would shout, "Make him get it up." It was easy to correct, but I had been doing it for three years in the minor leagues without anyone noticing it. Welcome to the big leagues!

Casey Stengel and Jim Turner, the pitching coach, brought me along very slowly. My first seven starts were against second-division clubs. I won all of the decisions. Finally they gave me a start against a first-division club, Detroit. We were battling the Tigers for the pennant. Going into Detroit for a vital three-game series in September, we led the Tigers by one game. We lost the first game and won the second, so the third game was still for first place. That's the game I pitched. After eight innings the score was tied, 1-1. Joe DiMaggio had homered for our run, and they scored on back-to-back doubles. I led off the ninth. I was sure he was going to pinch-hit for me. But he didn't. He let me hit. I walked and that started a seven-run rally. We won 8-1. I was happy because it was my eighth win in a row, and we remained in first place and stayed there for the rest of the year. We won the pennant by three games and I finished the season at 9-1. I felt great. At that point I knew I could pitch in the major leagues.

Casey gave me the start in the fourth game of that year's World Series. We were up three games to none at the time. Vic Raschi had won the first game, 1-0. Allie Reynolds had won the second game, 2-1, on a tenth-inning home run by DiMaggio off Robin Roberts. Tom Ferrick had won the third game in relief of Eddie Lopat, 3-2. Three one-run games. We hadn't exactly run them out of the park. In Game Four my teammates gave me a 5-0 lead going into the top of the ninth. But Willie Jones led off the inning with a single, and I hit Del Ennis with a pitch. Casey had Reynolds in the bullpen. He wasn't taking any chances. He wanted the sweep. But so did I. I got the next two hitters, and when Andy Seminick hit a fly ball to deep left, I thought I had the game and a shutout. But Gene Woodling lost the ball in the sun. Gene was a great left fielder, but left field is a tough sun field in October. A lot of great outfielders have found that out. Casey stayed with me, but when Mike Goliat singled, Stan Lopata, who was pinch hitting, represented the tying run. That's when Casey waved for Reynolds and got me out of there. The fans booed the hell out of Casey. Half of them were my friends and relatives. But he was right. I was getting tired and Lopata could reach the seats. Reynolds came in and blew Lopata away on three pitches. I don't think Stan ever saw the ball.

Casey wasn't an emotional man. He never said anything to you after a big game. He might wink at you but he didn't display his feelings. After he took me out of the 1950 World Series game, he didn't say he was sorry or try to justify his move. Ralph Houk would have. Tommy Lasorda would hug and kiss you to death. It just wasn't Casey's way. They booed Casey that day. But he didn't care. He knew what he had to do and he did it.

One day in Washington in 1954, President Dwight Eisenhower was attending our game so I wanted to do well. I did — against every hitter except Jim Lemon. He owned me. That day he hit three home runs off me. Fortunately no one was on any of the times, and I was winning 5-3 with two outs in the ninth. Then someone singled — I can't remember who — and Lemon, representing the tying run, was standing at the plate. Casey came out and I said, "Let me stay in, Case, I'll get him this time."

"What are you, crazy, out of your damn mind?" he said. "He's already hit three home runs off you. Do you want him to try for four?" So he brought Tom Morgan in, and Tom got Lemon, and we won the game. The Old Man wasn't afraid to make a move.

The best team I played on had to be the 1961 club. It had the greatest blend of offense and defense that I've ever seen. Initially I thought it was the 1950 team. But I was a rookie at the time and in awe of those guys. They might have had a better starting four-man rotation: Raschi, Reynolds, Lopat, and Tommy Byrne. Those four guys won seventy games that year. But they didn't have a closer like Luis Arroyo. He won fifteen and saved twenty-nine in 1961. That year someone would ask, "Who's pitching?" and another one would answer, "Ford and Arroyo." I didn't have anything to prove. I had led the league in complete games. I was more interested in winning games than finishing them. That year I won twenty-five games. He saved more than half of them. I was happy to hand a lead over to him and conserve my energy for the next game.

But I was talking about 1961. Where would you ever find a better infield? Bill Skowron at first, Bobby Richardson at second, Tony Kubek at short, and Clete Boyer at third. We had three catchers who combined to hit a total of sixty-four runs — Ellie Howard, Yogi Berra, and Johnny Blanchard. Granted, they played the outfield once in a while. Overall, the team hit a record 240 home runs. And we won 109 games — the 1950 club had won only ninety-eight. It was also the year of Roger Maris and Mickey Mantle. What a home run race! It was an unbelievable year and an incredible club.

Babe Ruth's record of twenty-nine and two-thirds consecutive scoreless innings? I never even thought about it back then. No one did. In 1960 I pitched two shutouts. I shut out the Pirates in Game Three, 10-0, and I blanked them in Game Six, 12-0. Bobby Richardson had quite a Series. In Game Three he hit a grand-slam home run and drove home a record six runs in one game. Overall, he drove home a record twelve runs. I remember that Mickey hit a couple of long home runs over the center-field fence in Pittsburgh, and that was a very deep center. I had pitched two consecutive shutouts, but no one was thinking about Babe Ruth's record at the time.

That all changed in 1961, when I pitched a two-hit 2-0 shutout in Game One of the World Series. It was against Jim O'Toole. Clete made sensational plays at third, but I was never in any trouble. Eddie Kasko singled for the Reds in the first, and Wally Post singled in the fifth. I walked Frank Robinson in the seventh. It was on a three-two pitch. I threw a sharp curve that broke right over the plate. It was beautiful. I was surprised that Frank didn't swing. He started to, but he had those strong wrists, and he held up. I was also surprised that the umpire didn't call the pitch a strike. But that was it. The Reds had only thirty batters that day, and only one of them reached second.

Now everyone was talking about the record. I needed only three more scoreless innings to surpass the Babe's streak. I got them in Game Four, which we won 7-0. I only went five innings. We were winning 2-0 at the time I left the game. Jim Coates finished up for the save. I was pitching well but I hit myself in the foot twice in the same inning with foul balls. It was very painful. Ralph could see that I was having some trouble with it, so he took me out and put Jim in.

In the record third inning I got Gordon Coleman on a ground ball to second. Then Darrell Johnson singled to left. But O'Toole hit into a force play, Elio Chacon grounded to second, and the record was mine.

In Game One of the 1962 World Series, I extended the streak to thirty-three and two-thirds innings before the Giants broke it. With two outs in the second inning, Jose Pagan scored from third on a swinging bunt by Willie Mays. I remember at the time I had no play at home and I had no play on Mays, but I threw to second attempting to get the force. If I had gotten it, I would have been out of the inning. I didn't care about the streak. As I said before, when we were talking about Luis, all I cared about was winning. We won the game, 6-2.

That's why I feel bad about the 1960 World Series. I had missed the first six weeks of the season because of a bad shoulder, and I didn't pitch well during the first half of the season. But I finished strong and wound up 12-9. I was very strong in my last four starts, so I figured I would get the opening-game assignment against the Pirates in the World Series. Casey held me back until Game Three. He said something about my pitching in the comfort of Death Valley. But I didn't agree with him. It's the only time I was ever annoyed with Casey. Holding me back till the third game prevented me from pitching three times. I pitched two shutouts. I was pitching the best ball of my life at that time. If he had given me three starts, I would have given him three wins, and we would have been the world champs again.

I was so mad at him that I wouldn't talk to him on the plane ride home to New York after the seventh game. But two days later I felt sorry about that. The Yankees fired Casey. So in the end Casey's move hurt him more than it did me. Overall, I enjoyed playing for him. It was the only disagreement we ever had. He let you go out and play, and if you did your job, he left you alone.

He could come out smelling like a rose, too. You like to play for a guy like that. I remember one day I was clinging to a one-run lead with one out and first and third in the ninth. Casey came out and said that he wanted Johnny Kucks, because Johnny was a sinkerball pitcher, and he thought Johnny might get the double play. He had already called down to the bullpen and said that he wanted "Kucks," but Darrell Johnson, the bullpen catcher, thought Casey said "Trucks." Casey almost died when Virgil hopped over the fence. Well, Trucks came in and threw one pitch, a ground-ball double play, and the game was over. But Casey never let the press know the wrong man came in. The Old Man had style.

Bill Skowron

Bill Skowron gave the Yankees nine productive years. In his first four years he batted over .300 each season. Overall, he did it five times. Four times he hit more than twenty home runs in a season for the Yankees. Ironically, New York traded him to the Los Angeles Dodgers after the 1962 season, one of his best. He had hit twenty-three home runs and driven home eighty runs. In fact, in his last three years in New York, "Moose" averaged twenty-six home runs a year and eighty-seven RBIs per season. The Yankees said that they did it to make room for a promising youngster, Joe Pepitone. But they also did it to allow Skowron to escape a messy divorce.

Skowron was a big-game player. In his fourteen-year career he batted .282, hit 211 home runs, and drove home 888 runs. In World Series play he batted .293, hit eight home runs, and drove home twenty-nine runs. He played in seven World Series in his nine years with the Yankees. Ironically, the year after the Yankees unloaded him, he played on a World Series winner with the Dodgers, who defeated — who else — the Yankees. Skowron led the Dodgers with a .385 average, and he hit one home run and drove home three key runs in the winners' four-game sweep. In all, Skowron hit eight World Series home runs, which is good for seventh place on the all-time list. His eight home runs also tie for the most by a right-handed hitter in Fall Classic play. Joe DiMaggio and Frank Robinson also hit eight.

Today Bill is a sales representative for Intercheck, Inc., a check-printing company in Naperville, Illinois. He has been with Intercheck for fourteen years, and says he is very happy. He credits the Yankees and his World Series checks for helping him to send his three children, two sons and a daughter, through college. He has remarried.

It's ironic that I got to the major leagues, because I never played baseball in high school. I went to a Catholic school in Chicago that didn't play baseball at the time. But my dad Bill was a semi-pro baseball player in Chicago for eighteen years. I was the bat boy. So I observed the game closely and got a lot of good advice. My dad taught me the game, encouraged me to play it, and followed my whole career.

Eventually I went to Purdue University on a sports scholarship, and in my sophomore year I played varsity football, basketball, and baseball. By the way, Hank Stram was my frosh football and baseball coach. Anyway, I won the Big 10 batting crown in my sophomore year with an average of .510, and Purdue sent me to Austin, Minnesota, that summer to play semi-pro baseball. Joe McDermott and Burleigh Grimes, scouts for the Yankees, saw me and, I guess, they liked what they saw. They offered me a contract. I quit school and signed for $25,000.

Casey Stengel started his Rookie Instructional League in 1951. Gil McDougald and Mickey Mantle and Jackie Jensen and Tom Morgan and Bob Cerv and Andy Carey were there, too. We all made it. In 1951 I played "B" ball under Mayo Smith with Norfolk, and in 1952 and 1953 I played "AAA" ball under George Selkirk at Kansas City.

In 1954, when I came up to the Yankees, Johnny Mize was gone. He had retired after the 1953 season. But Joe Collins and Eddie Robinson were still there. It was a great opportunity for me. Strangely, I had never played first base before I signed that first contract with the Yankees. I had always played third base. In 1951 they moved me to the outfield. But Casey told me, "Your quickest way to the major leagues is at first base." He bought me a first baseman's glove and, believe it or not, he sent me to dancing school. My feet were never that good, you know. But dancing school helped me around the bag, and one year in the minor leagues I batted .319. In my rookie year with the Yankees, we won 103 games. The Yankees under Casey Stengel had never won that many before, and they would never win that many again under the Old Man. But we lost the pennant to the Cleveland Indians. By *eight* games. That's the year the Indians won an American League record 111 games. I wasn't aware that the Yankees had won five consecutive World Series. I was thinking of 1954, and I was thinking 103 victories was enough to win. But it wasn't. I couldn't believe it.

I remember that in the final game of the 1955 World Series, against the Brooklyn Dodgers, we were losing 1-0 when Duke Snider laid down a bunt. I bent over to get the ball and I gave him a soft tag. Duke bumped into me and gave me an elbow in the side, and I dropped the ball. Gil Hodges eventually scored Duke and the Dodgers won, 2-0. That was the Dodgers' first World Series victory. As it turned out, even if I hadn't dropped that ball, they would have won. But it was a costly mistake and a valuable lesson. You can bet I never tagged anyone softly again.

In 1956 I took over the starting job at first. I loved it, especially because Casey had confidence in me. But he lost that confidence in that year's World Series. In Game One I went hitless in four at bats against Sal Maglie of the Dodgers. Sal beat Whitey Ford at Ebbets Field, 6-3. I guess Casey decided to go with the veteran at that point. He benched me for the next five games and replaced me with Collins. I was pretty mad, because I thought I had done the job all year long. But I thank Billy Martin for getting me back in the lineup in the seventh and final game, when Johnny Kucks pitched that three-hitter and shut out Don Newcombe and the Dodgers, 9-0. After we lost Game Six in ten innings, 1-0, Billy sat behind Casey on the bus, and he chewed the Old Man out. He said, "If you want to win this World Series, you better get (Enos) Slaughter and Collins out of the lineup for the seventh game."

Casey raised his eyebrows and said, "Oh, and who would you put in their place?"

"Ellie Howard in left and Skowron at first," Billy shot back.

Kucks, my roommate, pitched the shutout, Yogi Berra hit two two-run homers, Ellie hit a solo shot, and I hit a grand slam. It's a good thing Billy said something — and Casey listened!

I don't remember too much about Don Larsen's game in 1956. Just that we all sat in the same seat all game long. No one moved, because we didn't want to bother him. We were superstitious in those days. But nothing at all bothered Don that day. He was perfect.

In 1957 I hurt my back, lifting a window air conditioner. It was my own fault. In Game One of the World Series, against Warren Spahn of the Milwaukee Braves, I reinjured it running out a ground ball to first base. Harry Simpson took my place and went oh-for-19, or something like that. (*Actually it was one-for-twelve.*) In the last game I pinch hit for the last out of the Series. The bases were loaded at the time. We were down 5-0. I hit the ball right on the nose, and it almost went through, but it didn't, and Casey blamed me for the loss. "If Skowron was healthy, we would have won," he said.

I remember that fight in 1957. Art Ditmar knocked Larry Doby of the White Sox down, and Doby got up and charged Art. I tackled Doby to protect my pitcher. Well, there was a pileup and, I guess, a few guys hit Doby. Walt Dropo of the Sox thought I was hitting Doby when he was down, so he charged me and ripped my pants off. Boy, that man was massive. Slaughter came to my aid. That was a mismatch. By the time the storm was over, it looked like Enos had just barely weathered a cyclone.

I suffered a lot of injuries, too. The funny thing is, in high school and college I never did. Back, leg, and arm injuries bothered me the most. In 1959 I was off to a good start. I had fifteen home runs, a .298 batting average, and I was the runner-up to Harmon Killebrew when I broke my wrist and had to sit out the season. Coot Veal, a shortstop with the Tigers, hit a ground ball to Hector Lopez at third base. But Hector made a bad throw. He threw the ball into the runner and I tried to save it. I stuck my hand out and Veal ran over it. That ruined that year. Actually it was a bad year for a lot of Yankees. We suffered a lot of injuries, and we finished just four games over .500, fifteen games behind the league-leading White Sox. We were embarrassed. It was the first time Casey had finished as low as third with the Yankees. We vowed that it would never happen again. And it didn't. Not for the next five years anyway. From 1960-64 we rattled off five consecutive pennants.

I remember the home run I hit off Camilo Pascual in 1959. It gave Whitey Ford a fourteen-inning 1-0 victory. He struck out fifteen Washington Senators that night. That's the longest American League 1-0 game that's been decided by a home run. Pascual hung a curve and we all went home. Finally.

The next year (1960) I came back and led the club in batting with a .309 mark. I hit twenty-six home runs and drove home ninety-one runs. No, I never drove home a hundred runs in a season. For one thing, I never got enough at bats. For another, look at who I had in front of me in the order: Mantle and Berra and Maris. They didn't leave too many runners for me to pick up.

We never should have lost the World Series to the Pirates that year. What made the difference? Well, for one thing, the rock that caused Tony Kubek to get hit in the throat. But I think Jim Coates made the difference, too. In the seventh game Roberto Clemente hit a ball to my right. I back-handed the ball and looked for Coates, who should have been covering the first-base bag. But he was still standing on the mound. Then he challenged Hal Smith. He had him one-and-two and he challenged him with a fastball. Smith wasn't a home run hitter, but he *was* a fastball hitter. And he took Coates out. After Ralph Terry threw the home run pitch to Bill Mazeroski, the one that won the World Series for the Pirates, Coates came over to a slumped-over Terry in the dressing room and said, "I'm sorry for you. I'm happy for me. You got me off the hook." That's what he said. Can you believe it? He didn't care that we lost. All he cared was, Terry got him off the hook.

Well, that World Series loss was it for Casey. He had made up his mind to retire before the Series. That was it. The Yankees got Casey's word on it. And Ralph Houk was ready to move in. But when the Pirates won, Casey changed his mind. He wanted to come back. By that time, though, it was too late. The machinery to replace him had been put into motion.

There was no problem with the transition from Stengel to Houk, though. A lot of the younger players, like Bobby Richardson and Tony Kubek, had played for Houk at Denver. They knew his approach and they liked it. But, of course, we had the horses, too. We hit a record 240 home runs in 1961. Six of us hit twenty or more. That's one record I hope no team breaks. If they do, I hope they put an asterisk next to it. Why? We didn't have a designated pinch hitter.

I made the All-Star Team from 1957-61. We didn't do too well against the National League during those years, but we didn't worry about it, either. The American Leaguers at that time would have preferred to have the three days off.

My top salary was $37,000. Can you believe it? As Hank Bauer says, "The bat boy gets more than that today." I never dealt with general manager George Weiss. He only dealt with the real big boys, and I was never one of them. I negotiated with Roy Hamey, his assistant. But I wasn't bitter when Hamey traded me to the Dodgers after the 1963 season. I was going through a difficult divorce at the time. He told me, "Bill, I think it's better that you get out of town. We have (Joe) Pepitone and we expect a lot from him." They got Stan Williams for me but he came down with a sore arm. I didn't want to leave the Yankees. I had been in their organization for twelve great years. But I agreed with Hamey that I needed a change of scenery.

I thought Pepitone was one of the greatest rookies ever to come up with the Yankees. He had everything — except self-discipline. He lasted as my roommate for one night. My roomies had to be in before ten o'clock at night. He came in at two in the morning and found the door chained from the inside. He kicked the door down. Then he saw that he had to get through a bigger obstacle — me! That changed his mind. He left and asked for a new roommate the next day.

One day in 1962 he came up to me and said, "Bill, you'll never believe this, but last night two underworld figures who have taken a liking to me said, 'Joe, you want to be the starting first baseman for the Yankees'?"

"I said, 'Sure, but how? Skowron's there'."

" 'Just give us the word, and we'll break both of his legs with a baseball bat'."

"I told them, 'Heh, I don't want the job that bad'."

I just laughed. I didn't believe him. How could I? Then when his book, *Joe, You Could Have Made Us Proud,* came out, I became more interested. I read only that chapter. It was true. I laughed, this time dryly to myself.

The Dodgers experience didn't work out well for me. With them in 1963, I batted just .203 with three home runs. But fortunately I had a good Series against the Yankees. In Game One I got two hits off Whitey, and in Game Two I hit a home run off Al Downing. Overall, I batted .385, the team high, and drove home three runs, which tied for the Series high. Would you believe that three runs batted in could tie for the Series high? That shows how good Sandy Koufax, Don Drysdale, and Johnny Podres were.

Was I surprised with the Dodgers' four-game sweep? Well, I wouldn't have bet on it. I knew how great the Yankee lineup was. But I also knew how great the Dodger pitching staff was. I had marveled at them all year long. Koufax, Drysdale, Podres, and Claude Osteen were simply awesome. They had some command of their pitches. And Koufax was in his prime!

Koufax had class, too. Game Four was a pitching masterpiece between him and Ford. The two of them were titans of the game. Whitey gave up two hits, one a long home run by Frank Howard and the second a single in the decisive seventh inning, when Pepitone cost the Yankees the game by losing Clete Boyer's throw at first. Well, after the game, Koufax said, "I'm glad we won today, because that club was capable of coming back and winning four straight." Can you believe that? A lot of guys would have buried the Yankees in a spot like that, but Koufax gave them something to walk away with. I felt good afterwards when Mantle and Maris walked up to me and said, "If we had to be swept by anyone, we're glad it was a team with you on it."

Anyway, I didn't have a good overall year with the Dodgers. But there were some justifying factors. I was going through that divorce, I had some injuries, I had some problems adjusting to the new league, and Ron Fairly simply had a great season the year I was there. I've got to say, though, the Dodgers were a great organization, and I'm glad I spent some time with them.

To tell you the truth, though, I was glad to be back in the American League in 1964. It's tough to adjust to another league's pitchers. You just don't know them. In 1964 and 1965, with Washington and Chicago, I knew the pitching and I had two pretty good years. It's true the National

League was a fastball league, and the American League was a breaking ball league. It goes in cycles. But I think it's that way today, too. The umpires are a lot different, too. In the American League the inside fastball is a ball; in the National League it's a strike. I liked the ball away from me, out over the plate. Obviously I preferred the American League umpires' strike zone.

But I have no regrets. Look at the managers I played for: Casey, Houk, Lopez, Walt Alston, Bill Rigney, Eddie Stanky, and Gil Hodges. How many players can say that? Remember, in 1964, under Lopez, we lost the pennant to the Yankees by only one game. If we had won, I would have played on three pennant winners in three consecutive years for three different teams. That would have been a record. Don Baylor recently did it. But two of the teams he played on lost the World Series. I could have played on three World Series winners. Wouldn't that have been something?

In 1964 Phil Linz of the Yankees played the harmonica on the bus after a loss to us. Yogi told him to stuff it and it became a big story. There was a funny sidelight to it, I've heard the Yankees say. Linz with all the noise on the bus at the time couldn't hear Yogi, so he asked Mickey, who was sitting across the aisle, "What did he say, Mick?"

Mick, holding back a grin, said, "Play it louder."

Linz did and Yogi exploded. The Yankees also exploded. They won their last eleven games. We won our last nine. But we fell short by one game at the wire.

I had some big thrills, though. I hit .282 lifetime with 211 career homers. But if you look at my nine years with the Yankees, you'll find that I batted .298 with them. Also, I played in eight World Series in my first ten years. Five of those teams won the World Series. The three times we lost, we lost in seven games. In addition, I hit eight home runs in the World Series. The only right-handed batter before me to do that was Joe DiMaggio. The only one after me was Frank Robinson. Pretty good company, heh? And though I wasn't paid for my fielding, or my feet around first, I set a World Series record by playing in thirty-one consecutive games without committing an error.

All told, I played on five different teams, but I always felt like a Yankee, and I think I always will. We had a lot of togetherness on those teams. There was no jealousy or dissension. No one cared if you made more money than they did. All they wanted you to do was to play hard and to produce. One day, when I was a rookie, Hank Bauer and Gene Woodling took me into a corner and said, "Don't mess with our money. We like a new car every fall, and our wives like a mink coat." The World Series, in the minds of the Yankee players of that time, was a bonus, and it was worth working for.

But I was talking about my World Series home runs. Four of them I hit to right field and four of them I hit to left field. At Yankee Stadium I had to learn to hit to right field. I had hit too many on the track in the power alleys. Then there was one year I led the team in hitting into double plays. You didn't last long with Casey's teams doing that. Casey said to me, "If you don't learn to hit to right field, you're going back to the minors, and you're going to stay there until you learn how to do it." That was all the incentive I needed.

The only bad World Series that I had was against the 1962 Giants. In 1956 Casey didn't play me until the final game. In 1957 I was hurt. In the other Series I did pretty well. But in the 1962 World Series I went only four-for-eighteen against the Giants. They had a great pitching staff. Jack Sanford was tough. And don't forget Billy Pierce, Billy O'Dell, and Juan Marichal. I did make a contribution to our victory, though. In Game Seven I got a base hit and advanced to third on two walks. Then I scored the only run of a 1-0 victory when Tony Kubek grounded into a double play.

In the ninth Ralph Terry got into trouble. Matty Alou got on first and Willie Mays doubled him to third. Maris saved the game with a great cut-off. Alou was stopped by his coach at third. Richardson handled the relay and made a good throw to the plate. Actually, I was supposed to go out for the relay throw, but my shoulder was sore, and I couldn't make the throw. Before the game we decided that Bobby would go out for the throw. Not too many people knew that. But we didn't give too many secrets away.

Ralph Houk decided to go out to the mound to ask Terry how he wanted to handle the open base. I was sure they would put Willie McCovey on first base so that they could pitch to right-handed batter Orlando Cepeda with the bases loaded. So I was talking to the first-base umpire. While I was talking to him, Terry threw to McCovey, and Willie lined the ball to Bobby at second. If he had hit it to me, he would have taken my head off.

I enjoyed my twelve years in the Yankee organization, three in the minors and nine in the majors. I was fortunate to be in the right spot at the right time. But I had to produce, too. I had to put numbers on the board.

I'm fifty-eight years old and I feel great. The only thing that would make me feel better is if Mr. George Steinbrenner offered me a five-year contract with big numbers to swing at.

Bob Turley

Bob Turley in 1958 became the first American League pitcher to win the Cy Young Award. He had an awesome year. He led the American League in wins, winning percentage, complete games — and walks. Those bases on balls would turn out to be the bane of an otherwise exceptional major-league pitching career. Three times he registered more walks than strikeouts, and once they evened out. But in 1958 he put everything together and finished up a phenomenal year with an incredible World Series. In Game Five he pitched a complete-game shutout, in Game Six he got a save as the short man out of the bullpen, and in Game Seven he got a win as the long man in relief.

Born in Troy, Illinois, Bob lived in Dunwoody, Georgia, during his Yankee years, and now resides in Marco Island, Florida, with his third wife, Carolyn. They have been married for eight years.

Turley, who roomed with Bill Skowron, Andy Carey, and Ralph Terry with the Yankees, describes himself as one of the "lucky ones." After a year as the pitching coach of the Red Sox, he got out of baseball and became a stock broker and a life insurance salesman for a while, doing well and not so well, he says. Then, nineteen years ago, he and six others formed a business that became A. L. Williams, the giant life insurance and mutual-funds sales organization. It has now merged with Prime America, the parent company.

Once in a while, Bob goes to Old Timers' Day games to see his former teammates and recall his baseball past, when he was known as "Bullet Bob," a pitcher who won 101 major-league games, four World Series contests, and the Cy Young Award. That's where I caught up with him, at the 1989 Yankees' Old Timers' game, standing behind the batter's cage during pre-game warmups.

I came up to the Browns in 1951, and I was with them in 1953, too. Zack Taylor and Marty Marion were my managers there. The Browns were a party-time club. Boy, they were bad.

The Browns' franchise was moved to Baltimore in 1954. Jimmy Dykes was my manager there. Harry Brecheen was his pitching coach. He was good. I won fourteen and lost fifteen games in my only season with the Orioles. That wasn't too bad considering we won only fifty-four games. We lost one hundred. So I won twenty-five percent of our games.

I learned about my trade to the Yankees in October of 1954. I was watching the Jack Paar *"Tonight Show"* when a picture of me flashed on the screen and the story announcing the trade accompanied it. Don Larsen, Billy Hunter, and I moved to New York. For me it was a dream come true. The Yankees had a great defense and I knew I was going to become a better pitcher. It gave me the thrill of my life.

Walks were my Achilles heel. I walked a lot of batters. Three times I led the league. Your strikeout-walk ratio should be roughly two-to-one. But my bases on balls were always close to my strikeout total. Three times I gave up more walks than I had strikeouts. I didn't give up too many hits, though. I was always the league leader in least hits per nine innings. About ten years ago I was sixth or seventh on the all-time list. I don't know where I am now.

I went to the no wind-up delivery toward the end of the 1956 season. One night we were warming up down in the bullpen. Don Larsen was with me. It was late in the season and we were getting ready for the World Series. Jim Turner, the pitching coach, talked to Larsen and me. He got Larsen to go to the no wind-up because the other teams were stealing his signs. He was tipping his pitches. He got me to go to it to improve my control. I didn't sacrifice speed for control. But I gained rhythm. When you take a full wind-up, it's easy to lose your rhythm. There's a lot of motion in the full wind-up. I cut down my margin of error. I think some sixty-five percent of today's pitchers use it.

I only pitched two hundred innings in three seasons: with Baltimore in 1954 and New York in 1955 and 1958. I had 247, 246, and 245, respectively. But it wasn't because I was hurt a lot. Casey used a five- and six-man rotation. He had good relievers, too. We just didn't pitch that many games. Even Whitey Ford didn't win that many games when I was there. You know how many twenty-game winners we had in my time with Casey's Yankees? Two. Bob Grim in 1954 and me in 1958.

Later, when Ralph Houk brought Johnny Sain in as his pitching coach, that changed. They went to a four-man rotation, and Whitey won twenty twice. Ralph Terry and Jim Bouton won twenty, too.

I had a good year in 1955, my first season with the Yankees. I was 17-13 with 210 strikeouts. But I also led the league with 177 bases on balls. In 1956 I didn't pitch much and I was only 8-4. I have no complaints, though. Other pitchers were doing a better job. I filled in as a spot starter and did some relieving. Casey would go with whoever was hot. If you lost two or three straight games, he would get you out of there.

In 1957 I was 13-6 with a 2.71 ERA. My starts were down again. In 1956 I had twenty-one starts. In 1957 I had twenty-three. But I changed my style in 1957 and it helped me. I went more to the slider and the sinker and got away from the change and the curve. Basically I was always a power pitcher. The batters hit a lot of foul tips off me. Consequently I didn't get them out that quickly, so I threw a lot of pitches. Later I learned to pitch. I realized I didn't have to strike everyone out. I started getting the hitters on one or two pitches. The following year, 1958, I mastered the art of pitching. I was 21-7 with nineteen complete games. The wins, my winning percentage (.750), and my complete games were league highs. It was my peak year. I won both the Cy Young Award and the World Series MVP Award. Those are the two greatest honors a pitcher can receive. The reason I had so much success in 1958 was all of a sudden I could spot my slider and sinker. Suddenly I was getting double plays. Until that time I seldom did. If I didn't strike the batter out, he usually flied out.

In 1959 I dropped to 8-11. I also dropped in starts from thirty-one in 1958 to twenty-two. Everyone on the Yankees seemed to have a bad year at the same time. There were a lot of injuries, too. Nothing went right. On July 4 we were in last place. We finished just four games over .500.

Casey used me in the bullpen a lot in 1960, and I had a pretty good year. I was 9-3. He used me as a spot starter, too. But overall with the Yankees I did a lot of relieving. Casey used his pitchers that way. He would give you an extra day's rest between starts so that he could use you in relief once in a while. The year 1960 was a turning point for me. At the end of the year, in Chicago, I hurt my arm. It was a cold day and I heard my arm pop. But I didn't tell anyone, I continued to pitch, and I never complained. My arm was in bad shape in the World Series. It was bone chips. In that World Series I picked up a 16-3 win. I gave up thirteen hits and didn't strike out a hitter. It was the only time in my life that I threw so many innings and didn't strike out a batter. I started the seventh game but I didn't get out of the second inning. I didn't have a thing.

The following year, I had a sore arm all year. I still hadn't said anything. Finally I told the doctor and he found the bone chips. We decided to "gut it out" through the season and operate on it after the year ended. In 1962 my arm felt good again. But the Yankees had an outstanding pitching staff and there was no way to break into the rotation. I have no complaints, though. Houk handled the staff well. He gave me three or four straight starts, and I just didn't pitch well. After the season they traded me to the Angels, with whom I had good stuff. In one game against the White Sox, I pitched a one-hitter. Only one batter got on base. But the Angels released me and I finished up the season and my career with the Red Sox. They asked me to be their pitching coach in 1964 and I said, "Yes," but it turned out to be the most frustrating year of my baseball life. There was such turmoil! I never saw such division between front office management and the field manager. Johnny Pesky really had a tough time.

I had a .126 career average, and I remember a couple of my four home runs. One day I hit a home run off Satchel Paige to tie the score, but they scored a run in the ninth inning, and I ended up the losing pitcher. Another day I hit one off Pedro Ramos to win a 2-1 game.

I had a 101-85 career average. I would like to have won more games, but I'm pretty proud of my .543 winning percentage. There weren't too many pitchers at that time, like Ford, who had winning percentages of .600 or above.

I'm pretty proud of my World Series record. I was 4-3 with a 3.19 ERA. With a little luck I could have been 5-2. In 1956 I lost a ten-inning game to Clem Labine of the Dodgers, 1-0. I struck out eleven batters in one of the best games I ever pitched, but I lost it on a misjudged fly ball. Jackie Robinson hit a line drive at Enos Slaughter in left field. He would have caught the ball in his tracks if he had stood still. But he charged it and it went over his head. The defeat was devastating. I gave up just four hits — actually I could have pitched a no-hitter that day. Jim Gilliam hit a high fly ball that Slaughter lost in the sun. Then Labine hit a fly ball to the wall and Slaughter ran into it and fell down. The ball dropped right behind him. On the other play, a ball was hit pretty sharply to either Andy Carey or Gil McDougald. Whoever it was fumbled the ball and then dropped it. The scorer ruled the play a hit.

Of course the Series I'll always remember is the 1958 one. Going into Game Five, we were down three games to one. I won Game Five in a start, shutting out Lew Burdette, 7-0. Then I saved Game Six, and I got a win in relief in Game Seven. I don't know if any other pitcher has ever been involved in the last three decisions of a World Series. Maybe Rollie Fingers with the Oakland A's. In the 7-0 game I was close to coming out in the sixth or seventh inning. The score was 1-0 at the time. The Braves had a man on first. But Elston Howard came up with a great catch in left field. He ran hard, dove, and extended his arms. If he hadn't made the catch, one run would have scored and I would have come out of the game. In Game Six I relieved Ryne Duren with two outs in the ninth inning and two runners on, with us leading, 4-3. The batter hit the ball off my glove. It deflected to Gil McDougald at second and that was the game. In Game Seven I came in for Larsen with the score tied, 1-1. I pitched six and two-thirds innings and allowed just one run on a sixth-inning home run by Del Crandall. Ellie Howard hit a game-winning single in the eighth, and Bill Skowron then iced the game with a three-run homer. Overall, I pitched sixteen innings in the three games. In Game Seven I struck out nine or ten batters. I had a good curve and great control of it. The Braves didn't expect that from me.

I wish I had won more games and I wish my career had gone a little longer. But when I look back, I'm satisfied to see the total picture. I'd like to be remembered as a guy who gave everything he had, a guy who was well-liked and respected by both his teammates and opponents, and a guy who didn't sully the game with controversy. In short, I think that I gave back to baseball as much as I got from it.

It's great to come back for Old Timers' Day games. Looking at Mantle across the field, I'm reminded of a play he and Bauer made behind us one day. Harvey Kuenn was the batter and he lined a ball to right-center field. Hank raced for it but he couldn't get to it with his glove hand, so he reached out his bare hand and deflected the ball to Mantle, behind him, who caught it in full stride. They were running in stride and they took it in stride. When they got to the dugout, they said with deadpan faces, "That's a play we've been working on." It's a great feeling to put on the uniform again and see the guys — guys like Mick and Whitey and Clete and Moose. It's like putting a seashell to your ear. It all comes back: the memories, the emotions, the thrills. And it's just great.

Jim Bouton

It was sad and strange to see Jim Bouton pitching in High Bridge, New Jersey, on July 4, 1975, the first time that I interviewed him. At first I thought it was a big comedown for the former Yankee to pitch in front of a holiday crowd of just over a thousand people instead of the sixty thousand-plus crowds that had seen him lose a 1-0 decision to Don Drysdale in the 1963 World Series and watched him win 2-1 and 8-3 games in the 1964 Fall Classic.

But as Rose Kennedy, the mother of the former President, once said, "Attitudes are more important than facts." Jim Bouton's attitude is big-league all the way.

At the time, I was the sports editor of the Hunterdon County Democrat in Flemington, New Jersey, and I had arranged with the former major-league pitcher to sandwich an interview into his hectic schedule. While he was warming up before the game, he told me that he had to tape an interview in Battery Park in New York at 5:00 P.M. and do his CBS television sportscast at 11:00 P.M. But there was still time, he thought, to pitch an afternoon baseball game in High Bridge and drive two hours to his home in Englewood, before his workday began.

Bouton excused himself while he rushed his final warm-up throws, but suggested that I sit on the bench with him during the game and finish the interview. After he sat down the side in order in the first inning, I asked if he ever fantasized about pitching the way he did for the Yankees in 1963 and 1964. "I fantasize all the time," he said. "Once in a while I'll throw a good pitch and I'll say to myself, 'Why can't you do that again?' My pitches tease me. I throw just enough good ones to keep biting." He's been biting for twenty years, since he left major-league baseball in 1970.

Bouton wrote Ball Four, *a funny and irreverent bestseller, in 1970. In the same year he retired from baseball and became a sportscaster for WABC-TV in New York City. From 1971-77, he wrote a sequel to* Ball Four, *won good reviews in a movie called* The Long Goodbye, *joined WCBS-TV as a sportscaster, and created, wrote, and acted in a network situation comedy based on* Ball Four.

Now he has his own product development company. One product is Big League Cards — personalized baseball trading cards that are marketed nationally. He has been married twice and has three children, two sons and a daughter, from his first marriage, and two stepchildren, a son and a daughter, from his second.

In the summer of 1989, I spoke to Bouton several times at his office in Teaneck, New Jersey. He hadn't changed a bit.

No, I haven't been invited back to any Old Timers' Day games by the Yankees. By anyone else, either. Am I bitter? Well, let's just say I'm disappointed. But no, I don't intend to push it. I've heard that Mickey Mantle won't show up if I'm invited. I don't want to be the reason that fifty thousand people don't get to see Mantle. But I think the real reason why they don't invite me back is that I can still play this game, and they can't.

Actually I think it's funny as hell that they don't invite me back. It just reinforces what I said in *Ball Four.* Only baseball is worse than I made it out to be in my book. Yes, I think there's collusion. It's not only the Yankees. It's baseball, too. But hell no, I don't intend to do anything about it. I tell people it's my claim to fame. If baseball didn't have anything to worry about, they'd laugh at the book. The fact that they've blackballed me indicates that they are uptight and there are things to hide. It also tells me that I'm right and they're wrong. Their attitude toward *Ball Four* tells more about baseball than my book. And it gives me more attention than Old Timers' Day games would.

What are my thoughts of Mickey? Well, I remember when I won my first major-league game in 1962. When I came into the clubhouse after the game, there was a path of towels from the door to my locker. Mickey was putting the last one in place when I walked through the door. I'll never forget him for that. Also in my rookie year, in Kansas City one day, I was eating alone in a restaurant when Whitey Ford and he walked in. Mantle asked me to join them and picked up the tab. I'll never forget that, either.

Then there was Game Two of the 1964 World Series. The score was 1-1 going into the bottom of the ninth inning at the Stadium. I had driven home our only run with a single off Curt Simmons. Barney Schultz was pitching for the Cardinals in the ninth. He was a knuckleball pitcher, but he threw Mantle a knuckler that didn't knuckle. Mickey said after the game that the pitch just laid there, and he deposited it in the third deck to win the game. It was some shot. I never saw another ball get up there so fast. That was my first World Series victory.

But there are other things about Mantle that I can't forget, either: the times he pushed little kids looking for autographs out of the way, the times he made writers crawl for a minute of his time, and the times that he refused to sign baseballs in the clubhouse before the games. Everyone else had to sign, but Pete Previte, the clubhouse man, signed Mantle's signature. There are thousands of balls around the country with Mickey's signature on them, in Pete Previte's writing.

Then there was the time in Baltimore when he thought he was on the disabled list, but Ralph Houk had taken him off the list one day early. Mickey had gone out the night before, and I guess he got smashed, because he looked hung over, and he was sleeping at the other end of the bench when Houk told him to grab a bat and pinch-hit. He could hardly see. Hank Bauer, who was then an Oriole coach, knew that Mantle was hung over and told manager Billy Hitchcock, who sent his pitching coach out to the mound to tell his pitcher to throw nothing but high heat. Mickey staggered up to the plate and hit the first pitch to left for a tremendous home run to win the game, and then staggered around the bases. Bauer hung his head and shook it in wonder. We shook our heads in wonder, too. It was an incredible feat. We asked him how he did it. He said, "I saw three balls coming to the plate. I just swung at the one in the middle." Then he looked up at the fans who were giving him a thunderous ovation and said contemptuously, "Those people don't know how tough that really was."

There's humor and there's pathos and there's Herculean drama in that story. I alluded to it in one paragraph in *Ball Four*. Mickey and Whitey, in their many books, devoted pages to the incident. But I've been ostracized for my brief reference, whereas they've reveled in their descriptive accounts.

Yogi Berra and Ralph Houk were both good managers. Bobby Murcer summed up Houk best. He said, "Ralph won't interfere with a good team. He'll let it play its game. But the trouble with Ralph is he won't interfere with a bad club, either."

Yogi was a member of the old guard. You were supposed to look and act sad after every loss. Once in a while Joe Pepitone, Phil Linz, and I would giggle about something after a loss, and we would incur angry stares from the veteran players.

This was what was behind the famous Phil Linz harmonica incident in 1964. We had just blown a doubleheader and got swept in a four-game series with the White Sox, and we had dropped four and one-half games off the pace. Well, we got stranded in traffic on our way from Comiskey Park to O'Hare Airport. The day was unbelievably hot, and the air conditioner wasn't working, and we sat in traffic for about two hours. Tempers were short. That's when Phil's harmonica became a catalyst. Linz, who was sitting beside me, was upset because he had come into Chicago with a ten-game hitting streak, but he didn't get to play in any of the four games. Well, he pulled out a harmonica that he had bought that morning and, very respectfully and quietly, began to play "Mary Had a Little Lamb." The reason he played that song was that it was the only one he knew how to play. But under the circumstances it sounded like a funeral dirge. Phil had poured fuel on the fire.

Yogi, who was in the front of the bus, stood up and shouted, "Knock it off."

Linz didn't hear what Yogi said, so, according to legend, he leaned across the aisle and asked Mantle, "What did he say?"

"Play it louder," Mickey said. Linz didn't believe that but he continued to play.

Well, in a few moments Yogi was in the back of the bus, breathing hard and snarling. He said, "Shove that thing up your ass."

"You do it," Linz said, jumping up on the seat and flipping the harmonica at him. Yogi swatted the harmonica away, and it hit Pepitone in the knee. Immediately Joe went into his act. "Oooh, you've hurt my little knee," he said. All of a sudden everyone was laughing, even though you're not supposed to laugh after you lose, especially a doubleheader. In the middle of the hilarity, Frankie Crosetti, the long-time coach, stood up and in his squeaky voice screamed, "This is the worst thing I've seen in all of my years with the Yankees."

Well, the worst thing turned out to be the best thing. The incident was over in a minute, but it broke the tension on the club, and we went on to win sixteen of our next eighteen games, and won the pennant by one game over the White Sox.

I won two games in the 1964 World Series. I feel pretty good about that. I think about the 1964 World Series a lot. The 1963 Series, too. In 1963 I lost a 1-0 decision to Don Drysdale. I think about what would have happened if I had pitched the first game instead of the third game in 1963.

I would have defeated Sandy Koufax, even though he struck out fifteen batters and set a World Series record. In 1964 Yogi had to start Whitey in Game One, even though he had hurt his arm *before* the Series started. If he had started me and it had backfired, he would have come under a storm of criticism. But yes, I do feel I could have won three games in that Series. I was in peak form. They say that I set a record in that World Series. I lost my cap thirty-nine times. I used to lose my cap so much because I had a crewcut and I threw so hard. At the All-Star Game that year, I was only 5-8, but I finished the second half with a 13-5 mark. So I was pitching well at World Series time.

A couple of things about the 1964 World Series stand out in my mind. First, the game-winning home run that Mantle hit for me in Game Two. The second thing is Bill White, the first baseman for the Cardinals. He was a left-handed batter with good power. I usually threw left-handers a lot of change-ups, but in one of the games I didn't throw him any his first three times up. His fourth time up, I struck him out — on a change. The next day I read a quote of his in the papers. He said, "I waited all day for the change-up and he never threw it. Then I gave up looking for the damn thing and started looking for the fastball and here it came."

You've got to outthink the hitter up there. Johnny Sain was good at that. He was our pitching coach from 1961-63. The Yankees let him go after the 1963 season over two thousand dollars. It was a big mistake. Whitey won twenty-five games one season and twenty-four another while Johnny was there. Ralph Terry and I won twenty, too. Sain was a gentleman. And he had great insight. He also had great rapport with his pitchers. He never tried to impose his theories on you. But he would transpose himself into your body and your repertoire and say, "If I had your tools, I might do this." He was always trying to help you from *your* point of view, not *his.*

I'm glad I wrote *Ball Four.* Once in a while I take the family to the ballpark. It's a strange feeling to sit there and watch from the stands. The game looks easier than it really is. Fans can't see the up-close grunting and straining. Or when someone hits a home run, you can't hear the pitcher make little whimpering sounds. And it all looks so much more serious than it really is. You can't see any of the nonsense and the fun going on out there. When the manager goes out to talk to the pitcher, it looks very scientific. I don't ever want to forget what they're really saying. If it weren't written somewhere that a manager named Joe Schultz advised pitchers to "zitz 'em and go pound Budweiser" I might not believe it myself anymore. And I was there.

So why the anger? It couldn't have been that I said Mantle hung out in bars. The last time I flipped on the television, there was Mickey, in a bar, bragging about how much beer he used to drink. And it couldn't be that I said that Whitey used to scuff up the baseball. In his own book Whitey went into even greater detail on the subject. Maybe they're mad because they wanted the stories for *their* books.

You've got to be able to laugh. In fact, I laugh every time I think of Harry Walker. I hit .305, my major-league high, in my last year (1970) with Houston. Harry taught me quite a few things about hitting. He talked hitting with everyone, including the pitchers. Most managers are not good teachers. They're managers of men. Harry Walker may not have been a good manager of men. But he was a great teacher.

I liked Harry. The problem was nobody else did. He never stopped teaching. Sometimes he was a pain in the butt. You'd go to an afternoon movie, and you'd try to concentrate while Harry slipped into the seat behind you and whispered in your ear, "Now here's the way we're going to do it tonight." The players had this joke on the Houston club. Harry's wife, the story went, would lean over to Harry in bed at night and say, "Harry, tell me you love me." And Harry would say, "It's all in the stride. It's all in the wrists. Get those two things down and you've got it made."

What triggered my comeback with the Atlanta Braves in 1978 was that I had come up with a pretty good knuckleball, and I thought I could still get batters out. I met Ted Turner when he came to New York to accept the Yachtsman of the Year Award for winning the America's Cup and asked him for a try-out. He said, "Sure, I'll give you a chance to make one of my minor-league teams. So what if you're thirty-nine? I'm thirty-nine, and I don't think I'm washed up."

I got my chance and I made it all the way back to the majors. In the end I didn't win enough, but I got five starts, and I pitched much better than my record indicates. It was 1-3, but it easily could have been 2-2 or 3-1.

I'm pitching now with the Little Ferry Giants in the New Jersey Metropolitan League. I picked up a win recently with three and two-thirds innings of scoreless pitching.

Why do I continue to pitch at the age of fifty? Well, I explained that in my summation of *Ball Four*. One day in 1970 I was taking a cab to the airport in Cincinnati, and I got into a conversation with the driver. He said he had played against Jim O'Toole that summer in the Kentucky Industrial League. O'Toole was pitching for the Ross Eversoles. He said O'Toole was all washed up.

How ironic, I thought to myself. In the spring he and I had started out even, when we were both trying to make the roster of the Seattle Pilots. He ended up with the Ross Eversoles, and I wound up with a new lease on life. I thought to myself, *Would I do that? When it's over for me, would I be hanging on with the Ross Eversoles?* I went down deep and the answer I came up with was yes.

You spend a good piece of your life gripping a baseball and in the end it turns out it was the other way around all the time.

Luis Arroyo

I met Luis Arroyo at a Yankees' Old Timers' Day game on July 15, 1989. Phil Linz introduced us, and Arroyo told me to call him when he got back to Puerto Rico. I must have called fifteen times before I finally contacted him. Arroyo is a busy man, combing the playing fields of Puerto Rico and the Dominican Republic for the New York Yankees, who hired him as a scout in 1964, when he retired as a player.

For the first ten years he covered the whole Caribbean, but then he got sick, and now he limits his duties to Puerto Rico and the Dominican Republic. One of the many players he signed for the Yankees was Otto Velez. Today he collects his social security and pension checks, and he enjoys his part-time job.

"I'm grateful to the Yankees," he says. "When I hurt my arm in 1962, I went through a troubled time for two years. In 1963 I pitched in only six games. But they gave me a full share of the World Series money. The Yankees are class."

Arroyo ranks with the Yankees' all-time great relief pitchers: Wilcy Moore, Johnny Murphy, Joe Page, Allie Reynolds, Ryne Duren, Sparky Lyle, Goose Gossage, and Dave Righetti. In 1960 and 1961 Arroyo won a total of twenty games and lost just six. In addition, he posted thirty-six saves and compiled an ERA of 2.53. In 1960 he pitched and saved the pennant-clincher, when he got Pete Runnels of the Red Sox to pop up to Clete Boyer to end the game. In 1961, at one point in the season, he pitched in nine consecutive games, and he wound up being named The Sporting News' *"Fireman of the Year."*

Everything went right for him in 1961. He even batted .280. But he was a lifetime .227 hitter. Not bad for a pitcher. And six or seven times, according to his estimate, Roger Maris and Mickey Mantle hit game-winning home runs for him in the ninth inning.

When he was a youth in Puerto Rico, he dropped out of school in the eighth grade, but he encouraged his four children, three sons and a daughter, to get an education. He constantly reminded them of his difficult early days, milking cows, cutting sugarcane, and feeding chickens. His daughter and one son are doctors. A second son is an architect, and a third is a sergeant in the army. Luis is now married to his second wife, Judy.

When Fidel Castro came into power in Cuba in 1960, I got the biggest break of my life. I was pitching with the Havana Sugar Kings in the International League that year, and when Castro took over the government, the franchise was switched to Jersey City. But I spent only two weeks in Jersey City. The Yankees called me up to the big club on July 20, 1960.

At the time the Yankees were having trouble with their bullpen, and I was having outstanding success against Richmond, their franchise in the International League. Steve Souchock, our manager and a former Yankee first baseman and outfielder, recommended me to the Yankees because I was doing so well. One weekend we had a big series in Jersey City, and a lot of Yankees scouts were there to see me. I pitched in all three games and did an outstanding job. Later I heard that a couple of scouts said to Casey, "He's too old."

Casey said, "Can he pitch?"

They said, "Yes."

"Give him a contract then."

The next day Souchock said to me, "We finally got rid of you." He helped me a lot.

Well, on July 20, 1960, the Yankees bought my contract and told me to report to the Stadium for a three-game series against the White Sox. I was a little chubby at the time, and when I reported to the gate, one of the attendants said, "Who the hell are you?"

But another guy said, "That's Luis Arroyo. We just bought him. Let him in. I'll show him to the clubhouse." When I looked around and saw Mickey Mantle and Roger Maris, I got very excited. Then Casey came out and called me into his office. Roy Hamey, the assistant to George Weiss, was there, and he said, "How much are you making?"

I said, "I was making $10,000. Do I get more now?"

He said, "No, no more money."

I said, "Just give me the contract to sign."

I was thirty-three when I joined the Yankees. What took me so long to get to the majors? Well, I had been up briefly with three other teams, but I was always one pitch short. I had a fastball, eighty-seven or eighty-eight miles an hour, a curve that wasn't too good and I couldn't throw for a strike, and that was it. The fastball was my out pitch. In the beginning it was effective, but when the hitters realized I didn't have anything else, they waited for it, and Luis Arroyo was back in the minors.

It took me seven years to get to the big leagues, but once I got there, I won my first nine decisions. Harvey Haddix was the number one pitcher on the club, and I was number two at the time. But after the All-Star Game I had trouble with my mechanics and relied on my fastball too much. The hitters sat on my fastball, I won only two of my last ten games, and before spring training broke in 1956 I was sent down to Omaha. In a month I was recalled, and two days later I was traded to Pittsburgh, where I was 3-3 in 1956 and 3-11 in 1957. Between that time and the time I came to the Yankees, I bounced around with the Hollywood Stars, Columbus, the Cincinnati Reds, and the Havana Sugar Kings. Well, one day in the minor leagues I was warming up, and my manager, Al Hollingsworth, came up to me and said, "Louie, I think I can help you." He told me I needed another pitch, which I knew, and suggested the screwball. He gave me a few tips, I took it from there, and that made the difference.

When I joined the Yankees, we were six and one-half games out of first place. We lost that first game to the White Sox. The next day Casey used me in both games of a doubleheader, and I saved both games. Well, we went on to win eighteen of the next twenty-two games, I finished the season with five wins, one loss, and seven saves, and we won the pennant.

I didn't get to know Casey too well. I was only with him two months. But he treated me well. He couldn't pronounce my name so he called me "Yo-Yo." That wasn't unusual for him. He couldn't pronounce Johnny Blanchard's name, either. He called him "Butcher Boy." That first day, when I signed my contract with the Yankees, he said, "Are you ready to pitch?"

I said, "Yeah."

"Well, stay on the bench with Eddie Lopat. He'll go over things with you." That's what I did. Lopat was the pitching coach. Casey delegated authority to his coaches and kept his distance from the players.

He surprised me in that year's World Series, though. He used me in only one game, the fifth, for two-thirds of an inning. The writers asked me, "Do you have a sore arm?"

"No."

"Why aren't you pitching then?"

"Ask the Old Man."

There were a couple of times I thought I could have helped the Yankees in that series. One of them was in the seventh game. Jim Coates and I were warming up. Casey went with Coates and he gave up an infield single to Roberto Clemente and a three-run homer to Hal Smith. I thought I could have got Smith, but he didn't use me. When we were on the plane flying back from Pittsburgh, Casey was walking up and down. We both had had a few drinks. Casey said to me, "I don't think I'll be here next year, but I appreciate what you've done for me. Here's my phone number. If there's anything I can do, get in touch with me." He didn't say he was going to quit or he thought he would be fired. He just thanked me and offered to help me, if I needed a contact. I thought that was nice.

I was good in 1960, but 1961 was my real big year. I wish I could tell you what made the difference. In spring training Jesse Gonder hit me with a line drive and broke my arm. It was a chipped bone. They put my arm in a cast for three weeks. I got only ten days of spring training, so I was worried about my career. But it turned out that I had a super year. I was with the right team, in the right place, at the right time. Everything went right for me. For example, one day we were playing Detroit, and Ralph Houk brought me in with the bases loaded in a tie game. Al Kaline hit a grand slam, and the Tigers scored four more runs before Houk came out and said, "Get the hell out of here and get a shower." While I was in the clubhouse, we came back and scored nine runs, and I ended up the winning pitcher. In the World Series I came into Game Three in the bottom of the seventh, and we were losing, 2-1. But Blanchard hit a pinch-hit home run in the eighth, and Maris hit one in the ninth, and I ended up the winner, 3-2. In the ninth, by the way, Leo Cardenas hit a double off the scoreboard, and Gordy Coleman knocked a shot right back at me, but I knocked it down and threw him out at first to end the game.

I saved a lot of Whitey Ford's twenty-five wins that year. But let me tell you this: I've been in the game for forty years, and I've never seen another left-handed pitcher who was as good as Whitey for seven innings. And he was a total team player. If he got tired and no longer had his good stuff, he would tell the manager. He knew we had good men out in the bullpen. I was proud to pick up a save for him. Overall, I was 15-5 out of the bullpen with twenty-nine saves. The wins and saves were the league high for relief pitchers. I also picked up that win in the World Series. As I said, it was my premier year.

After the Series we were traveling back to New York by train, and everyone was having a few drinks. Hamey called to me, "Heh, little man, what are you doing tomorrow?"

I said, "I'm staying in New York for three or four days, and then I'm heading back to Puerto Rico."

"Stop off at my office at ten o'clock."

When I got there, it was obvious that he had a hangover. Houk was there, too. I had pitched for Ralph before, for a couple of years in San Juan. Hamey said, "What are you doing this winter?"

"I'm going to play winter ball."

"No, you're not. No winter ball this year."

"I've done this all my life. I'll hurt my arm if I don't. If I do, I can pitch three or four more years in the majors."

"Do you need money? You're making $15,000."

"Yes, but I can make an additional $9,000 for three months of winter ball," I said. He took out his checkbook and wrote a check for $9,000. I pushed it back and he got pissed. "I know my arm. It will hurt my arm if I don't pitch." But he wouldn't take no for an answer. So I took the check and said, "Heh, Roy, this isn't my raise for next year."

"We'll talk about it later."

"No, Roy, we'll talk about it now."

So anyway I took the $9,000 and a few dollars I had saved, and I had a few drinks, and I went to a few parties, and I put on fifteen pounds, and the next spring my arm was dead. Then I hurt it on Opening Day in Detroit. It was raining but they had forty thousand fans in the stands, and they didn't want to lose the gate. So they played the game. Whitey was pitching, but in the seventh inning the phone rang, and they said, "Arroyo, get up." I went in and saved the game. In the ninth inning the Tigers had first and second with one out and Kaline at the plate. I snapped a good screwball, and Kaline hit into a double play. When I let the pitch go, I heard something snap in my arm, but everyone was excited with the win, so I forgot about it until I woke up at one o'clock in the morning and couldn't move my arm. I called Gus Mauch, the trainer, and he told Houk, and the next morning they had me on a plane to New York to see Dr. Sidney Gaynor at Lenox Hill Hospital. He prescribed rest, and I was put on the disabled list for the worst month-and-a-half of my life. After that my arm felt pretty good, and I got into twenty-seven games, but I won only one game and saved seven.

After the season they said that I had chips in my arm, and that I might end up crippled for the rest of my life if I didn't have an operation, so I said,

"Okay." I missed virtually the whole season. They wanted to offer me a contract for 1964, but I said, "No," I would go to spring training without a contract. After two weeks of frustration, I said, "We're wasting our time," and I hung up my spikes. Since that time I've been scouting in Puerto Rico, and I feel real good.

My years with the Yankees were the best four years of my life. I've been in the game for forty years, and I've never seen another team as good as the 1961 Yankees. They didn't have one hole on the club. We had Skowron, Bobby, Tony, and Clete in the infield. Roger, Mickey, Yogi, Blanchard, and Lopez in the outfield. Ellie behind the plate. And a good pitching staff. Don't forget the defense. It was superb. Clete would say, "Let them hit it to me." He saved so many games for me. On that club a lot of poor pitchers, including Luis Arroyo, became good pitchers because of the offensive and defensive support we received.

I remember one game against the Orioles in 1961. We had returned to the Stadium after a series in Detroit, and we were a game and a half ahead. Well, I went through my mail at the Stadium, and one of the letters got my attention. It said, "If you walk into the bullpen tonight, you'll be shot."

I was a little worried, so I went to see Houk. He said, "Don't worry about it. Roger and Mickey get threatening mail all the time."

But I was still worried. There were FBI men and security people all over the place. In the first game of the series, Houk called me in to get the final out in the ninth inning. When I got to the mound, he said, "I'm getting out of here. I don't want to get shot. If *you* don't want to get killed, you better get this batter quick." I let the batter hit the first pitch to Clete at third, but I didn't wait around for any post-game congratulations. I bolted from the mound before the out was made at first base. The only guy in the clubhouse before me was Ralph.

Andy Carey

Andy Carey, who was born in Oakland, California, on October 18, 1931, is presently living in Anaheim. He's not currently married, but he has three children, two daughters and a son, from a previous marriage.

Carey batted .260 with sixty-four home runs in eleven major-league seasons. His best overall year was 1954, when he batted .302 with eight home runs and sixty-five RBIs.

Andy has been an entrepreneur since he got out of baseball in 1963. For fifteen years he was a stockbroker. For the past fifteen years he has had his own insurance company in Anaheim. In addition, he owned a commercial fishing company in Micronesia and a boy's ranch in Wyoming.

In recent years he's become involved in "Legends of Sport," which is sponsored by Fantasy Camps International. He did one with Whitey Ford and Mickey Mantle in Ft. Lauderdale, Florida. He did one on his own last year in Orlando, Florida. It ran from November 13-18. The name of the camp is "Boardwalk Baseball." He's presently looking at an additional site in Phoenix, Arizona, for the 1990 season.

Andy may soon be wearing a third hat. He is disgusted with the way that baseball is treating its old-time players, especially in respect to their pensions. "It's not right," he says. "There are too many inequities. Something's got to be done." When we spoke in late July of 1989, he mentioned some possible courses of action.

Remember the first time Casey Stengel held a Rookie Camp? It was 1951, in Phoenix, Arizona, the same year the Yankees broke away from St. Petersburg, Florida. The idea was to bring the rookies in one week before the veterans. It also gave us a chance to work on fundamentals and to get to know each other. I thought it was a good idea, and it worked out well. The Yankees had just signed me right off the campus of St. Mary's College for $60,000. Jackie Jensen was the only player who got more from the Yankees. He got $75,000. So they kept me around to give me a good look. There were some great prospects in that camp: Bill Skowron, Mickey Mantle, Bill Renna, Gil McDougald, Clint Courtney, Jim Brideweser, and Kal Segrist. Do you think the Yankees of today would like to invite rookies like those to one of their camps?

Well, I was assigned to the Kansas City Blues under George Selkirk. I didn't get off to a good start. After two months I was batting only .240. Then one day I dropped a pop-up with the bases loaded to lose a game. The third-base coach got all over me. He said, "You drop a pop-up like that again and you won't be here." Selkirk chewed me out, too. They made me so mad that I batted .400 for the next month, and my batting average climbed over .300. That was the turning point of my career.

I was invited to the Yankees' spring training camp in 1952. Selkirk told me, "Kid, go over there and take over third base." I took him literally. I went out to my position, and I drew a line between third and shortstop. Phil Rizzuto said, "What are you doing?" I said, "I'm drawing the line. Anything on my side of the line is mine, and anything on your side of the line is yours." Rizzuto had been there for eleven years, and he couldn't believe it. It wasn't ego on my part. I had worked hard to get there. I was just sending a message to the regulars that I intended to stay.

And I did — for three weeks. I had a good spring training, batting .400, so I went north with the club. The first time I saw Yankee Stadium, I was in awe of the structure. I had heard so much about it, and it didn't disappoint me. It was magnificent: the memorabilia, the flags, the history that permeated the playing field. Remember, I was a kid just out of college. I made an error in my first game. But then I was able to put things in perspective. The Yankees had won three consecutive world championships, and they wanted me to be a part of their club. I'm proud to say that I was a part-time member of the fourth world championship and a full-time member of the fifth. I wear the World Series ring from the fifth consecutive year, the one with five stones commemorating the five years, on my left hand.

In 1953, when we won our fifth consecutive championship, I batted .321. Casey used me sparingly, but that was the way Casey handled young players, unless you were Mickey Mantle, and remember, he sent Mickey out to Kansas City for a while in his rookie year. But it was hard to break into that lineup. Look at the competition. There was Joe Collins and Johnny Mize at first base. Billy Martin and Gerry Coleman at second. I got my break with the Yankees when Billy broke his ankle. That's the way the Yankees worked in those days. They had two guys, equally good, at each position, so if one guy got hurt they had a fill-in. Phil Rizzuto and Gil McDougald at shortstop. In fact, Gil could move all over the place. He played second, short, and third while I was there. Bobby Brown and me at third. Yogi was behind the plate. Ralph Houk and Charlie Silvera, too. The outfield was the same, very competitive. And the pitching was awesome. We had a better team on our bench than the other teams had on the field. In fact, I didn't even get into the 1953 World Series because Casey went with the veterans when the money was on the line.

But 1954 was a different story. Brown retired from baseball in early July to concentrate on medicine, and the third base job went to me. I got 411 at bats, I hit .302, and had sixty-five RBIs. I felt pretty good about that. We won 103 games. I felt pretty good about that, too. But we finished in second place, eight games behind Cleveland. I didn't feel too good about that. In my eight seasons with the Yankees, that was one of only two times we didn't win the pennant. And maybe we had our best club in 1954. But the Indians were awesome that year. We went into Cleveland with two weeks to go in the season, and we lost four straight in front of eighty thousand people each game. Their pitching staff was incredible. Early Wynn, Bob Lemon, Mike Garcia, Bob Feller, Don Mossi, and Ray Narleski. Every time we played the Indians, the hitters felt lucky if they got one-half the number of hits they would get in a normal series. And Al Rosen was incredible that year. The year before he was even better. He just missed winning the Triple Crown.

In 1955 I got more at bats, but my batting average slipped to .257. I did tie for the league lead in triples with eleven. Mickey hit eleven, too. But overall I had a pretty poor year. I don't know why. Maybe it was because I was getting married. I might have been nervous. After the season the Yankees represented our government in the Orient. Three of us were on our honeymoon at the time: Johnny Kucks, Eddie Robinson, and me. It was a fabulous six weeks.

I got only two at bats in the 1955 World Series, but I got nineteen in the 1956 Series. Don Larsen's perfect game, of course, was the highlight. There were three important defensive plays in the game. In the second inning Jackie Robinson ricocheted a hard one-hopper off my glove to McDougald at short, and Gil just nipped Jackie at first. In the fifth, I think, Mickey made a spectacular back-hand running catch of Gil Hodges' long drive to left-center field. Then in the eighth Gil hit a low line drive to my left. It was a half-check swing but it could have been trouble. I caught it just off the grass but I threw it to first anyway. I didn't want to take any chances.

There's an interesting story about Larsen's perfect game. My mom and dad were close to Don. They wanted him to do well in the Series. Before the fifth game they went down to Times Square in New York and had two newspapers printed. Don's nickname was "Gooney Bird," so one proclaimed, "Gooney Bird Picked to Start Fifth Game." The other said, "Gooney Bird Pitches No-Hitter." They tacked the papers to Don's hotel door, then took them down. They thought the headlines might turn out to be a jinx. But actually they were an augury. I still have one of them. I figured offensively in that game, too. Mickey homered for the first run. I singled, Larsen bunted, and Hank Bauer singled for the second.

From 1955-57 I struggled at the bat. For some reason I wasn't concentrating as well at the plate. Maybe it was because I was married. But in each of those seasons I got one RBI for every two hits I got. Selkirk used to tell me, "You've got to produce when the ducks are on the pond." I never forgot that. We had good power hitters on the club, but everybody produced in the clutch. We were drilled to score the runner in whatever way it took. Each individual player on those clubs could carry the team for one or two weeks. We had great offense, we had great defense, and we had great balance. And someone would always rise to the occasion and pick up the team.

In 1958 I got my act together and batted .286. Also I had twelve home runs, my high with the Yankees, and forty-five RBIs in only 315 at bats. I got a big hit off Lew Burdette in Game Seven, too. He defeated us three times in the 1957 World Series. He had a great sinkerball that really moved. That and a spitter, too. He would deny it but it was so. Anyway, in 1958 we hit him pretty hard. But he still started Game Seven. It was 2-2 in the eighth when we finally got to him. I led off with a single, and Bill Skowron hit a three-run homer. Ellie Howard got a big run-scoring hit, too, and we went on to win the game and the championship, 6-2. That was the Series when they had us down, three games to two, but they popped off after the fourth game, we got irritated, and we came back to win three straight. It was only the second time that that had been done.

After the 1958 World Series I came down with mononucleosis, and it affected me throughout the 1959 season. I had no opportunity to win the third-base job. I got into only forty-one games and got only 101 at bats. I was so out of it I was put on the disabled list for a couple of months. I would work out for half an hour and feel exhausted. I couldn't take batting or fielding practice. Before each game I had to take 1000 cc's of vitamin B-12.

Well, after four games in 1960, I was traded to the A's for Bob Cerv. I felt the trade coming. We had struggled in 1959, finishing in third place, just four games over .500, and I wasn't contributing. The year before I got to Kansas City, the fence in left field had been forty feet shorter. Charlie Finley had it moved back before the 1960 season. During my first week in Kansas City, I hit seven balls that would have been homers in the old park but were outs in the new one. Every time I ran back to the bench I would curse Finley, who was sitting behind our dugout. The old park used to be like Fenway Park. I would have paid money to play in it. Casey used to call me "Butcher Boy." I came up to the majors as a pull hitter, but late in my career they got me to go to right field more, and I ended up hitting a lot of 420-foot outs to center. Still, I ended up hitting twelve home runs, which tied my all-time high with the Yankees.

The following year, Kansas City sent me to Chicago, and I learned a lot from manager Al Lopez. I was hitting over .300 when I was healthy, but I hurt my back, then I played sparingly and I was traded to the Phillies. But I quit rather than report to Philadelphia. Finally I worked out a deal with the Dodgers that brought me back to California. We ended up losing the pennant in a playoff with the Giants. I would have given my eyeteeth to play against the Yankees in that year's World Series.

My biggest thrills were my first game at the Stadium, batting .302 in 1954, Larsen's perfect game, and my associations with great guys, great players, and Hall of Famers. Also, I had a five-for-five game at Fenway Park one day. I hit two home runs, a double, and two singles. And, do you know, I didn't know whether I would be in the starting lineup the following night. That's the way Casey was. But the bottom line was he had great talent, had great instincts, knew the parks, and knew the teams.

George Weiss was my favorite member of management, though. He liked me, kept me there, and treated me well. If I had any problems, he would take care of them. Every year I held out. I liked to negotiate. After I hit .321 in my second year, I held out for three weeks. Finally he would take over the negotiations from a subordinate. "What do you want, Andy?" he would say. I would tell him and I would get it.

That's one of the things that bothers me about today's game: the way they treat the old-time players. They are not being compensated in proportion to their contributions to the sport. There's a pension fund of $300 million dollars out there. If they took just the interest on that annually, they would have $30 million dollars a year to help out the old-timers and their widows.

Recently I read that Carl Hubbell was living on social security when he died. That's a great injustice. There are two thousand retired players out there, and quite a few of them are down on their luck. The modern-day player will retire with a pension of $90,000 a year. Warren Spahn gets less than a thousand dollars a month. That's just not right.

Ryne Duren

If you take a cursory look at Ryne Duren's lifetime statistics, you won't be particularly impressed. For example, he won just twenty-seven games and lost forty-four for a meager winning percentage of .380. In relief he won just twenty-two contests and lost thirty-five for a scant winning percentage of .386. He completed just two of thirty-two starts, pitched only one shutout, and batted a paltry .061.

But Duren's subsurface statistics are something else. In his glory years with the Yankees, 1958 and 1959, he posted back-to-back ERAs of 2.02 and 1.88. In his two World Series with the Yankees, 1958 and 1960, he registered ERAs of 1.93 and 2.25—a World Series ERA average of 2.03. Overall, he registered fifty-seven saves out of the bullpen, which evens the number of win-loss decisions he compiled in relief.

Duren's forte was coming out of the bullpen to get a strikeout when it was needed. In his career he recorded 9.1 strikeouts for every nine innings he pitched. And he was not as wild as batters thought. But hitters were intimidated by him. They feared three things: his spotty control, his poor eyesight, and his penchant for nursing a hangover. Duren threw his fastball around one hundred miles an hour, so just one of those attributes was cause for concern; all three combined were downright life-threatening.

Ryne Duren's reputation off the field was not good. But the former roommate of Andy Carey, Jim Coates, and Ralph Terry has gotten his life together in his post-baseball career. In Milwaukee, he studied growth and developmental problems with children. Then he became concerned about the drinking problems of children and their families. Ultimately he trained as a counselor and opened up a rehabilitation hospital. Since 1980 he has conducted workshops, given lectures, and been the keynote speaker for many meetings.

Ryne has one son and one grandchild from his first marriage, three step-children and six step-grandchildren from his second marriage. He and his wife of fifteen years, Diane, live in Middleton, a suburb of Madison, Wisconsin.

I spoke with him late on a hot, sultry Tuesday night in July, and found him to be just as his 1963 Phillie manager, Gene Mauch, described him — a "winner!"

I came up with Baltimore in 1954 but I broke my hand and got into only one game. I didn't go home, though. I just hung around for three weeks and drank with Don Larsen.

In 1957 I was back to stay. With Kansas City. I was 0-3 with them but I was an impressive 0-3. In my first start, against the Yankees, I lost 2-1. I drag-bunted our only run home. That day I had an intimidating fastball. Bauer and McDougald later told me that they went to Stengel and said, "Get him over here so we don't have to face him anymore."

I felt pretty good about my trade to the Yankees in 1957. One moment I was on top of the world. I was going to the first-place Yankees. The next moment I was back in the dumps. I learned the Yankees were sending me to Denver. It was a big letdown. But I went out to Denver and pitched up a storm and thought I would be brought up for the pennant drive. It looked that way for a while. But the Yankees decided to go with a veteran. They bought Sal Maglie.

The Yankees brought me up to the parent club in 1958. The first game I saved for them was amazing. Ralph Houk and I came out to the park early that day. I said to him, "Hit some balls back at me. I'm weak at fielding comebackers." He hit a lot of balls to me. Well, I came into the game with first and third and one out. The tying run was at third and Jim Marshall of the Orioles was at the plate. He hit a bullet back to me but I fielded it flawlessly and whirled and threw to Kubek, who pivoted and tossed the ball to first for the game-ending double play. So my first save with the Yankees was with my glove, not my arm.

I had a big year in 1958. I was 6-4 with a 2.02 ERA, and I led the American League with twenty saves. I had a lot of movement on my fastball, and the hitters swung at a lot of bad pitches. I was always grateful that they did, though my control got better in 1959. Until that time my control was marginal. In 1958 I was truly scared, because bases on balls are a defeating type of thing. If the batters had taken every pitch, they could have beaten me. But it didn't happen. Most of my strikeouts came on fastballs, and most of my fastballs were out of the strike zone. If they would swing at the first high one, I would throw the second one a little bit higher. And so on with the third.

They never clocked me. We didn't have speed guns in those days. NBC wanted to clock me and Dick Farrell with some electronic device, but the Yankees wouldn't go for it. Frank Scott, the agent, went to the Yankees and said, "Would it be all right if he does it after a game, when he's already warmed up."

The Yankees said, "Yes."

But NBC said, "No good. We have to promote the match."

The winner was supposed to get $1,000. Casey knew I was upset so he tried to pacify me. "I'll give you the $1,000," he said. But he never did. Anyway, I don't know how fast I threw, but I do know that Mantle told me I was the fastest he ever saw. And Tony Kubek said I threw harder than Nolan Ryan.

I used to throw my first pitch up on the screen. Accidentally at first, deliberately thereafter. As I said, the first time was an accident. I rushed my warm-ups. Turley had made the ground crew flatten the mound. The first pitch I threw, instead of dropping down, my knee came up into my chest. The pitch went high up on the screen. The fans got a kick out of it. The writers, too. Frankie Crosetti was a coach with us. He was always looking for an edge. He said to me, "Throw one every once in a while. You'll shake the hitters up a little." So I did, and I found out that it was a great intimidating force. Eventually I went one step further. You know, we used to have our bullpen in deep right field, and the visitors' dugout was on the third-base side. When I was really warmed up, I would hurl one out of the bullpen into the third-base dugout. That got their attention, I'll guarantee you that.

I had some impressive statistics in my three full years with the Yankees. In 1958 I pitched seventy-five innings and struck out eighty-seven batters. In 1959 it was seventy-six and ninety-six. And in 1960 it was forty-nine and sixty-seven. My ERA in 1959 was 1.88. In fact, on the day we were mathematically eliminated from the pennant race, it was 0.69. At one point I had gone more than thirty consecutive innings without allowing a run. There was only one problem with that. The Yankees went more than forty consecutive innings without *scoring* one. That Christmas Eve George Weiss sent me a contract calling for a $4,000 cut. Talk about Scrooge. Well, I went to spring training, but when we didn't resolve our differences, I decided to go home. There was no use hanging around. But Til Ferdenzi, the writer, urged me to stay.

I said, "I'm being fair. They're not. I'll tell you what, though; you get the writers together and poll them to see what I'm worth. Whatever you decide, I'll settle for."

Well, they did what I asked, and they printed their figure. It was closer to my figure than George's. I had gotten $16,000 in 1958. He wanted to cut me to $12,000. I ended up getting $17,500. It was all a ploy on his part. He didn't want to give me a raise. He wanted to sign me for the same figure I had gotten in 1958, but he ended up giving me a token raise. So I got the last laugh that time. I used to joke, "Weiss didn't sign me. The writers did."

Now Casey was something else. He was fabulous with me. We were both good for each other. He talked to me a lot. One day he said to me, "You're having dinner with me tonight." He built me up all evening. Another day in Washington, he used me in the first game of a doubleheader. Before the second game I was standing in the dugout. My glove and jacket were on the floor. He said, "Take them and walk down to the bullpen. You're getting to be a star. I won't use you in the second game. But I want you to get some exposure. There are some people here who didn't see you in the first game. I want them to see what a star looks like." Another day he called me into his office and said, "Just because I don't say anything to you about your performance doesn't mean that I don't appreciate you. You're doing a hell of a job." That would make me want to pitch for the man. He used to say, "When Duren comes into the game, everyone stops eating their peanuts." I thought that was a good line.

One year I wasn't doing too well.

The reporters said to Casey, "What's wrong with Duren?"

Casey said, "He's seeing too good."

"Well, what are you going to do about him?"

"I'm going to give him a dirty hanky to fuzz up those coke bottle glasses of his." That was another good line.

I had some physical problems with the Yankees. At the end of the 1959 season, I broke my arm. It was in a cast for eight weeks. In 1960 I didn't have the proper strength in it. By the end of 1960, the strength came back and it was strong in 1961. But by that time I was encountering other problems, and Houk decided to get me out of town. I was boozing quite a bit and my body was beginning to deteriorate. I've talked freely about my alcoholism in other forums. Alcoholism is a progressive disease and it was beginning to take its toll on me.

That's why the Yankees got rid of me in 1961. My drinking incidents — some reported, some not — were a source of embarrassment. Houk never cared for me, either. I think he saw some of himself in my Jekyl and

Hyde personality. His behavior was unique, to say the least, too. He did some crazy things. Maybe he just didn't want to be bailing me out anymore. Problem guys, when they're doing well, are okay. But when they're not, they're trouble.

Houk and I had had an incident in 1958 when we clinched the pennant. We were riding the Wabash Cannonball from Kansas City to Detroit, and I got smashed. Somehow I got into some physical contact with Ralph. I was drunk. I don't remember anything. But it wasn't anything that clubs hadn't seen a hundred times before, and most of the writers sat on the story. But Leonard Schechter, the guy who collaborated with Jim Bouton on *Ball Four,* blew it way out of proportion. He said that I provoked Houk, he pushed me, and we got into a big fight. When we got into different stations, George Weiss had detectives waiting for us. Bad ones. They ended up following the writers instead of the nightowls. In fact, a few of them followed Richardson, Kubek, and Shantz into a YMCA, where they played pool and drank malted milks. The other writers were accused of hiding printable material. They got into trouble with their editors. From that point on Schechter couldn't get a story in our clubhouse.

So I was glad to get out of New York. Luis Arroyo was pitching well. The Yankees were in good shape. And I needed a change of scenery.

But I left some good memories behind. I had some big days in New York. Especially in the 1958 World Series. I got off to a rocky start in Game One when I relieved Whitey in the eighth inning and lost to Warren Spahn of the Braves in ten innings, 4-3. There were runners on base when Billy Bruton hit a ball up the alley. There was no play on it. In Game Three we were still looking for our first win. Larsen pitched seven shutout innings, and I pitched two scoreless innings of relief to get the save in a 4-0 win. Hank Bauer drove home all of our runs, two with a home run and two with a single. In Game Six we had our backs to the wall again. We were down three games to two. I relieved Ditmar, who had relieved Ford, and pitched four and two-thirds innings of one-run ball. I had two outs in the ninth but I couldn't get the last out. Actually I had Johnny Logan struck out and should have been in the clubhouse, but I didn't get the call. Turley came in and got the last out of a 4-3 victory on a grounder to McDougald at second.

That was my day to shine. Jack Lescoulie of the "Today Show" was in the clubhouse, and he arranged a big interview with me. It went on forever. I got up the next morning and turned the television on, but I was extremely disappointed. They showed hardly anything. I complained to him at the park that afternoon. His defense was, "In all of the footage Yogi was running around bare-ass-and-balls naked. We had to cut most of it."

But we won the seventh and deciding game that afternoon, and that took the sting out of my disappointment. Turley pitched six and two-thirds innings of relief for the win. Skowron got the big hit, a three-run homer.

I pitched twice in the 1960 World Series. I pitched fairly well in two losses to the Pirates. I pitched two innings of scoreless ball in Game One and two innings of one-run ball in Game Five. The question, though, is why didn't I pitch in Game Seven, which we lost on Bill Mazeroski's sudden-death home run, 10-9. I should have been in that game. Everyone else was. In 1972 I was sitting with Casey at an Old Timers' Day game in Los Angeles, and he congratulated me on conquering my addiction and praised me for working so well with problem kids. He said, "You know the biggest mistake I made in the 1960 World Series? I brought that right-hander in in the eighth inning." He meant Jim Coates. He pitched to Hal Smith, who hit a three-run homer. "I should have brought you in instead." Actually the mistake he made was bringing Coates in, in a bunt situation, when he had the best fielding pitcher in baseball on the mound: Bobby Shantz. I think Bob Skinner was the batter. Shantz won Gold Glove awards from 1957-64.

Hindsight, of course, is twenty-twenty. But based on his overall record, Ford should have pitched the opening game of the 1960 World Series. Then he would have had three starts. Instead he got two, both of them shutouts. He was the best pitcher I ever saw in a big-game situation. I remember when, in 1960, Baltimore came to town for a four-game series. They were right in the race. Well, the day before the series, Whitey came down to the bullpen and threw hard. We wondered why. Then one of the guys said, "He thinks he's going to pitch the first and fourth games." That wasn't unusual for Whitey in big-game situations. And that's exactly what he did. He won both games and knocked the Orioles out of the race. He was smart. A team player, too. If he knew he had a guy like me or Arroyo out in the bullpen, and he was tiring, he'd get himself out of the game. Whitey didn't pitch for pride. He pitched for pennants. The intangibles made him great. He didn't have the greatest curve or fastball. He had the greatest control, though. And he could outthink the hitters. Quite often sluggers would look for his curve, and he would throw three fastballs right down the center of the plate.

My biggest thrill was a game I pitched against the Yankees after they traded me to the Angels in 1961. I struck out twelve batters and beat them, 5-4. The Angels started me fourteen times that year. That time I went up to the plate against Turley with the bases loaded and singled up the middle. Then Albie Pearson hit a grand slam. That was all the runs we scored, and it might have been the end of the line for Bob. Houk told me later, "That game finished Turley as a pitcher."

My arm was still strong, but my drinking problem was getting worse. I was still striking out a man an inning, but in my last five years I changed uniform five times. After the 1965 season I knew that I had to get on top of the alcohol, and I did. I took an active role in my personal rehabilitation. I think baseball should take a more active role, too. We need to put a different perspective to our kids.

I've seen so many of my former teammates die of alcoholism. So I've gone to the Commissioner's office twice and the Players' Association once, requesting permission to talk to the players in spring training. I've been rejected. Worse, I've been blackballed. I haven't been invited to an Old Timers' Day game in three or four years. I qualified for two this year but wasn't invited.

In Stoughton, Wisconsin, when I announced that I was an alcoholic, they wanted to run me out of town. Recently about fifteen guys from Stoughton came to me and said, "We don't drink anymore. You woke us up." These people once thought I disgraced them. Now they know that I helped them. Maybe baseball thinks I disgraced it. But I can help it now. If they let me.

Norm Siebern

When Norm Siebern was traded to Kansas City after the 1959 season, he left New York along with Marv Throneberry and a couple of institutions: Hank Bauer and Don Larsen. Of course, the Yankees acquired an institution in that trade, too: Roger Maris.

The Yankees went on to win five consecutive pennants, Siebern to have five prime years. He averaged eighteen home runs a season during that period. In 1962 he had his best major-league season when he batted .308, hit twenty-five home runs, and drove home 117 runs. It's easy to generalize and say that Siebern's numbers in New York would have been even better, with that inviting "short porch" in right field. But Norm might not have gotten the at bats in New York that he did in Kansas City. Roger Maris and Mickey Mantle were fixtures in the outfield. Managers Casey Stengel and Ralph Houk had a lot of skilled players on the bench, and they rotated them in left field. Hector Lopez is a prime example. He was Norm Siebern in reverse. He came to the Yankees from the Athletics in 1959, but never put up the big numbers on the board that he did in Kansas City. Siebern averaged 559 at bats in his four years with the Athletics. In Norm's case, things probably worked out for the best.

When I first called Norm in July of 1989, he told me to give him a call around 5:00 P.M., when he usually closed down his office. I called at the prescribed time, but his line was busy for an hour. "Business is good," he said, when I finally got through. It has been good since he set up his property and casualty insurance agency in Independence, Missouri, twenty years ago. Before that he had scouted for one year for the 1969 Atlanta Braves and for five years, part-time, for the Kansas City Royals. In 1981 he moved his agency, Southwest Florida Insurers, to Naples, Florida.

He and his wife of thirty-two years, Elizabeth, have three daughters and live in Naples.

It was a great feeling — a big thrill — to attend my first spring training with the Yankees in 1956. The team had won five consecutive world championships from 1949 to 1953 and six pennants in the previous seven years.

The Yankees were looking for a steady left fielder in 1956. That's why Casey Stengel gave me the shot. They hadn't had one since Gene Woodling left. They tried Bob Cerv out there but it didn't work out. They also had Irv Noren out there. The other Yankee players told me that he was a solid defensive player, but he hurt his knees and ended up having surgery on both of them. So Casey in 1956 thought that I might be the Yankees' future left fielder. He started me in the first thirteen games of spring training. The thirteenth was unlucky. I ran into the wall and cracked my kneecap. They sent me back to Denver and I didn't return until June 15. But if the Yankees hadn't traded me to Kansas City after the 1959 season, I just might have been the starting left fielder from 1960 to 1965, when they won five consecutive pennants. They tried everyone out there during that period. Yogi Berra, Elston Howard, Hector Lopez, Johnny Blanchard, and Cerv again. I often think of what might have happened if I had stayed around during that period.

Well, as I said, I got to come back up to the big club on June 15. Cleveland was a game or two behind at the time, but we went into their stadium and swept them in a three-game series, and we went on to win the pennant by nine games. I batted .204, hit four home runs, and drove home twenty-one runs in limited action. But I got to play on a pennant winner and a world title club. I even got one at bat in the World Series. It was a special thrill just to be on that bench, on that team, and seeing Johnny Kucks lock up the seventh game with a three-hitter, 9-0. Don Larsen's perfect game was a special thrill, too. We didn't even think about the possibility of one until the middle of the game, and there were no statements by any of the players in between innings. Don either sat on the bench or stood in the runway. He was very composed. Once I looked up and saw a big grin on his face. He knew what was going on, and he was enjoying it, too.

I remember my World Series at bat. I pinch hit against Don Bessent of the Dodgers, and I hit the ball well, a line drive to left center. Billy Hunter told me afterwards that just before Bessent threw the pitch, manager Walt Alston moved Duke Snider towards left center. It was an easy play for Duke, but I was happy that I had hit the ball well.

I was fighting that cracked kneecap all season. After the year was over, I had surgery on it, and Dr. Sidney Gaynor removed the crack. By spring training in 1957, I had pretty much recuperated, but they sent me to Denver, and I played the entire season for manager Ralph Houk. In 1958 I returned to the Yankees, and I batted a flat .300, with fourteen homers and fifty-five RBIs. It was a big year for me. Only two other Yankees hit .300. Elston Howard hit .314 and Mickey Mantle batted .304. Also, only two other players hit more home runs than I did. Mickey hit forty-two and Yogi hit twenty-two. That was the year I proved to myself that I could play in the major leagues, and when we won the World Series in seven games, I was over the hurdle.

I didn't have a good World Series. I went only one-for-eight with two runs batted in, and I hurt my chances to play more when I had a bad time in left field in Game Four. Even today, thirty-three years later, I don't like to talk about it too much. I lost two balls in the sun and Warren Spahn beat Whitey Ford, 3-0. Whitey should have had a shutout at the end of nine innings. It should have been nothing-nothing going into extra innings. After the game I said to the writers, "Report it as you saw it." I was reluctant to blame the sun field. I felt extremely bad for Whitey, because he had pitched a great game, and I felt extremely bad for the team, because I had put us in a big hole. We were down three games to one, and we had to win three straight to win the World Series. Only one team had ever come back from that deficit before. But the redeeming factor was that we came back to win, and we beat a great Milwaukee Brave club in doing so.

It was a great feeling to be there and to participate on that world championship club. Just like in 1956 — but this time I felt more a part of the team. The Yankees won nine pennants in ten years. No one else has done it. And I was part of it.

The following year was a bad one by Yankee standards. Anytime they didn't win in those days, you knew they were going to make changes. We finished only four games over five hundred, in third place. No one really had a good year. My batting average dropped to .271, but my home runs and runs batted in stayed about the same. But I heard that they were going to make changes, and I knew I was dispensable. I thought that I might be going somewhere.

On December 11, 1959, they traded Hank Bauer, Don Larsen, Marv Throneberry, and me for Roger Maris, Joe DeMaestri, and Kent Hadley. I was traded to Kansas City. I was actually happy with the trade because I was a Missouri native and had gone to college at Southwest Missouri State. Jerry Lumpe and I had played on two national title basketball teams there. I got the chance to play every day with Kansas City. With the Yankees I was strictly a platoon player.

I had some good years in Kansas City, especially in 1961 and 1962. In 1961 I batted .296, hit eighteen home runs, and drove home ninety-eight runs. The following year, I batted .308, hit twenty-five homers, and had 117 RBIs. I was very happy at the time. That's the period when I got married, when my three daughters were born, and when we bought our first home. It was a time of stability in our lives. And the Kansas City clubs were better than their won-lost records. We had some good hitters: Dick Howser, Jerry Lumpe, Gino Cimoli, Wayne Causey, and Manny Jimenez. But I guess we gave up more runs than we scored. The first year or two with Charlie Finley was great, but then he started fighting with the city fathers, and the situation rapidly deteriorated.

Mine did, too. I was on a merry-go-round during my last five years in the majors. In 1964 I was traded to Baltimore for Jim Gentile. It was a straight-up swap for first basemen. In 1966 I was with the California Angels, platooning with Joe Adcock at first. My final two years I spent with the Giants and Red Sox, primarily pinch hitting and playing some spot first base, once in a while for Willie McCovey.

Those were lowlights. But I had a lot of highlights, too. I played with Mantle when he won the Triple Crown in 1956, I played with Brooks Robinson when he won the MVP Award in 1964, I played with Carl Yastrzemski when he won the Triple Crown in 1967, and I played with McCovey and Willie Mays in San Francisco in 1967. I thought about my luck yesterday when I watched on television as Yastrzemski was inducted into the Hall of Fame in Cooperstown. You know, he was a great, great player. He got 3,419 base hits and hit 452 career home runs. And he got to play in two World Series. But he never played on a winner. I played in two World Series, and I played on two winners.

Jerry Lumpe

Jerry Lumpe was born in Lincoln, Missouri, on June 2, 1933. Today he lives in Springfield, Missouri, with his wife of thirty-five years, Vivian. They have three children, two sons and a daughter.

When I called Jerry in July of 1989 for the interview, I hooked into two coincidences. Jerry and Vivian had just celebrated their wedding anniversary, and that evening were celebrating the birth of their third grandchild.

Jerry, like Norm Siebern, was a standout athlete at Southwest Missouri State College. Both of them starred in basketball and baseball. Recently, Jerry was inducted into the Springfield (Missouri) Hall of Fame. His best friend, Siebern, was there to speak at the induction ceremony. So was Whitey Herzog, another Missouri man.

When Jerry and Norm were traded by the Yankees to the Athletics, they were both sorry to leave the Yankee organization and the Yankee players. They had spent some happy years in New York. But unlike Thomas Wolfe, they found they could go home again. They were returning to their native Missouri, and they were going to a team that would give them an opportunity to play. Jerry, like Norm, made the most of it. He had four solid seasons with the Athletics. The best was in 1962 when he batted .301, hit ten home runs, and drove home eighty-three runs.

In 1971 Jerry served as Dick Williams' first-base coach with the Oakland A's. Irv Noren, another old Yankee, was the third-base coach. "I enjoyed the field part, but not the off-time," Jerry says, "so I decided to get out. But I get to St. Louis a few times a year, and every time I do I see Whitey, so I stay in touch with the game."

Jerry was in the banking and insurance business, and, although semi-retired, is still pursuing both today.

I came up to the Yankees in 1956, as a shortstop. The year before, I had played shortstop at Birmingham, and I had a good year. In spring training I didn't think I'd get a chance to play. Gil McDougald was going to be the shortstop, and he was solid. But Gil got hurt, and the last two weeks of spring training I got a chance to play, and I played well. I played every inning of every game for the rest of spring training, and I opened the season at shortstop in Washington. Remember, Phil Rizzuto was still with the club. It was the first season since 1941, excepting the war years, that Phil didn't start. I was his heir apparent at the time, and I was in a state of shock. I was only twenty-two. But eventually I didn't play well in the field, and they sent me back to Richmond. I came back after September 1 and stayed in the majors for the next eleven years.

In 1957 I played sparingly. I got into forty games and had 103 at bats, and I batted .340. There were so many great infielders there, though, I didn't know what to do. I came back from Richmond as a third baseman, but I played some games at shortstop, too. Basically I platooned with Andy Carey at third. Yes, I felt good about hitting .340, and I felt great about playing in the World Series. I hit .286 in six games. Two of the hits were pinch-hits. That was one off the all-time record. One was off Lew Burdette, the other off Warren Spahn. I felt good about that, too.

I remember the one off Spahn best. Casey wouldn't start me in that game, because it was lefty against lefty. But before I came in to pinch hit, he put a lefty up to hit for Kubek, who was a lefty himself. I was in the bullpen at the time. The next hitter was the pitcher. Suddenly the phone in the bullpen rang. They wanted me to pinch hit for the pitcher. I ran in from the bullpen and I was very nervous. When I got to the bat rack, I had trouble picking up a bat. Well, Spahn threw two strikes to me, and then I lined a single to center. When I came back to the dugout after the inning, Casey yelled to me, "Go to shortstop for the rest of the game." I had played there only six games all year. How do you figure that? But, can you believe, that's my most memorable moment as a Yankee, that base hit and playing shortstop the rest of the game.

In 1958 I got more at bats (232), but my average dipped to .254. I remember that I hit three homers. One of them won a game for Bob Turley. But Casey wouldn't play me every day, and truthfully I didn't know whether I could play in the big leagues or not. He batted me almost everywhere: first, second, third, seventh, and eighth. But never ninth. That was something to be thankful for. When Don Larsen or Tommy Byrne pitched, one of the regulars batted ninth. They were good-hitting pitchers. In the World Series I played in six games and got two hits in twelve at bats. I was unsuccessful in three pinch-hit at bats. Nothing memorable about that. But we were down three games to one, and we came back to beat the Braves. It was my first and only World Series championship. That was memorable.

I enjoyed my time with the Yankees. They were a class act, but on May 26, 1959, I was traded with Johnny Kucks and Tommy Sturdivant for Hector Lopez and Ralph Terry. I had mixed emotions. I was sorry to leave such a great organization of great guys, but I was going home to Missouri where I'd get a chance to play every day.

You know, I ended up playing eleven hundred games at second base, one hundred and eighteen at third base, and one hundred and five at shortstop. But I never played one at second base with the Yankees. Not during the regular season anyway. In spring training Casey would occasionally put me at second. The first time I was there, Ryne Duren was on the mound, and he got a comebacker. You know what a heavy ball he threw. Well, he threw it to me and almost carried me out to center field with the throw. Anyway, when I joined Kansas City, Harry Craft, the manager, said to me, "You're going to be my second baseman."

I replied, "Then I better learn how to play there." But second base is the position that I should have been at all along, and it took them that long to find out.

I liked my Kansas City experience. Old Municipal Park was a great place to play. George Toma kept the field in great shape. He worked Super Bowls, you know. The park was suited for my hitting, too. I was a line drive hitter, from right center to left center. I didn't pull the ball. I probably should have, but I never ran into the right batting coach. My swing was back up the middle. I was a singles and doubles hitter. Talking about hits, though, I never had more than fifty-nine in my three years with the Yankees. In my four years with the A's, I never had less than one hundred and fifty-six. Shows you the difference playing every day can make. My best years were 1961 and 1962, when I batted .293 and .301. In 1962 I drove home eighty-three runs, which was twenty-four higher than my second-best total.

We had a pretty good offense in Kansas City, but we had no continuity. Charlie Finley was the owner and Frank Lane was the general manager. They were always moving personnel in and out. We had some successful managers, but they never hung around long enough to prove themselves in

Kansas City. And there were lots of things going on: mules, fire trucks, and flashy uniforms. I was the player representative with Kansas City. In September of 1961, I think it was, I was in town to sign a contract. Finley couldn't wait to show me his new gold-and-green uniforms. "Aren't these the greatest uniforms you ever saw?" he said. They were really bad, but I couldn't tell him they were the ugliest I ever saw, because I wanted to sign the right contract. Basically I really liked Charlie. He and I got along just great.

I closed out my career with the 1964-67 Tigers. I should have done better in Detroit. It was a hitter's park. But I was disappointed with myself and with the club. We both should have done better. In 1967 we lost to the Red Sox on the last day of the season. Going into the final Sunday game, four teams had a chance to win: the Red Sox, the Tigers, the White Sox, and the Twins. On the last two days of the season, we played back-to-back doubleheaders against the Angels. We split both days. Each time we won the first game and dropped the second. If we had won the second game on Sunday, we would have forced a playoff with Boston. But Detroit was a good town and a good hitter's park. In fact, over the last half of the 1967 season, my last year in the majors, I never hit the ball better in my major-league career. But Mayo Smith was the manager and he platooned like crazy. You just couldn't keep it going.

Basically I was a small-town kid from Missouri who was lucky to do what he did. I wish I had played longer in the majors. But how many people can say they played twelve years in the majors? A few thousand?

I feel special for another reason. Norm Siebern and I enjoyed uncannily similar careers. We both came from Missouri and we both signed with the Yankees right out of high school. We both played professional baseball with Yankee farm teams during the summer and college basketball with Southwest Missouri State during the winter. We were both on the second team but we both played on two small college national title winners. We both spent two years in the service before we joined the Yankees, and we both played in New York from 1956 to 1959. We both played in Kansas City from 1960 to 1963, and we both had our best years in 1961 and 1962. We both played in the major leagues for twelve years, and we both got into the insurance business when we retired. And we were and still are best friends.

Now *that's* a record.

Al Downing

Al Downing was born in Trenton, New Jersey, on June 28, 1941, and now lives in Santa Monica, California. The link between the East Coast and the West Coast was a 2-10 season with the 1970 Milwaukee Brewers.

When Downing came up to the Yankees in 1961, he was only twenty years old. Early signs indicated a phenom. In 1964, at the age of twenty-three, he struck out a league-leading 217 batters. He also won thirteen games, as he had the year before. But in his seven full years with the Yankees, he never won more than fourteen games in one year. He won the fourteen in 1967, when he hurt his arm. Of course, he had the misfortune of pitching with the Yankees when they were a dynasty in transition. The 1965-69 clubs were not five of the franchise's all-time best.

Overall, Al won 123 games, lost 107, and posted a winning percentage of .535 and an ERA of 3.22. Two times with the Yankees and three times with the Dodgers he posted ERAs beneath 3.00. Those are good stats. But quite often today Downing is remembered as the pitcher who gave up Hank Aaron's record-breaking 715th career home run. Al counters, "He didn't get to Cooperstown with any help from me. He made it all on his own." A few people might remember that Downing, in one 1967 game with the Yankees, struck out the side on nine pitches. No one has done it any better.

When I spoke with Al Downing in the summer of 1989, I understood why he was able to bounce back from a serious arm injury in 1967 to win twenty games with the 1971 Dodgers. He is very articulate and analytical. If he were interested, he would make an excellent pitching coach or manager. He remembers, as if it were yesterday, pitches that he threw twenty-five years ago, and he can tell you with precision and logic why he threw the pitch and why he would throw it again, even if it didn't work out well the first time.

Al is a lifelong bachelor and a physical fitness advocate. "It's a natural followup from my days as an athlete," he says. He gets up every morning at six o'clock and starts off the day with a workout. For ten years he was the play-by-play man on Dodger Cable TV, but the system was sold in 1987, and Al was out of a job. "Timing's important in this industry," he says. In 1983 he began hosting a radio talk show. He's on before and after Dodgers games. If it's a night game, he goes on radio two and one-half hours before the game and follows it up with an hour show.

The future? "I'd like to do play-by-play again," he says. "I thought I was good." And the talk show? "Yes, so far the subject matter has been restricted to baseball. But I'd like to branch out. I think I'm diversified enough."

Anyone who knows Al will tell you he's right.

Bill Yancey had the greatest influence on my early baseball career. Later Johnny Sain and Elston Howard had a profound influence on me. Yancey played for the Lincoln Giants and the New York Yankees in the black baseball leagues. He also played professional basketball for the Harlem Renaissance. He had a lot of insight. He taught me how to conduct myself and how to discipline myself. He was from Moorestown, New Jersey, which is right outside Philadelphia. At the time he was a scout for the Phillies, and he was following me. One night I was playing in the North-South All-Star Game at Roosevelt Stadium in Jersey City. Between the two clubs there was a lot of competition for state supremacy. The North Stars got all of the publicity, so we really wanted to beat them. In the sixth inning I got into the game and struck out the side. Then I got a base hit and stole second base. He was very impressed that a pitcher was acting like Willie Mays on the base paths. I told him, "When I'm on the mound, I'm a pitcher. When I'm on the bases, I'm a base runner." Well, I went to Muhlenberg College right out of high school, and Bill and Roy Hamey, who was the general manager of the Phillies, moved to the Yankees. That's how I signed with the Yankees.

I came up to the Yankees on July 16, 1961, and stayed for the season. I had just turned twenty. In fact, it was my first year in organized ball. That year I had been assigned to Binghampton in Class A ball. I was 9-1 at the time I was brought up. It never should have happened. It was an early sign of the coming decline of the Yankees. They didn't have any promising left-handers in their system. I was only two years out of high school. I had watched a lot of Yankee games, though they weren't my favorite team. The call-up had a tremendous effect on me. I was overwhelmed. I said to myself. "Why me? Now I'll have to go up there and win twenty games." There was a lot of pressure on me. That disappointed Bill Yancey. He knew that the Yankees had rushed me to the big leagues.

In 1961 I got only one start. It was against the Senators in Washington. I got knocked out in the second inning. The veterans must have been saying to themselves, "What's he doing on the ball club?" They were right. I was asking myself the same thing. Well, Ralph Houk came out to the mound and said, "You're just a little nervous. You'll get another start." But it never happened. I was used in mop-up situations. No one said anything about next year. It was obvious that I was over my head.

In 1962 I was assigned to Richmond in Class AAA ball. I was still two steps ahead of where I should have been. At the end of 1962 I went into Reserve Training, and I didn't get out until the middle of March. When I went to spring training, I was three weeks behind the other pitchers, so I was reassigned to Triple A. It was the best thing for me. It was also a sign of the times. In those days a promise was a promise. They told me, "If you go to Triple A, you'll be the first guy called back." They fulfilled that promise. And the extra seasoning paid off. In 1961 I had had control problems. I wasn't wild. I was just trying to do more than I was capable of. In slightly more than a half a season, I won thirteen games and lost five, with an ERA of 2.56 and 171 strikeouts. I was always a strikeout pitcher. If you believe you're going to strike hitters out, and you have the tools, you're going to succeed.

But I wasn't conceited. Even after my successful season in 1963, I didn't think that I had necessarily made it. There were too many stars on that club. They had Mantle, Maris, Howard, Kubek, Tresh, Richardson, Ford, and so many others. I said to myself, "Okay, you've had a pretty successful half season, and you've played in the World Series. Let's see what you can do next year." I didn't feel that I belonged until 1967. Today a rookie has a good first month and he acts like a seasoned veteran. It's got something to do with the way today's writers perceive the young player. The old writers were different. You had to prove yourself to them. Do you remember Bob "Hurricane" Hazle? He came up with the 1957 Braves and hit .403. He was a ball of fire. But one year later he was gone. Bill Yancey was an intelligent tutor. He taught me to keep Hazle in mind. I never felt I had it made.

We got swept in the 1963 World Series. The Dodgers had sensational pitching, and good defense, too. They made the plays behind their pitchers.

We had a good defense, but one or two plays hurt us. Take the game I pitched against Johnny Podres. We got beat 4-1, but the game was decided with the game's first batter. Maury Wills singled up the middle. On the first pitch to the next batter, he took off for second. I threw behind him to Joe Pepitone at first. Tony Kubek was waiting for the throw at second. But Bobby Richardson cut in front of him, his momentum taking him too far across the bag to make the tag. Then Willie Davis hit a fly ball toward the line in right. Maris slipped, hurt his ankle, and the ball dropped with two runs scoring on the play. That was the game. One mistake compounded another.

In 1964 I was 13-8. In some ways I was dominating. I led the league in strikeouts, walks, and — wild pitches. That year I struck out 217 batters, the most I ever did. But I didn't pitch as well as I thought I could. I don't think I had the intensity I needed for a full season. It might have had something to do with the fact that I had never before spent a full season anywhere. Maybe it was simply that I wasn't yet acclimated. But I should have struck out more batters, and I should have won more games. I was still trying to do things that I wasn't capable of doing. If a pitcher doesn't have his best stuff, he has to finagle. I still hadn't learned that.

There was a reason why my strikeouts dropped to 179 in 1965. I had established myself as a strikeout pitcher. The hitters knew that so they didn't want to get in the hole. They started swinging at the first and second pitches. Also, I got very analytical, thinking, "If I try to strike everyone out, I'm not going to last. I'm going to throw too many pitches." Of course, if you throw six or seven pitches to everyone you strike out, you're not going to last. But if you throw only three or four, you will. I started to try to get batters out with one or two pitches.

I pitched the key game of the 1964 World Series. Game Four. But I don't think the pivotal play took place in the fifth inning. It occurred in the first inning. We had a 3-0 lead at the time, and we had the bases loaded with no outs. But we didn't score any more runs in the inning. And we didn't score any more runs in the game. My key pitch of the game came in the fifth inning. Let me set the record straight on that pitch. I know it has caused a lot of controversy. First, I shook Ellie Howard off. He called for a fastball. I wanted to throw a change-up.

Let me set the scene. There were two outs, the bases were loaded, and Kenny Boyer was at the plate. The change was my strikeout pitch. It was an important part of my repertoire. I didn't have a good curve. My plan of attack against right-handed hitters was a fastball and a straight change. I thought Boyer was looking for a fastball, and I didn't want him to get his bat out in front and hit a homer right inside the foul pole. I had two balls hit the foul pole that year. I thought I could either lead him off with a strike or get him to get out in front and pop up. It didn't happen. He hit a grand-slam home run to win the game. But I still think it was the logical pitch to throw. The scouting staff thought so, too.

Everyone says that the Yankees' decline in 1965 was sudden and unexpected. But remember, I said it was foreseeable in 1961. There were no good young left-handed pitchers in the system. What was unforeseeable was the rash of injuries. Mantle was operated on early in the season, Ellie came down with a sore arm, Maris got hurt early, Ford wasn't healthy, Bouton came down with a sore arm, Kubek didn't play, and Richardson didn't *want* to play. He wanted to retire after the 1964 season, but he stayed on because Tony was injured. Then when Tony retired after the 1965 season, management convinced Bobby to stay another year. They didn't want to lose the middle of their infield at the same time.

But the Yankees made a lot of bad changes at that time, too. Remember, Ellie had a bad arm. Frank Fernandez was the number-one replacement for Ellie, but the Yankees took Jake Gibbs, who was a shortstop and third baseman, and converted him into a catcher. Also, they had switched Tommy Tresh from short to the outfield. Phil Linz came up as a shortstop and they moved him to third base. In addition, they moved Pedro Gonzalez out of the system. Richardson and Kubek were leaving and we didn't have anyone to replace them. That was strange, because the Yankees always had moved their second baseman and their shortstop up through the system together. They had done that with Bobby and Tony. But for some reason they stopped. They were giving away a lot of young players, too, and they weren't replacing them. It didn't make sense then, and it doesn't now.

In 1965, I was 12-14. I had a good year. It wasn't the same caliber of club, though, and I didn't have the same intensity. I take a lot of the blame. I wasn't completing enough games. I would pitch one good game and one bad game. I didn't have any continuity or consistency. Also, suddenly I was supposed to be a leader. But I didn't feel that way. I was thrust into that role. How could I be the leader of the pitching staff? Whitey was still there. It wasn't my time.

A pitcher's arm is never sound, but I didn't hurt my arm until 1967, right before the All-Star Game. I was 9-5 at the time and having a good year. We were in Baltimore. I called Ellie out to the mound.

"What's wrong?" he said.

"I think I hurt my arm," I said. "There's a burning sensation going up and down it."

"What pitch did you hurt it on?" I told him. "Well, let's stay away from that one." I finished the game, but in the last two or three games of the year I could hardly throw the ball. The injury was never diagnosed that year. The front office didn't think I had a bad arm. They thought I was just disappointed because they had traded my roomie, Ellie, to the Red Sox. Remember, Ellie went to Boston that year and caught with them in the World Series.

In 1968 I reported to spring training late, because I was upset with my contract. Well, anyway, I was pitching in Mexico City, and I couldn't even throw the ball up to home plate. The doctor diagnosed my problem as a torn ligament. They sent me to the Mayo Clinic and therapy was prescribed. They didn't operate on it. I think, in retrospect, that was a mistake. Today with the sophisticated equipment that they have, they would operate. I would have been out for a year, I know. But at age twenty-six I could have afforded that.

I wasn't the only one who had injury problems. Maris had had a bone break in his hand, but it didn't show up on the x-ray. They took another x-ray at the end of the year, and then it did show up. It's hard to say if the Yankee management didn't believe Roger, or if they felt they needed him for the gate. Also, Joe Pepitone broke his arm on a throw from the outfield. It was a hairline fracture. They didn't believe him, either.

Anyway, I had another holdout in 1968, because the Yankees thought that I should be able to pitch. The last two years in New York were bitter years, so when they traded me to Oakland in 1970, I didn't feel too bad. It was time to part. I needed a change of scenery.

In 1969, when I was still with the Yankees, I had had a good game against the A's. I'd struck out a lot of batters. But in spring training in 1970, they found out that I couldn't throw hard. They couldn't believe it. They said, "You threw hard against us last year."

I said, "Yes, but that was just one game. Once in a while I can throw hard, but I never know when that time is going to be." So they traded me to Milwaukee and brought up Vida Blue. I guess that was a good move on their part. It was good for me, too, because I got a chance to pitch, and people saw that I could still do the job. One who didn't think so was Frank Lane, who had become the general manager. He wanted me to strike out ten or eleven batters a game, and I couldn't do that anymore.

He said, "I have a chance to trade you to either the Cardinals or the Dodgers. Where do you want to go?"

I said, "Send me back to the Coast."

I was lucky that time. I could have won fifteen games for Oakland in 1970, but it didn't happen. But the 1971 Dodgers team was the best I had been on since the 1964 Yankees. I spent the first two weeks in the bullpen, but then I got a chance to start, and I ended up 20-9 with a 2.68 ERA. The players got accustomed to playing behind me, and I got into a groove. Also, my arm was healthy for the first time since 1967. I had thrown a lot to build up strength, and it paid off. Of course, I could never again throw as hard as I could in 1967. Red Adams was my pitching coach with the Dodgers, and he was a lot like Sain. He would say, "You're the pitcher and you know what you want to do. I'm here in case you get off track."

Too much has been made of the fact that I threw Hank Aaron's 715th home run. He broke the record. I was just an accomplice. After all, he hit a record 755 home runs. I just threw one of them. He hit 754 more. If baseball gives him his proper due, he should go down as the greatest player in the history of the game.

I'm not satisfied with my 123-107 lifetime record. I should have won a lot more, considering the number of years I played.

But there were a lot of thrills along the way. Just getting to the major leagues was one. Associating with the caliber of people that I did was another. Pitching with pennants and World Series on the line was a third. And watching the children of fellow players develop was a fourth. One of Ruben Amaro's kids wound up playing ball for Stanford. Tito Francona's son, Terry, made it to the big leagues. So did Bump Wills, Maury's son. Those are the things you savor. The wins and losses, and the walks and strikeouts, come and go. But the healthy relationships go on forever.

That's why I often think of my days in the Bronx. There was a special relationship between the fans and the players. We don't have that in Los Angeles. Out here it's Freeway City. The players don't know the fans. But when I think of my Yankee days, the thing I think of most fondly is the neighborhood — the Concourse, 161st Street, the hustle and bustle of activity. Of course, the Pinstripes and nostalgia, too. Going to the Stadium, I was just another kid. I would listen to the fans talk. Boy, they were interesting. I was fine-tuned with the fans. That was healthy, too.

Johnny Blanchard

When I first called Johnny Blanchard
in the summer of 1989, he was out of town at a charity golf tournament. Golf is
one of his avocations. Another is fishing. When he was a Boy Scout many years
ago, his father took him each winter to Lake Minnetonka, where they built an
ice house and spent two weeks together. He looks forward to the summers when
he can take his sons out to the lake, where the sunfish are biting.

When he was young, Blanchard was an all-around sports star in Min-
nesota. He left college to sign a pro basketball contract with the Minnesota
Lakers, and was later lured away from them with a $30,000 contract by the
New York Yankees.

But Johnny was a catcher, and the Yankees had two of the best backstops in
baseball history, Yogi Berra and Elston Howard, so he had to switch to the
outfield, where Roger Maris and Mickey Mantle were in residence, and settle
for utility work. He performed his role well. Overall, he hit seven pinch-hit home
runs, ninth on the all-time list, and hit one round-tripper every eighteen times
he went to the plate — an incredible statistic.

In 1961 he amassed fifty-four RBIs with just seventy-four hits. In the
1960 World Series he batted .455; in the 1961 Fall Classic, .400; and overall
in post-season play, .345. From 1961 to 1963 he had more RBIs than any other
Yankee off the bench. In fact, he was often called the best tenth man in baseball.

Today he is a salesman for T.C. Johnson, a company that sells heavy-duty
cranes for laying railroad track. He and his wife Nancy have been married for
thirty-four years.

My call-up to the Yankees in 1955 was funny. I had played at Binghampton that season, and I'd had a good year. After the season my wife and I were in a pizza parlor one night around midnight when the guy behind the counter said, "You've got a phone call."

I couldn't believe it. Who would be calling me at a pizza parlor at that hour? "Hello," I said.

"This is George Weiss of the Yankees," a voice said. "I want you to report to Yankee Stadium tomorrow morning."

"You're full of it," I said and hung up the phone.

But the phone rang again and Weiss convinced me that he was who he said he was. Well, we went home, packed, drove all night and reported to the Stadium in the morning. The Yankees were on their way to Boston, so we went up there, I played one game, got three at bats, hit the ball hard, but took the collar. That was it. I was just up for a cup of coffee.

In 1956 I played with Birmingham, and in 1957 and 1958 I played with Denver. Ralph Houk was my manager in 1957 and Andy Cohen, the old Giant second baseman, in 1958. I had played for Ralph before in Puerto Rico. In 1957 under Ralph, we won the Junior World Championship at Denver. I had good Triple A years, but in those days there were only sixteen major-league teams, so there wasn't much room on major-league rosters.

In 1960 I finally got back to the Yankees. I got only fifty-nine at bats, twenty-eight of them as a pinch-hitter. When I think of 1960, though, I think of Bill Mazeroski. His home run still wakes me up in the middle of the night. Gino Cimoli of the Pirates said it best: "They set all the records, but we won the World Series."

Mickey Mantle felt really bad about the loss. He said, "We had the better team and we deserved to win. We beat their brains out. But they won the Series." I don't know, it's easy to second-guess and say "if." There were some questionable moves. But we just got beat. It wasn't in the cards. Personally, I did pretty well. I got five hits in eleven at bats and hit .455. Two of the hits were doubles. I remember one of them. I missed a home run by about three inches against Vinegar Bend Mizell. I felt pretty good about that. He was a tough lefty.

My banner year was 1961. I batted .305 and hit twenty-one homers with just 243 at bats. But everyone had a banner year in 1961. The club was awesome. We hit a record 240 home runs. I think that the home-run derby between Maris and Mantle had a lot to do with the super performances that everyone else turned in. I've got two theories. One, we were left alone to do our own thing. There was no pressure on us. Consequently, we played relaxed. Two, it was like a golfer playing with a partner who is a few strokes better. It forces him to reach a little and two things happen. First, the subconscious relaxes and the creative juices flow. Second, you say to yourself, "You're doing it. Let us do it, too."

We had three catchers on that club who hit more than twenty home runs that year. Yogi hit twenty-two. Ellie and I hit twenty-one. That's pretty amazing. That's sixty-four home runs at one position. Of course, we could play other positions, too. Yogi could play left. I could play all three outfield positions. I even played first base once. Ellie could play left, right, or first. Sometimes Ellie caught, Yogi played left, and I played right in the same game. I would go behind the plate if Ellie or Yogi was hurt or needed a rest. The Yankees had great flexibility in those days. They were multi-dimensional. That was the key.

I hit four consecutive home runs in 1961. That's a record. I think only four guys have done it. The first one I hit was in Boston. One night we were down 9-7 in the ninth, with the bases loaded. It was a key situation. We were out of first place by two games, and we needed a shot-in-the-arm to get going. Well, Ralph sent me up to pinch-hit, and I hit a grand-slam home run to win the game, 11-9. The next day we were playing an afternoon game at Fenway Park. I think the score was 1-1 in the eighth when Ralph sent me up again. I hit another homer and we went on to win the game. The next day Houk started me against the White Sox, and I hit homers my first two times up at the plate. That tied the record. My third time up I almost broke it. I hit a high fly ball to right. I knew I didn't hit it right. I got under it, but I thought it had a chance to carry. Floyd Robinson went right back to the wall, leaned against the rail, and caught the ball with a lot of white showing. But I took my four straight and went home happy.

The 1961 World Series was another good one for me. We beat the Reds in five games. In the eighth inning of Game Three, it was pretty tense, though. The Yankees and Reds were tied at one game apiece, and we were losing, 2-1. Mickey was hurt with that abscessed hip, and it was doubtful whether he'd be back in the Series, so there was a lot riding on the game. Ralph called on me to pinch-hit in the eighth. I went back to the bat rack to grab a bat, and Mickey was standing there. I said to him, "What in the world is he (Bob Purkey) getting you out with?"

Mickey said, "He's going to throw you a slider on the first pitch for a strike. Then he's going to throw you knuckleballs. He's got a good one today. Don't take the first pitch. Jump on the slider." If Purkey had thrown the first pitch up in the press box, I would have swung at it. But fortunately he threw the slider down over the plate, and I cranked it. Then Roger hit a solo shot in the ninth to win it, 3-2. But it just goes to show you how important it is to ask questions. Sometimes it gives you an edge.

In Game Five, which decided the Series, we had a scrambled lineup. Mickey was hurt so Roger was in center. I was in right and Yogi was in left. But he got hurt diving for a ball in the first inning, and Hector Lopez took his place. All Hector did that day was hit a three-run homer and a two-run triple. I had a good day, too, and I didn't think I would even play. I'll get to that in a moment. I went three-for-four and got on base all five times. First I hit a two-run homer. I think Bobby Richardson was on base at the time. Then I hit a double, single, got on on a walk, and reached on an error. You know, recently I heard Tony Kubek and Bob Costas on the "Game of the Week" talking about players who set a World Series record by getting on base five times in one game. Heh, I was captain of the scrubinis. I can't afford to be left out when I deserve to be included.

Before, I said I didn't think I would play that day. Joey Jay was pitching. Earlier in the Series, I took a nice oh-for-four collar against Jay. After the game I said to myself, "At least I can tell my kids that I started a World Series game." But let me tell you one thing about that game against Jay. You've heard a lot about the shadows at Yankee Stadium at that time of year. As the game wears on, the shadows extend halfway out toward the mound. The ball starts out white from the mound, and then halfway toward the plate it turns black. Well, to make a long story short, I hit four ground balls that day off Jay. I was sure I wouldn't start again.

But before Game Five in Cincy, Kubek came up to me and said, "Holy cow, you're batting fourth!"

I said, "Stop pulling my leg."

"No, honest, I saw the lineup."

Well, I went to look at the lineup, and sure enough, it was in Ralph's handwriting, but I still thought it was some kind of mistake. It was the truth, though. Then I went through a mental readjustment. I told myself if Ralph had enough confidence in me to play me and hit me fourth, I was going to have to play beyond myself and justify that confidence. And everything worked out beautifully — for him and me. You know, I never batted fourth before or after.

In 1962, 1963, and 1964 I didn't get too many World Series at bats. A total of eight. But that was all right with me. I was a scrubini, a fill-in.

My numbers started going down after 1961. I hit thirteen home runs in 1962 and sixteen in 1963, which wasn't too bad for the number of at bats I got. I didn't know until you told me that I averaged one home run for every eighteen times I came to the plate in my big-league career. That's a pretty good average, but I never think how many homers I might have hit if I had gotten 600 at bats in a season. I got all the mileage I could out of my limited ability. I didn't say "play me or trade me," the way they do today. I was used in my proper role. I wouldn't have done the same if I had played every day. I would have hurt the club. I accepted my role. It was no problem. But though my home runs per time at bat were still good, my batting average was going down. It dropped from .305 to .232 to .225 and then leveled off at .255 before I was traded to Kansas City.

Rollie Sheldon and I were traded to Kansas City for Doc Edwards on May 3, 1965. I felt lower than I had ever been before. The trade was a shock, a traumatic blow. The Yankees had been my life. I had always been a winner. In fact, I had left college to sign a professional basketball contract with the Minneapolis Lakers. I had always been a front-runner. Suddenly I went from first to last. I was stunned.

My Kansas City experience stunned me, too. I never knew what Charlie Finley would do next. He had painted the sheep beyond the outfield fences green-and-white, the team colors. One night I had my catching gear on and was ready to go when the umpires came out to home plate, then walked back to the dugout. I didn't know what was going on. Then the grounds-keepers wheeled a forty-inch cake out to home plate. I still didn't know what was going on. Suddenly the center-field fence opened, and they walked a donkey around the track to home plate. It was the donkey's birthday. I had been psyched up and ready to play, but I had to wait an hour before play began. Twenty-four players went out to the mound to sing "Happy Birthday" to the mule. I couldn't do it. They told me I would be fined but that was okay with me. I might have been playing in Kansas City, but my heart was still in the Bronx.

Another day we were playing the Red Sox for last place on the last day of the season. Finley staged a "Cellar-bration," anticipating that we were going to win and finish the season a half game in front of the Red Sox, in ninth place. If we had won, he was going to put twenty-five dollars in separate envelopes and put them in our lockers. There were no cigars that night. It looked good for a while, though. We were winning in the ninth, 2-1, when Fred Talbot tired. Haywood Sullivan, our manager, came out to the mound and waved for Catfish Hunter, but Cat didn't move.

"Do you think he can see us?" Sully said to me.

"Sure, he's not that far away," I said.

Well, the reason Cat didn't move is because he was sitting on top of a mule. He was waiting for the attendants to open the gate so he could ride the mule to the mound. When I saw them coming, I said, "Sully, c'mon." He just lowered his head, and sadly shook it. That wasn't the end of it, though. When the donkey got to the infield, he must have smelled the popcorn and he walked toward the first-base boxes. You should have seen Cat yanking on the mule's neck to steer it toward the mound. The mule's eyes almost jumped out of its head. Well, Cat threw two pitches, the second of which was a home run, and we lost, 3-2. The "Cellar-bration" was canceled. The A's had finished in tenth place again.

Another time Charlie rented a limo, filled it with players, and drove the starters to their positions. When the announcement was made, the player would step out at his position. I don't think the people liked Charlie's gimmicks. Kansas City was a good baseball town. They had a rich heritage as a Yankee farm team. The fans stayed away from the ballpark when Charlie was there. That had a lot to do with the club moving to Oakland.

Still, I played in five World Series, and I got two rings for world championship teams. I hit two home runs in the World Series and a record four in a row. I was part of the Yankee family of that era, and I hung around with Roger and Mickey and Whitey and Moose and Yogi and Bobby and all of those other great Yankees. And, believe it or not, I set World Series records for the most pinch-hit at bats — ten — and the most pinch-hit safeties — three.

Not too bad for a scrubini, eh?

Johnny Kucks

*Johnny Kucks, a product of Dickinson
High School in Jersey City, New Jersey, went to the Yankees in 1955 at the age
of twenty-one and played on four consecutive pennant winners. Six years later,
at the age of twenty-seven, his major-league baseball career was at an end.*

*Some players would have been bitter to see something so promising end so
soon. But Kucks had everything in perspective. "It was disappointing," he says,
"but it wasn't the end of the world."*

*In 1960, his last major-league season, Kucks, seeing that the end of his
playing days was near, took a correspondence course and earned his license as a
stockbroker. From 1965-72 he worked for a brokerage firm in New York City.
Then he took a position with Sealand Service, a steamship service company, and
stayed with it until 1987. At that time he switched to his present firm, Lykes
Steamship Company in New York City.*

*The biggest influence on Johnny's early baseball development was Howard
Whimpy, a milkman from Jersey City. I remember Howard Whimpy. When I
was a boy pitching for St. Peter's Prep in Jersey City in 1954, he was always
around the practice field. That's because another protégé of his, Jim Brady, was
on our team. Jim signed with Detroit and played with the Tigers in 1956.*

*Kucks married his childhood sweetheart, Barbara, in 1955. They have two
daughters.*

I was just an average pitcher. I
didn't have over-powering stuff. Control was my forte. If I didn't have it, I
would make a quick exit. I was just lucky to be in the right place at the right

time. I played for a great organization. I had a great team behind me. I was surrounded by great guys. And I played on pennant winners and World Series teams my first four years in the majors. How many other major-league players can say the same thing? Elston Howard was the only other one in my day.

I was born in 1933 in Hoboken, New Jersey, but I grew up in Jersey City, rooting for the Giants. There I met a milkman by the name of Howard Whimpy, who became a great influence on my baseball career. He taught me motion and mechanics, how to think along with the game, and how to outthink the hitters. He was very instrumental in my early development as a pitcher.

Suddenly in 1955, at the age of twenty-one, I was a member of the New York Yankees, pitching in Yankee Stadium, playing my first major-league season. So many important things happened to me in 1955. I pitched in my first major-league game, I picked up my first win, I put together a record of 8-7, I played on a pennant winner, and I got the opportunity to pitch in a World Series. As a matter of fact, I got into two games. Everything went all right there until Duke Snider hit a three-run homer off me in Game Four. But Duke had a hot series. He hit four altogether. The icing on the cake was my marriage to a Jersey City girl on October 6. My wife Barbara and I then had an unusual six-week honeymoon. The government and Pepsi Cola sent the Yankees on a goodwill tour after the Series. We visited Hawaii, Japan, Okinawa, Guam, and the Philippines. It was unforgettable.

The following year was my big season in the majors. I got my break when Tommy Byrne, who was supposed to start a game at the Stadium, came down with the flu and had to be hospitalized. I took his place and that got me on a roll as a starter. I finished the season 18-9 with three shutouts. We won the pennant again and this time we won the World Series. And I got the chance to start, complete, and win a World Series game.

I've read that Casey primed me for my seventh-game start by using me twice in relief. But that's just not so. The reason I didn't start before the seventh game is that I tailed off toward the end of the season. I simply hadn't pitched as well as I had in the first three-quarters of the season.

Going into the seventh game, we didn't know who was going to start until an hour before game time. In those days the starting pitcher knew he was working when Frankie Crosetti, our coach, walked over to him in the clubhouse before the game and put a ball in his shoe. An hour before the game Crosetti came over to me and put the ball in my shoe. He didn't say anything to me; there was no need to. I was a little excited, but it was my second full year, and I already had won eighteen games that season. I knew what I had to do.

We had an idea of the strengths and weaknesses of the Dodgers. We had gone over all of that in the scouting report before the Series. I wasn't concerned about pitching at Ebbets Field. I had pitched many times at Fenway Park, and I knew what it was like to pitch in a small park. Basically I was a sinkerball pitcher. I tried to keep the ball down. If my sinkerball was working, and I had control, I always had a decent chance. You always need support, though, and I got a lot of it that day. Yogi hit a two-run homer in the first and another two-run shot in the third. Both of them were off Don Newcombe. In the fourth inning Ellie Howard hit a solo shot, and before I knew it, I was up, 5-0. Bill Skowron finished off the scoring with a grand-slam home run in the seventh, and we won, 9-0. I pitched a three-hit shutout for the win. In any normal game everything revolves around the number of runs you're working with. I was working with a big lead that day, so I gained confidence early, it built, and eventually I got loosey-goosey. After the game people were jumping all over me. I was only a twenty-three-year-old kid, remember, so naturally I was pretty excited.

But I came back to earth quickly. In 1957 my record dropped to 8-10, and then it evened off at 8-8 in 1958. Actually in 1957 my stats were better than they were in 1956. But my record was much different. Luck plays a major role in your record. The difference could be going out of a game with an 8-7 lead, going out with an 8-8 tie, or going out with an 8-7 deficit. Records can be very misleading. But Casey had to make a decision. I was just 8-10, so he sent me to the bullpen, and I became an occasional spot starter. I got a good break in getting into the starting rotation. I might have gotten a bad break in being removed from it. I guess things balance out.

Before, I mentioned that I broke into the majors on four pennant winners. That meant I picked up four World Series checks when I was just a kid. The key to that was timing. I was in the right place at the right time. You can bet that luck plays a role in that, too. In my early Yankee days, my wife and I were living in a furnished apartment in Jersey City. The owner of the apartment was a realtor. I told him to keep his eye open for the house we wanted and described to him. He found the exact house we were looking for in Hillsdale, and we bought it with my World Series winnings. We still live in it.

I was disappointed, of course, about my trade to Kansas City in 1959. I had always been in the Yankee organization, I had fine memories, and I had been associated with fine people. Also, Barbara was expecting at the time. That was the really hard part, going home and telling her. But the Yankees were in last place at the time, and there were a lot of rumors going around. I knew that they weren't going to fire Casey. Someone else had to go. Well, one morning I got a phone call and was told to be at Yankee Stadium shortly. When I got there, I was told to go upstairs, and Casey told me, "The club needs to solidify a couple of positions. So we've made a three-for-two deal with Kansas City. You, Sturdivant, and Lumpe are going there. Hector Lopez and Ralph Terry are coming here." But I've got no complaints with the way I found out. They phoned me at home, they told me about the transaction in a business-like manner, and they told me the right way.

The deal was made on May 26. I went over there and won eight of nineteen decisions for a seventh-place club. Harry Craft was the manager and he used me as a starter. The following year, Bob Elliott was the manager. I got seventeen starts but I only completed one. I was lousy. I ended up the season in the bullpen with a 4-10 record. In spring training the next year, there were a lot of changes. Frank Lane came in as the general manager and Joe Gordon was named the manager. A new broom sweeps clean. I got caught in the spinning wheel, and I was sent to the Rochester Red Wings of the International League.

For four years I bounced around the minors, trying to get back to the majors, but it didn't happen. In 1962 I had a spring training tryout with the Mets. That was the first year of expansion in the National League. Casey was the manager. There must have been fifty thousand people there trying out. In 1963 and 1964 I went to spring training with the Cardinals. But I didn't make the clubs.

My major-league career was over at twenty-seven. If a pitcher's career ends because of an injury, he has no recourse but to accept it. But mine didn't. I never had an arm injury in the major leagues. I guess that's why I went down to the minors. I thought I could still pitch. But after 1960, my last season in the majors, I prepared for the future. I took a correspondence course and ultimately got my stock broker's license. I've been in the field ever since.

But baseball helped me to get started in life, and it's still helping me. I don't use my name with my clients before I close the deal. But afterwards, when they find out who I am and what I've done, they say, "You're Johnny Kucks, the pitcher with those great New York Yankee teams, and you didn't mention it, you didn't use it to make the sale. Why not?" I just smile. A little humility goes a long way.

Hector Lopez

When Hector Lopez was a boy in Panama, the Yankees were his favorite team, particularly after they visited Panama during spring training in 1947. Lopez went on to play with the Yankees of his time: Roger Maris, Mickey Mantle, Yogi Berra, and Whitey Ford. Together, from 1960-64, they played on five consecutive pennant-winning teams.

Lopez began playing professional baseball in Panama. In 1951 he played in the Canadian League. The next two seasons he played independent baseball, and he eventually signed a working agreement with the Philadelphia Athletics. In the meantime, though, the Philadelphia franchise was transferred, so Lopez came up to the major leagues in 1955 with the Kansas City Athletics. Lopez enjoyed good years in Kansas City. Three times he hit .283 or better, and three times he hit fifteen or more home runs. In his first five seasons in the majors, spent primarily in Kansas City, he hit eighty-three of his 136 career homers. In 1959 he split the season between the Athletics and the Yankees, and he put the best numbers of his career on the board.

The Yankees moved him to left field in 1960, and from that point on he became a dependable part-time player. He could bunt, he could hit behind the runner, and he could score runs. In his major-league career he averaged almost one RBI for every two hits he made. Lopez was a clutch player. In five World Series he batted .286. Ironically he batted .286 as a pinch hitter (two-for-seven) in post-season play, too.

When the Yankees hit bottom, tenth place, in 1966, Lopez was given his release. He hung on in Triple A ball for two years, hoping that someone would pick him up. In 1967 he batted .293 for the Hawaii Islanders. But it didn't *happen, so in 1970 he took a position as a recreation specialist for the Hemstead, Long Island, Town Board. He has been there ever since.*

He and his wife Claudette have been married since 1960. They had four boys, one of whom is now deceased, and they have five grandchildren.

Lopez asked me to dispel a common misconception: that he was a defensive liability. It is true that he led the league in errors at his position in three of his first four seasons in the majors, and that his fielding percentage with the Yankees was never very high. But it is also true, as Lopez suggests, he never spent enough time at one position to master it.

I'm going to call upon Jim Bouton in Ball Four *to come to Hector's defense: "I also remember the time I won my first major-league game. It was a shutout against the Washington Senators, in which I walked seven guys and gave up seven hits and had to pitch from a stretch position all game. They were hitting line drives all over the place, and Hector ('What a Pair of Hands') Lopez bailed me out with about four leaping catches in left field."*

How's that, Hector?

I like my job here. I've been with Hemstead and West Hemstead for the past twenty years as a recreation specialist and supervisor. We have two swimming pools, gymnastics, and daily educational programs. When I first came, we had a baseball league. But the interest has switched to basketball. The kids don't hang around in the summers. Their parents send them to camps — get them away from the streets.

I enjoy working with kids. I like to see them laughing. You have to keep them busy if you want to keep them away from drugs. The streets are nothing but trouble. You've got to keep them swimming, running, throwing, shooting, something. I like showing them a few fundamentals. I'm always looking for a baseball prospect. I'd like to see it do for them what it's done for me.

The memories, the desires, the feelings that I have for baseball have never died. The game stays with you like your first romance. Sometimes I'll be on the softball field or next to the pool and I'll see a plane fly over. I say to myself, "I should be on that flight. With the guys. I should be heading to Cleveland or Detroit for a game."

I was surprised in 1959 when Kansas City traded me to the Yankees. I had my best major-league season. I hit twenty-two home runs, drove home ninety-three runs, and batted .283. I had four and one-half pretty good years with the Athletics. I played a lot of games, I didn't get hurt, and by

1959 I got to know all of the pitchers in the league. I had better years in Kansas City than in New York because I got more playing time and the park was smaller — especially left field. It was 457 in the power alley when I played in New York. At the same time, though, I was happy to go to the Yankees. They were my favorite team when I was a boy in Panama. So I was surprised to be traded, but it was a pleasant surprise.

I got a World Series check in each of my first five full seasons in New York. Of course, they weren't as big as they are today, but they came in handy. I bought a house in West Hemstead with one of the checks. I still live in it.

Of course I didn't like the reduced playing time, but I adjusted to it. My family and my mother were in New York, so I did whatever manager Ralph Houk said. He always told me how important to the club I was, so I didn't want to let him down, and I did as much as I could.

The Yankees of that era were unbelievable. They could run, they could hit, they could play excellent defense, and they had better than average pitching. In 1961 we hit 240 home runs. That's an all-time record. But not too many people know that defense was our strength. There weren't too many four- or five-out innings with that club. Everyone in 1961 had an outstanding year. Everyone, that is, except me. It was just one of those years. That's the year I got married, so I put the blame on my wife Claudette. She just laughs. She doesn't take me seriously.

I had four different managers with the Yankees: Stengel, Houk, Yogi, and Johnny Keane. Each one had a different style. Casey had been around for a long time, so he made a lot of moves and kept everyone on their toes. Houk was a great motivator. Everyone wanted to play and win for him. Yogi was laid back. He just let you play. That's the way he must have been when he was a player. Keane was always changing things. He played a National League game. He looked for one run all the time. We were used to the big inning. He would say, "You can't bunt, you can't do this, you can't do that, you'll do it my way, or you won't do it." Houk was my favorite. He knew exactly what to tell you. There were never any surprises, so you were always ready.

I had a rough year in the field in 1959. That one year has stayed with me the rest of my life. Look at my records and you'll see that coming up through the system, I was never a hitter. I was a fielder. That was my forte. Joe DeMaestri and I led the league in double plays one year in Kansas City. He was at short and I was at second. But they kept moving me from one spot to another. If the team had a weak spot, they would say, "Put Hector there. He can do the job." I didn't care. I just wanted to help the team.

Well, you know Casey. He liked the two-platoon. So my first spring training, he made me an outfielder. That year I was concerned about my fielding, especially in left field at Yankee Stadium. So I concentrated more on my defense than my hitting. It hurt me a little bit, but I still had a good year. I batted .284 and hit nine home runs.

Lou Boudreau with Kansas City taught me everything I knew about hitting. I thought I'd never make it, but he taught me when to go to the opposite field and how to hit behind the runner. Thank God for Lou Boudreau. Baseball helped me to grow as a human being. I overcame my language handicap, and I learned how to overcome obstacles and deal with challenges.

But 1961, as I said, was not one of my better years. I started off wrong, and some of the other guys had super seasons. My number of at bats dropped to 243, and from that season on my batting average started to decline. In the early days I wouldn't have been able to handle that adversity. But I had grown as a man, so I adjusted and acclimated myself to a utility player role.

I was a good World Series player. All the Yankees of that time were big-game players. In the 1960 World Series I got only seven at bats, but three of them were hits. I was two-for-two as a pinch hitter. I wasn't disappointed with my playing time. Everyone was healthy, and I wanted them to stay that way. I just did what I was supposed to do. The one thing I was disappointed in was losing to the Pirates. I shouldn't say this, but I will anyway. Casey made some unusual moves in that Series. He started Art Ditmar in the opening game. I'm not taking anything away from Ditmar. He was a very good pitcher. But he wasn't Whitey Ford. Whitey was our meal ticket. If he had gotten three starts, instead of two, we would have won. Then Casey used Ralph Terry in relief in the final game. Terry was no reliever. Bill Mazeroski hit that game-winning home run off him. Ryne Duren was out in the bullpen. There were other good pitchers he could have used, too.

The 1961 World Series was my moment in the sun with the Yankees. No matter what happens to me for the rest of my life, I'll never equal what I did in the final game against the Reds. I made the Yankee fans forget Maris and Mantle for a while. For that one game I was "Mr. Yankee." Mickey had an injury — he was out of the lineup with an abscessed hip. Maris started the game in center, Blanchard was in right, and Yogi was in left. I didn't even start the game. But Yogi got hurt when he tried to make a shoestring catch and jammed his sunglasses into his eye. He had to leave the game. I took his place and got a couple of good opportunities. I hit a bases-loaded triple against Jim Maloney. He was a young flamethrower at the time. Then

I hit a three-run homer against Bill Henry. I felt very good. Everyone was happy for me. I was the runner-up to Whitey for the MVP Award. That was the year he extended his consecutive scoreless inning streak to thirty-two.

In 1962 they started to platoon me with Roger Repoz and Tommy Tresh in left. But in 1962 and 1963 I continued to have productive seasons. Those two years I got a total of two hundred hits, and I drove home one hundred runs, many of them in the clutch. Yankees of that era didn't care about batting averages. They cared more about clutch hitting. The fans knew who was producing. If Ralph put someone else in left, the fans would first boo and then chant, "We want Hector, we want Hector."

In the 1962 World Series I got only two at bats, though. It was just personnel. Most of the games were tight and there weren't many moves. Everyone was healthy and Tresh had such a good year that he won the Rookie of the Year Award. He also hit a big three-run homer and made that great catch on Willie Mays in the Series.

The 1963 World Series was devastating to us. After it was over, we couldn't believe that we hadn't won at least a couple of games. I got two doubles in eight at bats. It must have been against Johnny Podres, because I didn't do anything with Sandy Koufax, and I only started against lefties. In fact, I made the last out of the Series, against Koufax. There was a man on first and we were losing 2-1. I hit a ground ball to Maury Wills at short. That was the game in which Pepitone lost Clete Boyer's throw in the sun. He got hit on the chest. Mantle homered for our only run. Give the Dodgers credit, though. They had a great pitching staff and their pitchers all had great years at the same time. And Moose Skowron, my buddy, had a great Series for the Dodgers. He hit the ball all over the park.

Now the 1964 World Series, like the 1960 one, was one we should have won. We had the better team but we just didn't get the job done. Whitey hurt his arm in Game One and didn't pitch again. That hurt us. There were two big plays in Game Four, too. We got the jump on them that day. We went up 3-0. It could have been more. But Mickey made a couple of base-running mistakes. In one of them, he got picked off second by Dick Groat on the hidden-ball trick. That shifted the momentum of the game. The other big play was Ken Boyer's grand-slam home run. It gave the Cardinals a 4-3 victory. I know some of my teammates have questioned Ellie Howard's call and Al Downing's pitch to Boyer. But that was the plan. They were supposed to change speeds on him. They didn't do anything on their own. But Whitey was probably the biggest factor. He was such a good pitcher. He had all that savvy, he challenged the hitters, and he threw strikes. Remember, we had that great defense behind him.

I knew we were slipping, but I didn't think our decline would be that fast or that sharp in 1965 and 1966. A lot of things contributed. One was the new rule affecting the draft with respect to bonus babies. You could no longer protect them in the minors. You had to keep the kids on the team. It was one of those rules that was put in because of the Yankee dominance over the previous thirty years. It seems like a small thing, but it was important. We had to let a few guys go, and it weakened us. Everything went downhill in 1965.

There were two big thrills. In 1957, when I was with Kansas City, I hit three home runs in a game against Washington. In fact, I hit them off three different pitchers. I drove home seven runs in that game. I also drove home seven runs in the 1961 World Series. After the bad year I'd had, it was a very satisfying experience.

I miss baseball. There was such togetherness with the Yankees. I was more than an individual. I was part of a team. We didn't need coaches around because we had spirit — Yankee spirit. We believed in the uniform, the tradition, and each other. It was beautiful to see men so close. I've tried to recapture that feeling outside baseball, but I haven't succeeded. I guess I never will.

You know, I carry my Yankee uniform around in the trunk of my car. It keeps me close to that special feeling I knew. Once in a while I'll open the trunk and say to myself, "I used to play for the greatest team in the world."

"No one can ever take that away from me."

Billy Hunter

*Billy Hunter was born in Punxsutaw-
ney, Pennsylvania, on June 4, 1928, and now lives in Luthersville, Maryland,
with his wife, Beverly. They have two sons and three grandchildren.*

*After Hunter retired from professional baseball, he spent a couple of years in
scouting and had an insurance agency. Then he hooked up with the Baltimore
Orioles on a full-time basis. He wore many hats with the Orioles. He was a
minor-league infield instructor, a coach in the Rookie League, a scout, and a
public-relations speaker. During this time he told the Orioles, "If a coaching job
is available, I'd appreciate it if you would consider me."*

*That coaching position opened up in 1964, and Hunter was given the job.
He became the third-base coach. Gene Woodling was the first-base coach.
Sherman Lollar and Harry Brecheen were on the coaching staff, too, and Hank
Bauer was the manager. Hunter remained in that position for more than
thirteen years, and got into four World Series during that time, one under Bauer
(1966) and three under Earl Weaver (1969-71). The Orioles won two of the
four world championships.*

*In 1977 Hunter became the fifth Texas manager of the season, and he
guided the Rangers to a second-place finish in 1977 and a third-place finish in
1978. He and his wife did not want to relocate, though, so in 1979 he became
the head baseball coach at Towson State College in Maryland. In 1984 he
became the school's athletic director as well as its baseball coach. Two years ago
he gave up baseball to concentrate on his athletic director's responsibilities. "It's
a full-time job," he says.*

We had five managers at Texas in 1977. Frank Lucchesi started the season, but he got fired. Then Connie Ryan served as an interim manager before they signed Eddie Stanky. Stanky didn't really want the job, but I think Eddie Robinson talked him into taking it. When Eddie got to Texas, he saw that things were different than when he'd been a manager before. He lasted just *one* day. I talked to him before he left. He said, "What am I doing here?" The next morning he called upstairs and said, "Get a manager. I'm going home." So Connie Ryan served as the interim again.

Brad Corbett, the owner, then called me and said, "Would you be interested in the job?"

I had been a coach with the Orioles for thirteen and one-half years, and I thought I was ready for the challenge, so I said, "Sure."

"Okay, good. But we're also talking to Harmon Killebrew and Don Drysdale. We'll get back to you, okay?"

I said, "Fine." Well, they decided on me and it was a good experience. In 1977 my manager's record was 63-30. We had some talent but we didn't have any relief pitchers. We didn't have a real stopper. But we finished in second place with ninety-four wins in 1977, and we won eighty-seven games in 1978. We would have won both years if we had had a stopper.

After the 1978 season Corbett offered me a three-year contract. Then he upped it to five years. But my wife wasn't interested in moving to Texas, so I said, "That's all." I had been in the game twenty years as a player, coach, and manager. It was a good time to make a break. I told Corbett that I would manage for one more year, but he thought that as long as he had to find a new manager, he might as well do it then. So we parted amicably.

There were a couple of other reasons to get out. It was just at the onset of the drug problem. I found out later that we had some people involved in it. And there were about eight players with five-year contracts. It was impossible to motivate them. I told Brad that one day.

He said, "I'll give you a ten-year contract."

I said, "That won't solve the problem. I'll just have to put up with it longer."

I've been connected with Towson State College since I left the big leagues. First as their baseball coach and now as their athletic director. I gave up the baseball job two years ago. I found out I couldn't do both at the same time.

I think I would liken college coaching to coaching in the Rookie League, which I did in 1962 and 1963. One of the products that I had there was Mark Belanger, who turned out to be quite a major-league shortstop. I had the pleasure of coaching him with the Orioles, too. But a college coach has so many things to worry about. His players' grade-point average. The schedule. Who you're playing that day.

Marty Marion was the perfect manager for me to break into the majors under. When I was a kid in Indiana, Pennsylvania, my father would take me to Forbes Field in Pittsburgh whenever the Cardinals came to town. Marty Marion was my idol. In my rookie year with the Browns, 1953, I told him that. He appreciated it, but he said, "You play more like Pee Wee Reese than Marty Marion."

I said, "Pee Wee Reese is the reason I'm here."

I signed initially with the Dodgers. The Dodgers had a lot of good young shortstops at the time. But they either traded or sold most of them. The reason was Reese. No one could push him out of the position. I roomed with Dom Zimmer in the minors. We were called the "heirs apparent." I used to tell Zimmer that he would be the next Dodger shortstop, because he was a few years younger than I was and he had more pop in his bat. But we both ended up elsewhere. The Dodgers sent me to the Browns for four players and $90,000. Bill Veeck told me the next year, when we were in Baltimore, "I'm still paying for your trade." (*The St. Louis franchise was moved to Baltimore following the 1953 season*).

I was involved in two other massive deals. Seventeen players, including Don Larsen and Bob Turley, were involved in the deal that sent me to the Yankees. Eleven players were involved in the deal that sent me from New York to Kansas City. I went from an eighth-place team to a first-place club to a seventh-place squad. Let me tell you, there was a big difference in those teams. St. Louis and Kansas City had good individual talent, but never enough pitching depth. The Yankees, on the other hand, were winning regularly, and you could just about rely on getting an annual World Series check. George Weiss and Bill DeWitt took that into consideration when they were negotiating your contract. I had already signed with the Yankees for the 1957 season when I was traded to Kansas City. I told Kansas City that I wanted an adjustment in my contract, because I had originally signed it with the stipulation that my World Series check was part of it.

They just said, "No, sir." They had the best of both worlds.

But I enjoyed my two years with the Yankees. They got me because Phil Rizzuto was coming to the end of the line. In fact, they released him the next year, on Old Timers' Day. I got ninety-eight games of playing time in 1955. But around August 5, we were playing the Indians, and Casey took me out of the game in the sixth inning. I remember that Herb Score was pitching. He told me that he was sending me to Denver. I was very upset.

We had just come off a western trip, and I had gone fourteen-for-twenty-eight. My confidence was sky high. I thought I was really coming into my own. He had just picked up Enos Slaughter for the stretch run, and he had to open up a roster spot for him. They had to sign Enos before September 1 so he would be eligible to play in the Series.

I was so disappointed that I refused to report to Denver. Instead I went home for three or four days. But eventually Ralph Houk, who was managing at Denver, called me and convinced me to report. I played only thirteen games there, though. One day I slid into second and broke my ankle. I watched that year's World Series from the stands. The next year I reported to the early camp. Casey called me aside one day and said, "You'll be here all year long. We owe you this."

But I opened the season on the disabled list. Irv Noren was on it, too. One day, before the training deadline, they staged a race between Irv and me to see which one of us would be activated. I won by about ten yards. In order to open a roster spot for me, they sold Eddie Robinson to Kansas City. I felt bad about that. He was my roommate.

Well, two-thirds of the way through the season, Casey sat down next to me in the dining car and said, "Pick out the pitchers you want to play against for the rest of the season. I want you to hit .300."

I said, "Thanks, Casey, but I can't do that. I need to play every day to hit .300." Well, I didn't play every day, but I hit .280, which was my best average in the big leagues. That year I was in uniform for the Series, but I didn't get into one of the seven games. I remember the day that Larsen pitched the perfect game. Joe Collins, who was playing first that day, would throw the infield ball to me. This one inning, when I got up, Mickey Mantle sat in my spot. In those days, remember, we were very superstitious. When I came back, I said, "Mick, you can't sit there. You've been sitting on the steps all day long. You can't change the luck now." He got up without a word and sat again on the steps, in the corner, where he had been every inning. I never saw Casey as animated in the dugout as he was in the seventh, eighth, and ninth innings of that game. He wanted that perfect game. Frankie Crosetti was really into the game, too. He was usually low-key. But that day he shouted all day long.

I had good speed and a strong, accurate arm. I played deep because I liked to charge the ball and it enabled me to go deeper into the hole. But I wish I had been a better hitter. I had some of the best hitting coaches one could have — George Sisler, Frankie Frisch, Bill Dickey, and Joe Gordon. They all said the same thing: "There's no reason that, with your hand-eye coordination, you shouldn't hit .300." But I never did. My biggest problem was the strike zone. I swung at too many bad pitches. I didn't strike out much but I didn't hit the ball as solidly as I should have.

But I got in six seasons in the majors, and I played on two pennant winners. I'm grateful for that. I also coached in four World Series — one under Hank Bauer in 1966 and three straight under Earl Weaver from 1969-71.

I remember Casey at the 1969 World Series. I loved to hear him talk to sportswriters. They loved it, too. I can still see Casey that year in the Hospitality Room sitting behind a long table with the reporters lined up six-deep listening to him.

Casey would often play hunches. I remember a game in Chicago in 1956. It was a Saturday afternoon, and we had scored two runs in the first inning before I came to the plate with the bases loaded. He pinch hit for me. Remember, we were the visiting team, so I hadn't even gotten a chance to take the field. He pinch hit for me in the top of the first inning! That day we had five shortstops in the lineup, and none of them got to bat. He pinch hit for all of them.

The following day we played a doubleheader. I played all nine innings of the first game, and the whole second game, too. Whitey Ford and Billy Pierce were hooked up in one of their typical one-one games when I came to bat in the tenth inning. We had two outs and there were dark clouds overhead. Everyone knew that this was going to be the last inning, because of the rain. Well, I got two strikes before I realized Casey wasn't going to pinch hit for me. I hit a line drive between Jim Rivera and Minnie Minoso that bounced hard off the wall, for an inside-the-park home run, and we won, 2-1.

I told the reporters after the game, "That's why he pinch hit for me yesterday. He wanted me to save all of my energy for Sunday, so that I could run out my game-winning inside-the-park homer."

Enos Slaughter

When I spoke with Enos Slaughter in
July of 1989, he was preparing to go to Cooperstown, New York, to see Carl
Yastrzemski and Johnny Bench inducted into the Hall of Fame. "It's the
greatest honor that can be bestowed upon a baseball player," he told me. "A lot
of people moan and groan because they have to wait so long to get in, but once
they do they never bother to go back and honor their successors. I do. I go back
every year."

Enos was married five times, has five daughters, and has been single for the
past ten years. When his playing career ended in 1959, he wanted to stay in
baseball, so he managed Houston in the Texas League in 1960 and Raleigh in
the Carolina League in 1961. He and Johnny Mize were supposed to be co-
managers of a team in the newly-founded Continental League, but the loop
aborted before it got off the ground. Enos found more stability in college baseball.
He coached Duke University's baseball team from 1971-77.

Enos also has been a farmer since the 1930s. Originally he had 240 acres,
but the Public Utilities Company took eighty and converted them into a lake.
Since he retired from college coaching, he has grown tobacco and vegetables.

At the age of seventy-three, he still plays baseball, too. This past year he
attended Whitey Ford's and Mickey Mantle's Fantasy Camp from November 4-
11, then made the transition into Andy Carey's camp from November 11-17.
One day later he was booked on a cruise. Enos is still on the run.

When he's not running, he lives in Roxboro, North Carolina, where I talked
to him one summer evening.

Some people in New York accused me of showboating when I ran everything out. Well, there was a story behind that. One day in 1946 I ran in from the outfield after the third out and walked from the foul line to the dugout. Eddie Dyer, the manager of the Cardinals at that time, said to me, "Are you tired? If you are, I'll get you some relief out there." I've been running ever since. Running's easy. And it's necessary to a ballplayer's health. Today everyone's pulling hamstring muscles. They're not in shape. I've had only one charley horse in my entire life.

That's how I ran out all those triples I hit. I had ten or more three-base hits in nine consecutive years. Might have been twelve, if I hadn't missed those three years in the service. Got a lot of them when the right fielder didn't play the carom off the wall in St. Louis right. Also, in Forbes Field in Pittsburgh. Dead center was 457 and the power alleys were 425. Of course, later they shortened left with Greenberg Gardens and Kiner's Korner. That took a few away from me.

I'd have to say my best years were 1942 and 1946. In 1942 I batted .318, led the league with seventeen triples, hit thirteen home runs, and drove home ninety-eight runs. I'll never forget the World Series that year. In five games, we defeated a Yankee team that had won twenty-nine of its previous thirty-three World Series games. The lone Yankee win came in Game One when Red Ruffing beat us, 7-4. That was his seventh World Series victory, a record at the time. He had a no-hitter for seven and two-thirds innings. That was another record at the time. Terry Moore broke up the no-hitter. In the ninth inning Ruffing needed one out to get a shutout. But a succession of hits and walks drove him from the game. Spud Chandler took his place. We ended up with a chance to win it. We had Stan Musial at the plate with the bases loaded, but Stan made out. The comeback was a big psychological boost. In the clubhouse after the game, we told ourselves, "We can beat them," and we did. Another turning point in the Series came in Game Two. Bill Dickey singled, and Tuck Stainback ran for him. Buddy Hassett hit a ball into the right-field corner, I played the carom perfectly, and gunned down Stainback at third. I had a great arm, you know. One year I had twenty-three assists. Career-wise, I had 152. I dared them to run on me.

In 1946 I batted .300, hit eighteen home runs, and drove home 130 runs. The homers and RBIs were career highs. Of course, when I talk about 1946, everyone wants to know about the winning play of Game Seven. It happened in the bottom of the eighth inning, and it enabled us to defeat the Red Sox, 4-3, and win another world championship. Actually it was set up by earlier plays in the Series. In one of the games, Mike Gonzalez, the third-base coach, held me at third on a critical play. The relay was bad and I could have scored if I had gone. We lost the game. Manager Eddie Dyer came up to me after the game and said, "If you find yourself in a similar situation in this Series, I want you to use your own judgment. I'll take the responsibility." The other play occurred in the top of the eighth inning in Game Seven. The Red Sox scored two runs that inning to take a 3-2 lead. But a critical play in that rally took place when Dom DiMaggio doubled and sprained his ankle sliding into second. Leon Culberson ran for him and took his place in center field. In the bottom of the eighth, I led the inning with a single off Bob Klinger. Whitey Kurowski popped out to third and Del Rice flied out to left. Then Harry Walker lined a base hit to left center. They gave him a double on the play, but it was only an ordinary single. When I was on first base, I made a mental note. I reminded myself that Culberson was now in center, and he couldn't run or throw like DiMaggio. When I got to second, I said to myself, "I can score," and I did. I ran right through Gonzalez' stop sign. Johnny Pesky went out for the relay with his back to the infield. They made him out to be the goat because he paused briefly before he threw home. But I don't blame Johnny at all. I blame Bobby Doerr, the second baseman, and Pinky Higgins, the third baseman. They didn't give him any help. They didn't tell him where to go with the ball. In fact, Pesky pivoted towards second, looking for a play on Walker. If he had pivoted toward third, I might have been out by ten feet at the plate.

I played nineteen years in the big leagues and ended up with a lifetime batting average of .300. I would have had twenty-two years except for those service years. I'm grateful for every year I got to play, especially those years after the war. I was thirty when I got out. Everyone thought that I was an old man, over the hill. But I had eight more great years with St. Louis.

In December of 1953 I signed another Cardinal contract. It was the first one Augie Busch signed after he bought the club. He said to me, "You're a credit to the game. You'll always be with us." Four months later I was traded to the Yankees. My heart broke. That was when I found out how cold-hearted baseball can be. Their justification was I was thirty-eight, and they had Wally Moon waiting in the wings. But they had been predicting my decline for eight years. Every spring they had some new prospect challenging me, and every summer he'd be returned to the minors. The same thing would have happened with Moon if I had stayed with the Cardinals. After the shock wore off, however, I got to thinking. If the Cardinals didn't want me, obviously the Yankees did. And they were a great organization, too. I decided I would go to New York and help the Yankees win some pennants. That's what I did. I played on three pennant winners and two world title teams in New York.

In 1954 Casey Stengel used me as a utility outfielder and a pinch-hitter. That's the year I ran into the wall and broke my arm in three places, so some adjustments had to be made. For the first time in my career I wasn't a full-time player. One day I went up to Casey and said, "I want to play more."

He said, "You'll play when I want you to. If you can accept that, you'll be around for a long time." He was right. I played until I was forty-three. If they had had the designated-hitter rule at that time, I could have played until I was fifty.

Around that time we used to say that Kansas City was the Yankees' farm system, because the Yankees and the Athletics were always exchanging large numbers of players. The Yankees sent Johnny Sain and me to Kansas City in 1955. I guess they thought I needed some more seasoning. I had a pretty good year. I batted .315 and was named the club's MVP. On the last day of the season, they gave me a Chrysler Imperial.

The following season, 1956, Norm Siebern and Bob Cerv each had a bad leg, and Joe Collins had a bad back. They needed a left-handed hitter, so they got me back on August 25, for the waiver price. I'd say that deal paid dividends. I joined the club in Detroit for a doubleheader and went five-for-nine in a sweep. Then we went into Chicago. I hit a home run off Dick Donovan in the twelfth inning to give us a win.

I haven't gotten too much credit for that game-winning home run in the 1956 World Series. We were down two games to none at the time, and we were down in the game, 2-1, in the bottom of the sixth. That's when I hit the three-run homer. We went on to win the game, 5-3. If I hadn't hit that home run, we would have been down three games to none, and you can bet that we would have lost the Series. No one has ever come back from a three-game deficit in the World Series.

If they didn't give me too much credit for turning the Series around, they gave me a lot of criticism for a play I didn't make in Game Six. The score was nothing-nothing in the bottom of the tenth at Ebbets Field. Bob Turley and Clem Labine were hooked up in a heck of a ball game. Junior Gilliam led off the inning with a single and was sacrificed to second by Pee Wee Reese. That brought Jackie Robinson to the plate. I played medium distance, anticipating two possibilities. If he hit the ball to the wall, I could get back to it. If he hit a ground-ball base hit, I could charge it and throw out Gilliam at the plate. Robinson hit a hard liner to left center, I jumped for it, but it landed three feet over my glove, against the left-field wall. The New York sportswriters jumped all over my case, saying that I had misjudged the ball. But it was a base hit all the way.

That's when Billy Martin went up to Casey after the game and said, "If you play your National League buddy tomorrow, you're going to blow the World Series." When Casey sat me the next day, it was all right with me. I wanted us to win the world championship any way we could. I played for eleven managers and whatever way they wanted to play, I played.

Casey and I got along just fine. He followed my National League career and knew what I could do. He had confidence in me against tough lefties like Billy Pierce and Herb Score. I could always hit lefties. I played for a long time with one of the best left-handed hitters who ever lived, Stan Musial. I remember when he came up to the majors: August 17, 1941. I had broken my collarbone and Terry Moore had gotten hit in the head. That's why they brought him up. He hit .421 the rest of the season. Every series we played we would see two left-handers. Like Johnny Vander Meer and Lee Grissom of the Reds. But I hit them all. I had very good success, as a matter of fact, against Carl Hubbell of the Giants. Frankie Frisch, when he left the Cardinals and went over to Pittsburgh, said, "Stop Slaughter and Musial and you stop the Cardinals."

Casey ran the club. I just sat on the bench and followed my instincts. When I knew that a left-handed pinch hitter would be needed, I would go to the clubhouse and do my preparation. You had to be on your toes at all times with Casey. One day he sent me up to bat for Rizzuto in the first inning. Another day he had me pitching batting practice before the game for fifteen minutes. I was very hot. Then he came up to me and said, "You're playing left field and leading off." I got three hits — against Herb Score. You know, I was a .306 lifetime pinch hitter. I tried to help the ball club any way I could. If Casey sent me up to pinch hit, I would take two strikes and try to get a walk. If the pitcher threw strikes, I would try to get a hit. Anything to start a rally.

The Yankees weren't going anywhere in 1959. That's why Casey got rid of me the second time. But he did me a favor. Let me reconstruct the story.

One day I fouled a ball off my left ankle and hurt it. It still hurts, forty years later. It was off Russ Kemmerer of the Senators. I didn't rub it but I was out of a couple of series. The club went from Washington to Baltimore and then came home. Casey came up to me and said, "We're going to finish third so I'm going to move you. The Braves are in a pennant race with the Dodgers, and they need a left-handed hitter. Wes Covington busted his knee." So I joined the Braves and the first day I was there, I pinch hit a single for Bob Purkey, and Fred Haney, the manager, put a runner in for me. But then we went on to the Coliseum for an important series against the

Dodgers — in fact, the pennant was on the line — and he played me, though I was hopping every step, every game. In one of the games I got a base hit to beat Don Drysdale. That's the series when Frank Dascoli, the umpire, took the pennant away from us. Joe Adcock hit a ball over the screen into the street for what should have been a homer. It would have given us the pennant if Dascoli called it right. But he blew the call — he ruled it a ground-rule double — and the Dodgers beat us in the next inning. The season ended in a tie, forcing a best-of-three playoff. We were short on arms about that time. Haney was forced to start Carl Willey, who hadn't started since July. He was doing a good job, winning 2-1, until John Roseboro beat him with a two-run homer. We blew the second and pennant-deciding game, too. We were winning 8-4, but they rallied for five runs to win the pennant. Haney used every pitcher he had except Bob Buhl in that game.

I'd have to say that the 1942 Cardinals were the best team I was on. We had desire and determination and the will to win. We could be eight to ten runs down and we still believed we could come back and win. The Yankees had great teams, too. I didn't play on the clubs that won five consecutive World Series. They must have been great. I can't knock the Yankee teams that I played on. They were great, too. And they treated me well. Let's just say that I went from one great organization in the National League to another great one in the American League.

I still see some of those Yankees. At Whitey Ford's and Mickey Mantle's Fantasy Camp. I still play. And I'm seventy-three. Last year I was two-for-two in one game, when I hit a ball in the hole. I beat it out but I pulled my Achilles' tendon. This year I'm going back to play some spot outfield and pinch hit. I can't go full-time anymore. My running days are over!

Bobby Shantz

Bobby Shantz was born in Pottstown, Pennsylvania, in 1925. He was only a little guy, five feet six inches and 139 pounds, but he lasted in the major leagues for sixteen seasons. His overall record was 119-99 with a 3.38 ERA and sixteen shutouts. Nine of those shutouts came in 1951 and 1952. He hurt his arm in 1953, but he was still able to hang on in the major leagues for twelve more years. Six times he had ERAs of 2.79 or less, and eight times he won the Gold Glove Award for his position. The Gold Glove Award was started in 1957 and Shantz won it every year until he retired after the 1964 season.

Bobby lives in Ambler, Pennsylvania, with Shirley, his wife of forty years. They have four children, three sons and a daughter, and four grandchildren. Shantz for a while owned a bowling alley, then bought a dairy bar he ran for twenty-two years. He sold it two years ago. Now he lives on his social security, baseball pension, and savings. He stays in the public eye by attending baseball card shows and Old Timers' Day games. Bobby enjoys playing golf, especially with baseball friends Curt Simmons, Robin Roberts, and Granny Hamner. Simmons and Roberts own their own course in Prospectville, Pennsylvania. "We have a lot of fun," says Bobby. "We like to talk about the old days in Philadelphia, and we still like to compete. We enjoy taking each other's money."

But Shantz enjoyed his years with the Yankees the most. "Geez, those years were great. I can't begin to tell you how much fun we had. Playing in Yankee Stadium — what a thrill. And I had Bauer, Mantle, Berra, Kubek, and Richardson in the lineup. I knew I'd get runs, and I knew they wouldn't give too many away. My father was a glazier, and I thought I'd end up working in a sawmill for seventy-five cents an hour. But I pitched sixteen years in the big leagues, and I played in two World Series with the Yankees."

That's not bad for a little guy.

I had a good infield when I broke into the majors with the Philadelphia Athletics in 1949. In fact, a great one. Ferris Fain was at first, Pete Suder at second, Eddie Joost at short, and Hank Majeski at third. Buddy Rosar behind the plate was a good defensive catcher, too. They made a major-league record 217 double plays in my rookie season. They called them "The Million Dollar Infield." Maybe we pitchers gave them a lot of chances.

Connie Mack and I got along. There were never any problems. But he was old when I came up, and he didn't say much. His son Earle sat next to him in the dugout, Connie gave the signs to Earle, and Earle gave them to us. I was nervous before my pitching turns when I was young. Jimmy Dykes would never tell me I was starting until the day of the game. He didn't want me worrying all night about it. Of course, I had a good idea when I was going to pitch, but I never knew for sure until Dykes put the ball in my locker before the game.

I started to find a groove in 1951. That year I was 18-10. I didn't have a good first half, but after the All-Star Game, I got in the groove. I know what the difference was. I started changing speeds. From that point on, I started to win.

I always pitched well against the Yankees. That's the reason, I believe, they traded for me. I remember one game in 1952 that I pitched against them. I beat them in fourteen-innings, 2-1. I went all the way. That was one of my biggest thrills. Not too many pitchers were going fourteen innings in those days. Today they have trouble going nine. Of course, we didn't have the bullpens that they have today.

My biggest year was 1952. I was 24-7, and I led the league in wins and in winning percentage. My 2.48 ERA was good, too. Everything went right. Ground balls and line drives went right at someone. It was one of those lucky years. But I had some bad luck, too. Three weeks before the end of the season, I broke my wrist. I could have won a few more games. It hurt me more long-range than short-range, though. Then in spring training the following year, I picked up some shoulder problems that stayed with me the rest of my career. The doctor said that I was favoring my wrist. From that point on I could never snap my curve the way I had.

The next four seasons were lost years. I was 13-26 during that period.

Actually I didn't pitch much. I couldn't. I was taking a lot of cortisone shots. Years later, in the National League, I was still taking them. When I was with Houston, in 1962, the doctor said he wouldn't give me any more. He said I would have a reaction later in my life. I don't know what kind. I didn't ask. So far, so good. I've got a little stomach trouble, but I don't think that's the problem. When I was traded to the Cardinals later that year, they resumed the cortisone shots. Overall, I guess, I had some forty to fifty shots. But as I said, so far, so good.

I thought my trade to the Yankees in 1957 was great. Who wouldn't want to have that club behind him? It was the greatest club I ever pitched against or for. They were awesome at the plate and colossal in the field. There were eleven men in the deal. The Athletics gave up five; the Yankees, six. Art Ditmar and Clete Boyer went to New York with me. The Yankees gave up some big names. But none of them ever had good years again. I'd say the Yankees made out on that deal.

When I came over to New York, I didn't think I'd start. They had two good lefties, Whitey Ford and Tommy Byrne. I figured I would be assigned to the bullpen and I was right, but Whitey came down with a bad arm, and Casey gave me a start. I won nine games in a row. Then Whitey got better and I went back to the bullpen. I didn't start another game that year, even though I led the league with a 2.45 ERA. I didn't like it. But what could you do? Whitey was the big guy in New York. He would be anywhere. He could really pitch.

In the 1957 World Series, my first year with the Yankees, I got the start in Game Two against Lew Burdette. He won three games in that Series. Casey told me I was going to start the game the day before. By that time I could handle my nerves better, but I was really nervous before the game. There was a lot of excitement. I think there were two hundred reporters covering the Series. They were all over the clubhouse. Well, I got knocked out in the fourth inning, and we lost, 4-2. It wasn't my day. Johnny Logan hit a home run off me right down the line. Three hundred and twelve feet. When I saw him at an Old Timers' Day game in Buffalo recently, he reminded me of his homer. He said, "Thanks, you made a star of me." In the same game Wes Covington took a home run away from me. He was a bad fielder, but he stumbled into the left-field stands to make the catch. I really hit the ball hard. Later in the game Yogi tagged up on a fly ball, and Wes threw him out at the plate.

Casey would remember everything. He didn't miss a trick. He and I got along all right. It was funny, though. I don't think he could even remember my name. Maybe he did. But every time he came out to the mound, he would say, "Hang in there, little fellow." That's all he ever called me, "little fellow." Once in a while he would sleep at the end of the dugout. His eyes were often closed. But he had so many great coaches he could depend on. Bill Dickey, Frankie Crosetti, Jim Turner. Quite often Casey would be out with his writer friends until three o'clock in the morning. They say he didn't need much sleep, that he would be up by seven. I guess he compensated by taking a few catnaps on the bench during the game. As shrewd as he was, he could afford to.

I didn't pitch in the 1958 World Series. A week and a half before the season ended, I got hit by a line drive that broke my finger. The Yankees had a bad year in 1959. I don't remember too much about it. I had a pretty decent season — I was 7-3 with a 2.38 ERA — but it seemed that I spent the entire season in the bullpen. I don't even remember my four starts or my two shut-outs.

Enos Slaughter — there's a guy with a fantastic memory. I think he remembers every hit he got, and he got a lot of them. I've been two or three places with him in recent years. Card shows, you know. I roomed with him up in Toronto. He wouldn't shut up. He knew everything he was going to do for the rest of the year. He even knew all of the airline stewardesses' names.

I don't think the bullpen prolonged my career. It might have shortened it. I pitched better when I started, but the way my arm was, I had no choice. Out in the bullpen you throw so much every day that you wear your arm out. But I didn't care. I was just happy to be in the major leagues.

The only game I remember in the 1960 World Series is the seventh game. The important one. We were down 4-0 when I came into the game in the third inning. I pitched four scoreless innings, and we got back in the game. In the top of the seventh, Yogi hit a three-run homer to give us a 7-4 lead. The roof fell in, in the bottom of the seventh. Gino Cimoli, who batted for Roy Face, led off the inning with a single. Bill Virdon then hit a double-play ball to Tony Kubek, but it took a bad hop and hit Tony in the throat. It was the turning point of the game. Tony had to leave the game, and the Pirates suddenly had the momentum. Dick Groat followed with a single between short and third, and Cimoli scored. That made the score 7-5 and Casey made a move. He brought Jim Coates into the game. It might have been a bad move. Bob Skinner was up and it was a bunt situation.

Anyway, Skinner advanced the runners to second and third, and they stayed there when Rocky Nelson flied out to Roger Maris. Then there was another key play. Roberto Clemente chopped a little ground ball to Moose

Skowron's right. It should have been the third out, but Coates never moved off the mound. It was a critical mistake. The score was 7-5 and the Pirates had two runners on. Maybe Coates lost his concentration. He knew he had made a mistake. Well, he made another one. He threw a three-run homer to Hal Smith and suddenly the World Series turned around. The Pirates were up 9-7. We tied the score in the top of the ninth, but Bill Mazeroski won it in the bottom of the ninth. It was an unbelievable turnaround. I remember the clubhouse after the game. It was as quiet as a tomb. Casey didn't say anything. He took everything in stride.

Expansion came in 1961. Washington picked me up but traded me to the Pirates for Bennie Daniels, Harry Bright, and R.C. Stevens. Suddenly I was pitching for the team that beat us in the previous year's World Series. They didn't tease me about the Series. They won the games they had to. But I sensed that they thought they had been lucky. They knew we had the better team.

Phil Linz

Phil Linz was at loose ends when I first spoke to him two years ago. He had been in the night club business for twenty-three years, but his lease had just six months to run, and he was thinking of making a clean break. He recently did just that, and now he works for Schlott Realtors in Stamford, Connecticut. He may move back to Baltimore, Maryland, where he grew up.

The second time I spoke to Phil was at the Yankees' Old Timers' Day game in 1989. He didn't play for the Yankees that day. He played for their opponents, who represented the National League. Phil, you might remember, concluded his major-league career by playing for the Philadelphia Phillies and the New York Mets. In the visitors' clubhouse, after the game, he introduced me to Pedro Ramos and Luis Arroyo, two other Yankees I interviewed for this book.

Phil played in the majors for seven seasons and batted .235. Ironically, he batted .235 in two World Series, also. But Phil earned a permanent niche in Yankee lore and legend when he played a children's tune, "Mary Had a Little Lamb," on his newly bought harmonica one day in the late summer of 1964. The Yankees were in reverse at the time, but the harmonica incident put them in gear. They ended up winning the pennant by one game.

Phil and his wife Lyn, a stewardess for Eastern Airlines, have been married for nineteen years. They have a son, Phillip, who is a switch-hitting shortstop. There are a lot of similarities between father and son. "The one difference," Phil says, "is he can hit."

I grew up in Baltimore. I liked the heat there. I stayed there until I graduated from high school. Then I was away playing ball every year, so I decided to stay in New York.

All of a sudden, in high school, scouts were looking at me. I couldn't believe it. It was like God tapped me on the shoulder and said, "Come follow me." I went to the Yankees' Rookie Camp in 1957 and went on to have some good minor-league years. In 1960, with Greensboro, North Carolina, I batted .321, led the league, and won the MVP Award. In 1961, with Amarillo, Texas, I batted .347, led the league, and won the MVP Award. I'm the only Yankee product to lead two leagues in hitting.

I went to spring training with the 1962 Yankees. Tony Kubek was in the service so I was competing against Tommy Tresh. Kubek came back late in the season and reclaimed his job. They moved Tresh to the outfield, and he went on to make a sensational catch against Willie Mays in the World Series. He also hit a three-run game-winning homer in Game Five. Overall, he had a great season and he was named Rookie of the Year.

When I first made the Yankee club in 1962, I was awestruck. I had a lot of inner confidence but I was overawed about being there. In fact, I was worried that they would send me back to the minors. At the end of spring training, Ralph Houk, the manager, took me aside and asked me, "Do you want to go back to the minors and play every day or do you want to stay here and be a utility player?"

I said, "I want to stay here." It was good for me then but bad for me in the long run. I lost my competitive edge. I needed to play every day to get in a groove.

I didn't hit too many home runs. Eleven, I believe. I hit one of them in my rookie year. I even remember the pitch — a high slider by Dan Pfister of Kansas City. Overall, my rookie season wasn't too bad. I played three infield positions and the outfield, and I batted .287.

In 1963 I got almost two hundred at bats and I batted .269. By 1964 I started to feel established. A lot of people were hurt and I was the only utility infielder. I could play three positions. That meant the club could carry an extra pitcher. So I got into 112 games and got 368 at bats, my most in a major-league season. My average dropped to .250 but I hit five home runs and drove home twenty-five runs, also a major-league high for me. That's the year I hit two homers in the World Series. I hit the first homer off Barney Schultz in Game Two. We beat Gibson that day, 8-3. Mel Stottlemyre got the win. That was the only time we beat him. He won his other two decisions, including the seventh game. Schultz pitched in each of the first three games. In Game Three Mickey Mantle hit that awesome upper-deck shot off him in the bottom of the ninth to decide a 2-1 game. I hit my home run off Gibson in the ninth inning of Game Seven. Clete Boyer hit a homer, too, right before I did. There were two outs and two strikes on me when I hit it. Gibson was tired. Then Bobby Richardson got on. Roger Maris was up with that short porch in right-field. We still had a chance to tie it. The next spring in my first at bat I hit another homer off Gibson. That was the last hit I ever got off him. I think I made him mad.

Gibson was a great pitcher. But I batted against Sandy Koufax in the 1963 World Series and got a single. It was my only hit of the Series. But I only had three at bats. Koufax had a great fastball and a sensational curve. I never saw anyone who was similar to him. The 1963 loss to the Dodgers was hard to take. We were thoroughly beaten, swept in just four games. But the 1964 loss to the Cardinals was even tougher. We thought we were the better team, but we played bad baseball. We had never played a team like the Cardinals. They were always playing for one run. But we would have won if we had played good defense. Richardson made a couple of pivotal errors, and I made a bad play on a double-play ball in Game Seven. Also, I picked up a couple of errors on bad throws from Bobby. I guess I was coming across the bag too soon. He was probably used to working with Tony Kubek at short. Tony was a much better shortstop than I was, but he had a bad back. There was something wrong with his spine, and he didn't play in the World Series.

A crucial play in that World Series came in Game Four. We were up two games to one, and we were winning 3-0 at the time. Al Downing was pitching for us and Ken Boyer was up with the bases loaded. Ellie Howard called for a change-up with the bases loaded. I saw him wiggle his finger. I couldn't believe it. I wanted to call timeout and run to the mound, but I didn't do it. They hadn't hit a fastball all day, and it was hard to see at the plate, because of the haze and the shadows that come late in the season. The off-speed pitch allowed Boyer the chance to get his bat out in front. He hit the ball right down the left-field line for a grand-slam home run. That gave them a 4-3 lead. That's how the game ended. God, I should have called that timeout.

The harmonica incident happened in 1964. The White Sox had just swept us four straight games, and they were two and one-half games in front of us. There were fifty to sixty thousand fans there for all four games. The days were very hot and there were showers, too. After the game we were sitting in the bus, stalled in traffic, and it was extremely hot. In retrospect, I have to admit that I was feeling resentful. They had pitched lefties and I was a right-handed hitter who had a ten-game hitting streak going, and had always played well against the White Sox. But Yogi had put Boyer at third and benched me. Well, we had been sitting on that bus for about two hours, and I had just bought the harmonica that afternoon. Kubek and Tresh had been with me at the time. It was one of those Marine Band-type harmonicas, with a song sheet. I was playing by the numbers. "Mary Had a Little Lamb." Very basic.

Yogi was hot. He yelled, "Shove that thing up your ass."

I didn't hear what he said. I asked Mickey, who was seated across the aisle from me, "What'd he say?"

"Play it louder," Mick said.

Everything happened so quickly. But I played it again and I played it louder. Yogi charged me. I stood up on the seat and threw the harmonica at him. He threw it back at me. It hit Joe Pepitone, who was seated nearby. He started rolling on the floor, like he was half dead. That didn't make things any better.

"What are you yelling at me for?" I yelled at Yogi. "I give a hundred percent." After about five or ten minutes I finally sat down.

Well, the UPI writers used to ride on the bus at the time. I had sat down and Yogi had sat down. I thought to myself, *That's it.* We got on the plane and we got to Boston and we opened the newspapers and we couldn't believe the headlines. They covered the whole page. I went in to see Yogi, apologized, and we ended up shaking hands.

He said, "I've got to fine you $250. The writers have blown this thing out of proportion."

I said, "Fine." I understood. But I got that back — and more. The Hohner Harmonica Company called me and gave me $5,000 to endorse it. All of the stores in New York City sold it out in a hurry. It was a big joke at the time. Pepitone said, "You should have carried a piano on the bus. You would have made more money."

Thank God it happened, though. It became a rallying point for the Yankees, and I played great the rest of the way. We won the pennant by only one game. Thank God it happened for personal reasons, too. No one today would remember me if it hadn't.

Some people say Yogi lost control of the club in 1964. I don't feel that he did. It was easier to play for Yogi. We had been teammates. There wasn't the austere discipline there would have been under another manager, an outsider. We understood that. We also understood that he was a good guy. He had always been good to me. In my rookie year he often took me out to dinner. You couldn't cross a guy like that. But that feeling of friendship probably caused me to blow off at him. I wouldn't have done it with another manager — like Johnny Keane.

The idea of the game is to win. We wanted to do that. Yogi didn't have Kubek, and in the World Series he didn't have Whitey Ford. We were hurting in the bullpen, though Pedro Ramos had a great year for us. We didn't have our best team but he worked great with the pitching staff. Heck, he still won ninety-nine games. Casey in twelve years won more than that only once. Yogi was fired because he wasn't good with the writers. He wasn't articulate enough. He didn't give them good stuff to write. But he was an excellent manager. He proved that with the Mets, but he was fired there for the same reason.

The players did take advantage of Yogi, though. It was only natural. One day he was our teammate, and the next he was our boss. But basically the Yankees were loyal and committed to fellow Yankees. Take what happened to Hector Lopez at Newark Airport in 1965. The bartender wouldn't serve Hector. We all got upset and some nasty words were exchanged. The reason that the bartender wouldn't serve him was because Hector was black. That was almost twenty years after Jackie Robinson had gone through the same thing. It shouldn't have happened. No one was drunk. No one had more than three beers and there was no hard stuff. But the papers blew that story up, too. They made it sound like we were all drunk.

We had a bad year in 1965. We dropped from first to sixth under Keane. The big reason was that Mick and Roger were no longer Mick and Roger. Our left-handed power was depleted. We'd needed them more than we had realized. The pitching wasn't all that good, either. But give credit to Minnesota. The Twins had a great year. Zoilo Versalles won the MVP Award. Harmon Killebrew and Bob Allison had productive years, too. The Yankees were just getting old together.

Johnny Keane didn't respect us as players. He had a National League approach. For him, each game was the *only* game. We always felt that if we could stay close in a game, we could win it in the late innings, and if we could stay close in a pennant race, we could win it in the stretch. Keane would panic. There was mutual resentment. He didn't like us and we didn't like him. On the other hand, Houk used to say, "You guys are great. I'm just pushing buttons." We were used to that approach.

After the season I decided to open a night club. The Yankee organization advised me not to. When I didn't take their advice, they traded me to the Phillies for Ruben Amaro. I made $20,000 with the Yankees in 1965, $18,000 with the Phillies in 1966. I couldn't believe it when I opened their letter. Talk about not making a newly acquired player happy with a trade! I got into only forty games with the 1966 Phillies. In 1967 I got into only twenty-three. Before the 1967 All-Star Game I told manager Gene Mauch that I was going to quit. He said that he didn't want me to quit, that he would work out a deal for me. He traded me to the Mets for Chuck Hiller. I was very happy with the trade. I platooned at second with Ken Boswell. But I had lost my ability.

I regret that I didn't lead a cleaner life. I was single at the time and dating a lot of airline stewardesses. I opened the bar, Mr. Laffs, in 1965. It was the first singles' sporting bar in New York. Bob Anderson, the All-American halfback at Army, was my partner. The Mets used to come in. We had the World Series championship celebration there in 1969. I still have the same spot. Now it's called Avenue One. But the lease runs out in six months and I'm going into something different. I was never a big drinker, but when you keep late hours, you lose the edge. Consequently, when Gil Hodges asked me to come to spring training in 1969, I said, "No, Gil, I'm going to devote more time to my night club." But the grind wears you down. I work from nine in the evening to four or five in the morning Thursday, Friday, Saturday, and Sunday nights. I used to drink till seven or eight in the morning with the employees. But I don't do that anymore. I've stopped drinking permanently.

I'd like to be remembered as a guy who did the best with what he had. A guy who gave one hundred percent. A guy who loved to play the game of baseball, especially with the Yankees. A guy who did what he could to help the team. A guy who had some big thrills, especially those World Series homers. A guy whose biggest thrill was being a Yankee and being a part of the Yankee success story.

I've never really had a job. I never considered baseball a job. All I've ever done is the night club. But there have been pluses, too. I've enjoyed the time I've been able to spend with my son Phillip. At twelve he's a pretty good Little League player. He's a shortstop, like his dad, and a switch-hitter. In last year's division champion All-Star Game he hit two home runs. I've helped to coach the team and I've followed his progress. It's been great.

So if you run into anyone who's looking for a coach or a manager, tell them to give me a call. I could always play the "Star-Spangled Banner" on my harmonica.

Art Ditmar

Entering the 1960 World Series, Art Ditmar was on top of the world. Coming out of it, he was on the bottom, and the world was going to get worse before it got better.

Ditmar in 1960 had had his best overall season. He was 15-9 with a 3.06 ERA. Then Casey Stengel made a decision that would change his fate and alter Art Ditmar's destiny too. He and his coaching staff selected Art to pitch the opening game of the 1960 World Series against the Pittsburgh Pirates. It was an unorthodox move for Casey. From 1949 to 1953 he'd picked Allie Reynolds to start every World Series with the exception of 1950, when the Philadelphia Phillies surprised the baseball world by opening with Jim Konstanty, who had not started a game all year long. Casey always wanted Reynolds to pitch against the other team's best pitcher. The Phillies' best pitcher was Robin Roberts. He was scheduled to start Game Two. That's when Reynolds pitched. He defeated Roberts in ten innings, 2-1, on a Joe DiMaggio home run.

When Reynolds retired after the 1954 season, Whitey Ford took his place as the bellwether of the Yankee staff. Whitey got the nod for the opening-game start in every series from 1955-58. But in 1960 Casey and his staff deviated from tradition and form. They tabbed Ditmar for opening-game honors. Why not? He had had a better year than Ford. But the skeptics said that Ditmar had never won a World Series game, and Whitey, of course, would go on to win ten, the all-time high. Casey had left himself open for the second-guess. But that was nothing new. A big part of his success in baseball had been his ability to rely on a hunch. Joe Ostrowski of the 1950-52 teams once told me, "He always came out holding a bouquet of roses." This time he didn't. Art started two games, lost both of them, and pitched a total of only one and two-thirds innings.

Ford, on the other hand, pitched two shutouts in his only starts.

The Yankees lost the Series in seven games, Casey was done, and so was Ditmar. He never won more than two games in another major-league season. But Art was victimized by bad luck, seeing-eye hits, and a hard infield in 1960, and the worst was yet to come.

I spoke with Art by phone two summers ago. He was very congenial, a likable guy. For the first eight years after he got out of baseball, he was an assistant basketball coach at American International College in Massachusetts. Then for fifteen years he was the recreation department director in Brook Park, Ohio. He is divorced from his first wife, with whom he had four children, three sons and one daughter. (All of the sons have played baseball.) Now Art is retired and lives with his second wife, Diane, in Myrtle Beach, South Carolina, where he spends his time playing golf and tennis.

My brother George, who was two years older than I, influenced me to play baseball. My father had been interested, too, but he hadn't played sports because he'd had to work. George taught me through high school. He knew all the fundamentals. When he was at Williams College, he was the leading basketball scorer in the Northeast, and he was a starting pitcher on the baseball team for four years. By the way, a couple of years ago he went back to a reunion and had a picture taken with a classmate who'd become a big name in baseball — George Steinbrenner. Well, at any rate, he taught me pitch delivery and a curve. Then he followed my career through the pros. Whenever I was having problems, he would write to me, and invariably he would straighten me out. He had that kind of technical knowledge.

I signed with the Philadelphia Athletics at the end of 1947, after I graduated from high school. In 1948 in "C" ball, with Moline, Illinois, of the Central Association, I was the top pitcher (9-9) of a last-place club. In 1949 and 1950 I pitched with Savannah, Georgia, in the Southern Atlantic League. That was "A" ball. I was 7-6 and 14-7. The next two years, 1951 and 1952, I spent in the service at Fort Jackson in South Carolina and Camp Atterbury in Indiana. I got the chance to play with Frank Lary and Tom Brewer in the service. When I got out, I was assigned to Ottawa in the International League. But I had a bad year with them. I was only 2-13, so they optioned me back to Savannah, where I was 7-0 with a 2.01 ERA. We got to the playoffs and we got to the championship game, but we lost to Jacksonville in fourteen innings, 2-1. Hank Aaron was with Jacksonville, by the way. I got promoted to the A's spring training camp in 1954, but I was optioned to Ottawa. Late in the season the A's called me up to the big team. I got into fourteen games and pitched thirty-nine innings. I lost my first four decisions, two of them coming in relief. But I won my first major-league game on the last day of the season — against the Yankees! They had Yogi Berra and Mickey Mantle in the infield and Lou Berberet catching. They had a completely left-handed lineup that day. But they were pretty awesome. Remember, that's the year they won 103 games, but finished eight games behind the Indians. I pitched six innings and Mario Francona picked up the save.

In my first spring training that year, there was a lot of turmoil. Eddie Joost, the manager, had problems. Old players like Gus Zernial wouldn't go along with him. I remember one game I was winning against the Red Sox, 4-2. But Joost took me out and the reliever blew the lead. We just didn't know how to win. Philadelphia was not a good experience. We were really bad, we were constantly losing and the fans were constantly angry. The switch to Kansas City in 1955 was a blessing, a good experience for me. We finished sixth and the people were happy. There was no pressure. I got a chance to pitch often and ended up 12-12. One of my wins was a one-hitter. Twelve wins was a confidence-builder for me. A young pitcher needs that. You can't go out to the mound with negative thoughts. The following year, I won twelve games again. But I lost twenty-two. In sixteen of my twenty-two losses in 1956, the A's scored two runs or less. One day I was leading Detroit after seven innings, 1-0. But Al Kaline hit a two-run homer to beat me. That was typical of the season. But that's why the Yankees got me. I had a good arm, I was strong, and I pitched a lot of innings. Wherever I was, I eventually worked my way up to the best pitcher on the staff.

I didn't get too much support in Kansas City, but I had a lot of positive experiences. Lou Boudreau, my manager, was one of the best baseball strategists I ever played for. He's the guy who invented the Ted Williams shift. And the Mantle shift, too. He was constantly trying to find a way to beat you. I never could decide why Cleveland let him go. He was an excellent manager. He thought baseball twenty-four hours a day and did the best with what he had. We'd play Mantle deep, and he'd do us a favor and bunt for a base hit. I told him, "I'll give you five bunt hits if you want them." We didn't want him to swing away.

George Susce, the pitching coach with the A's, taught me the sinker. He came over from Cleveland with Oscar Melillo. Susce had taught Bob Lemon the sinker at Cleveland. We threw it the same way, with a fast rotation, like a knuckleball, off the seams. It's the closest thing you'll see to today's split-finger fastball. Vic Raschi taught me the slider and how to relax on the mound. He dressed in the locker next to me. He was a quiet, unassuming guy. He never bragged about his big days in the Bronx. We both came from the same area — Springfield, Massachusetts. We became good friends. I know there are stories that he was a tense competitor, that he always had sweat in the palms of his hands when he was out on the mound. Well, if he was tense on the mound, he never showed it. To me, he always seemed very poised.

In my days with the A's, the team was referred to as the Kansas City shuttle. They were always, it seemed, trading quality young players for quantity. We finished last in 1956 and after the season I was involved in one of those big trades with the Yankees. On February 19, 1957, I went to the Yankees along with Bobby Shantz, Jack McMahan, Wayne Belardi, Curt Roberts, and Clete Boyer. The A's got Billy Hunter, Rip Coleman, Tom Morgan, Mickey McDermott, Milt Graff, and Irv Noren. The writers said at the time that it was a "steal" by the Yankees. But I don't know. At the time I thought it was a reasonable trade. Shantz had a bad arm and Boyer was a young player. Kansas City, on the other hand, got a ball club. But in the long run it turned out right for the Yankees — and for me.

With the Yankees in 1957, I was 8-3. I worked mostly out of the bullpen, where I won six games, lost only one, and saved six. Sometimes I was a spot starter. That's what they wanted from me. We had nine starters on the team. They wanted me to pitch against the Tigers and the White Sox, teams I had pitched well against with the A's, and to miss the Red Sox, a team I hadn't pitched well against.

Casey knew what you did against other teams. One day he put me in to pinch hit against Tom Morgan. When I was with Kansas City and Morgan was with the Yankees, I hit a home run against him one day. Well, this day with the Yankees, we were down seven runs in the ninth, but we had a rally going. Casey said to me, "I know you can hit this guy." I doubled down the right-field line. That tied the score. Joe DeMaestri singled to win the game. Casey had a great memory for situations. That was the most admirable thing about him. He got on you when you won, left you alone when you lost. He was a great psychologist. We got along great. He second-guessed me at times and we had some confrontations, but he helped me, too. One night on a train, he convinced me that I would be a better pitcher if I threw more inside. He was right. He also got me raises. My highest salary was $30,000. But they figured your World Series check into your salary. They figured if they gave you a contract for $30,000, they were really paying you a salary between $40,000 and $50,000.

Until 1958 I had always thrown away from the hitters. Then, that night on the train, Casey said, "There's some talk that you're going to be traded back to Kansas City. It's you or Bob Grim. But I'm sticking with you. I want you to pitch inside to hitters, though. If you do, you'll do much better." And I did. In the World Series against the Braves that year, I relieved Whitey Ford with the bases loaded and two out, busted the hitter on the hands, and got out of the jam with one pitch.

Most people think that my best year was 1960, when I was 15-9 and got to start the first game of the World Series. I think 1959 was my best year. I was 13-9 with a 2.90 ERA. Most of the Yankees had sub-par years in 1959. There were a lot of injuries, too. We finished just four games over .500, in third place.

My pitching coaches with the Yankees? Jim Turner was there through 1959. He was good. So was Eddie Lopat, who was there for only one year. He taught me the fast slider and the off-center slider. All of Casey's coaches were good. He also had Bill Dickey, Frankie Crosetti, and Jim Hegan. Once in a while Casey would catnap on the bench, but that didn't take away from the quality of his thinking. He knew what he wanted to do, he knew he had an excellent coaching staff, and he delegated authority to it. Turner took care of the staff. He always knew how many pitches you had thrown. But he was quiet and he never got the credit he deserved. That was the Yankee way. They constantly told us, "Don't worry about your average. Just move the runner along. If you do that, you'll all get raises." That was the Yankees. When the team won, everyone won.

My role changed in 1959 because the situation changed. They decided they wanted only four or five starters and a couple of dominant closers. They wanted us starters to go seven innings, and they wanted Luis Arroyo and Ryne Duren to finish it off. In the bullpen I would throw five days in a row and not be used, then I would be used on the sixth day. That's tough on your arm. But I didn't care whether I started or relieved. The important thing was that I was with the Yankees. There was a big difference between Kansas City and New York. I was a sinkerball pitcher so I depended on my infield. If balls went by my infielders, I was in trouble. That's what happened in the 1960 World Series against the Pirates. In Kansas City I would be done in by a walk, a double play that wasn't made, and a seeing-eye hit through the infield. In 1960, with the Yankees, I gave up twenty-six home runs, but twenty-four of them were with no one on base. The big hit didn't mean as much in New York.

To me, Mickey Mantle was the greatest player who ever lived. Some say Willie Mays was better. I disagree. Mantle was a total player. He did it from both sides of the plate. He could field, run, and hit. He played hurt and he played big in big games. He could do it all. They threw at his ankles and legs all the time, but he never complained. He just produced.

That reminds me of Larry Doby. In his book he called me a racist. That wasn't so. He also said that he broke my jaw. That wasn't so, either. He just knocked my cap off. He was probably more of a racist than any white player at that time. You threw tight to get the batter off the plate. They threw at Mantle all the time. Was it because he was white? Doby felt that if you threw him tight, it was because he was black. It would be stupid for a pitcher to do something like that. He'd just get behind in the count. The purpose of a close pitch is to get the batter off the plate. Well, the pitch I threw to him was a foot over his head. In fact, it got past Ellie Howard or Yogi, I forget who, and went back to the screen, so I had to cover home plate. When I got to the plate, Doby said to me, "If you do that again, I'll put a knife in you." Larry Napp, the plate umpire, heard him say it. When he made a move at me, Bill Skowron tackled him. A big melee followed. I was the only one in it who wasn't thrown out of the game. Al Lopez, the White Sox manager, wanted to know why. Napp mentioned Doby's comment about the knife and Lopez just turned and walked away.

By the time 1961 rolled around, I was an established starter. Then Johnny Sain came in as the pitching coach. He had some good theories. He believed in putting rotation on the ball. But I got away from what I won with. My bread-and-butter pitches were the sinker and the slider. All of a sudden, I'm going to the curve ball. I won my first two games but then I started having problems, and Ralph Houk, who was a rookie manager, lost confidence in me. At the trading deadline I wasn't going well. In fact, I lost a little confidence in myself. But Ralph told me I wouldn't be traded. You know, the old vote-of-confidence cliché. I went out and pitched five hitless innings in Cleveland, and they traded me back to Kansas City the next day.

I was told by the traveling secretary. That was disappointing. We'd had some confrontations, but I wasn't an also-ran. I won forty-seven games for them. The trade was a hard thing to accept. Coming off my best win season (fifteen) and an opening-game start in the World Series, I won only two games for a team that hit a record 240 home runs. Can you believe that? I can't. But things immediately went from bad to worse. I went over to Kansas City after my best major-league season, pitched nine hitless innings in two relief appearances, and Joe Gordon, the manager, came up to me and said, "I don't know why the trade was made. We don't need starting pitchers. You can't pitch for us." That was ridiculous. No wonder he didn't last as the manager. But he was replaced by Hank Bauer in September, and I didn't pitch an inning for the rest of the season. In one year I had gone from the sublime to the ridiculous. It was a nightmare.

The following year, the nightmare got worse. I hurt my shoulder in spring training. I came down with tendonitis and the A's released me. To make things worse, I gave up half my salary. I could have held them to my contract, but I listened to them when they said, "Many clubs will want to pick you up." The bottom line was they didn't want to pay me what they owed me — $25,000.

Well, no one picked me up. I worked out with the Yankees in August, and they said that they would sign me, but they signed Skinny Brown instead. In spring training in 1963, I took x-ray therapy and my arm felt all right. The Yankees were hoping for a three-for-two deal that would open up a spot on the roster for me, but it didn't work out. There were no Tommy Johns at that time. At thirty-two I was done. The only club I didn't contact was Kansas City. That turned out to be a big mistake. Eddie Lopat was their manager then. He later asked me, "Why didn't you get in touch with me? We could have used you."

I said, "Well, Kansas City released me in 1962. I didn't think you were interested." I probably messed up but that's the way things were going in my life at that time. Was I bitter? You bet I was.

I still have regrets. I regret not being able to come back and get the opportunity to pitch. They said I had tendonitis. It might have been a rotator cuff. But the x-ray therapy during spring training in 1963 helped my shoulder. I was totally healthy and ready to pitch. No one would use me. It wasn't right; I wasn't at the right place at the right time. But there were more pluses than minuses. If I had come up through the Yankee system, I might not have gotten the chance to pitch with the Yankees. They might have traded me away. The Yankees had a winning attitude. You knew that you were going to win three-quarters of your games. Winning breeds success. Losing breeds losing, too. That's the way it was at Kansas City. We tried to keep the score close. The Yankees didn't think about losing. Consequently, it was a shock to them when they lost. The A's always thought about losing. They were shocked when they won.

I always tried to do my best, and I never offered excuses. Also, I pitched the way they needed me: middle relief, short relief, starter. I pitched hard and I pitched hurt. I didn't complain. And I've got a lot of good memories. My home run against Morgan. My other one against Camilo Pascual. It gave us a 1-0 lead in Washington. Pascual went crazy on the mound, then walked off the hill. My second time up that day, I singled with the bases loaded. That made the score 4-0. After the single Pascual threw his glove in the air.

Sandy Amoros of the Brooklyn Dodgers makes the key play of the 1955 Series. The Yankees had runners at first and second base with no outs in the bottom of the sixth inning of Game Seven when Amoros gloved Yogi Berra's slicing fly ball toward the left-field line, pivoted, and threw to shortstop Pee Wee Reese. Reese relayed to first baseman Gil Hodges for the critical double play which dashed the Yankees' hopes and gave the Dodgers their first world championship.

(Above) Enos Slaughter's three-run homer in the bottom of the sixth inning of Game Three turned the 1956 Series around. At the time the Brooklyn Dodgers led the Series, two games to none, and the game, 2-1. The Yankees went on to win the game, 5-3, and the Series, 4-3.

(Left) Tom Sturdivant, who won 16 games in both 1956 and 1957, pitched a six-hit 6-2 win in Game Four of the 1956 Series. He was part of a fivesome that pitched a record five consecutive complete games in Fall Classic play: Whitey Ford, himself, Don Larsen, Bob Turley, and Johnny Kucks.

(Right) Gerry Coleman takes a toss at second base. Yankee players from that era say that no other second baseman was as good as Coleman in making the double play.

(Above) In the fifth game of the 1956 World Series, Don Larsen (left) pitched the perfect game, Babe Pinelli called the perfect game, and Yogi Berra caught the perfect game.

(Below) In Game Seven of the 1956 Series, Yogi Berra hit two two-run home runs against the Dodgers' Don Newcombe. Bill Skowron (14), who was getting ready to greet Yogi, hit a grand-slam home run, and Elston Howard hit a solo clout in the Yankees' 9-0 rout of the Dodgers.

(Above) Johnny Kucks, who won 18 games in 1956, pitched the seventh game of that year's Series. He pitched a three-hit 9-0 shutout against the Dodgers to avenge the Yankees' defeat at the hands of Brooklyn in 1955.

(Below) Whitey Ford follows through on the first pitch of the 1957 Series to Milwaukee Braves lead-off hitter Red Schoendienst. Ford went on to pitch a five-hit 3-1 win. Andy Carey delivered the game-winning hit with a sixth-inning single against Warren Spahn.

(Above) Tony Kubek, who is greeted by Mickey Mantle at home plate, tied a rookie record when he hit two home runs in Game Three of the 1957 Series. The Yankees won, 12-3. Charlie Keller of the 1939 Yankees had set the record.

(Below) Elston Howard's three-run pinch-hit home run in the top of the ninth inning of Game Four in the 1957 Series tied the score at 4-4. But in the bottom of the tenth inning Eddie Mathews hit a two-run homer to give the Braves a 7-5 victory. The blow evened the Series at two games apiece.

(Above) This play proved to be pivotal in the seventh game of the 1957 Series. In the third inning, with the bases loaded, Johnny Logan hit a double-play ball to Tony Kubek at third base. Instead of getting out of the inning, though, the Yankees were victimized by Kubek's high throw to Gerry Coleman at second base. Milwaukee's runner Bob Hazle was safe at second and Logan was safe at first. The Braves went on to score four runs in the inning en route to their Series-clinching 5-0 victory.

(Left) Hank Bauer springs off the right-field fence in pursuit of Hank Aaron's game-tying double in the eighth inning of the opening game of the 1958 Series. The hometown Braves went on to win the game in ten innings, 4-3. Bauer went on to hit in 17 consecutive World Series games.

(Right) Elston Howard made the play that turned around the 1958 World Series. The Yankees were down in games, three-to-one, and up in the score 1-0 when Howard made his sparkling play in the top of the sixth inning. Billy Bruton had led off the inning with a single for the Braves. When Red Schoendienst hit a slicing fly ball to left, Howard made a diving catch and doubled up Bruton, who had rounded second on the play.

(Above) *The three heroes of the fifth game of the 1958 Series enjoy a satisfying moment after their 7-0 victory. Elston Howard (left) made a scintillating catch and play in the sixth inning, Bob Turley (center) picked up the win, and Gil McDougald hit a home run and a double.*

(Below) *McDougald connecting on a homer to left in the same game.*

(Above) Three of the happy heroes of Game Six of the 1958 World Series celebrate the Yankees' win that evened the Classic at three games apiece. In the 4-3 victory Hank Bauer (left) hit a homer, Ryne Duren (center) picked up the win in relief, and Gil McDougald hit a homer in the tenth inning.

(Above) Third baseman Jerry Lumpe dives to stop first baseman Bill Skowron's throw as Billy Bruton of the Braves slides back to the bag. Wes Covington had tapped a ball in front of home plate, Yogi Berra threw him out at first, and Skowron tried to throw behind Bruton after he had advanced from second to third and had overrun the bag. The Yankees went on to win the seventh game of the 1958 Series, 6-2. Lumpe played in six of the seven games, as a pinch-hitter, third baseman, and shortstop.

(Above) In spring training of 1959 (left to right) Tom Sturdivant, Art Ditmar, Whitey Ford, Bobby Shantz, and Yogi Berra compare notes. The 1959 season proved to be the only one during this period in which the Yankees failed to win the pennant. Besieged by injuries, they finished just four games over .500.

(Left) They might have been putting Casey Stengel "out to pasture" when this picture was taken at spring training in 1960. In that year Casey went on to win his tenth pennant with the Yankees, but he was fired by the club's brass shortly after his Bombers were defeated by the Pittsburgh Pirates in seven games in the World Series.

(Right) During the Yankees' 2-0 victory over the Cincinnati Reds in the first game of the 1961 World Series, Bill Skowron hit a solo home run in the sixth inning.

This 1961 photo says it all. Roger Maris (seated at left) hit a record 61 home runs, Ralph Houk (standing in the middle of the dugout) led the Yankees to 109 victories in his first season as a manager, Yogi Berra (standing at right) was one of three Yankee catchers to hit more than 20 home runs, and Mickey Mantle (seated at right) hit 54 round-trippers.

(Left) Clete Boyer gets an assist and a putout as Wally Post of the Cincinnati Reds tries to go from second to third base on Darrell Johnson's bouncer to the third-sacker in the fifth inning of the opening game of the 1961 Series. Whitey Ford pitched a two-hit 2-0 shutout.

(Right) Ralph Terry, who won 23 games in 1962 and won the final game of that year's Series, 1-0, warms up here under the watchful eye of pitching coach Johnny Sain.

Johnny Sain says that the 1961-63 Yankees had the best coaching staff in the history of the game. During the 1963 spring training season they posed (left to right) for the cameras: manager Ralph Houk, Jim Hegan, Sain, Yogi Berra, and (kneeling) Frankie Crosetti.

(Above) Stan Musial throws out the first ball at the 1963 World Series opener while Joe DiMaggio and Commissioner Ford Frick (seated) smile their approval. The Dodgers defeated the Yankees in four straight games as Sandy Koufax did some throwing of his own.

(Left) Pitching coach Johnny Sain (left) and Luis Arroyo talk pitching. In 1954, Sain's last full year with the Yankees, he led the American League in saves with 22. In 1961 Arroyo led the American League in saves with 29.

(Right) Mickey Mantle proudly displays his 1962 MVP Award, which was presented to him on Opening Day at Yankee Stadium in 1963.

(Above) Casey Stengel visits with manager Ralph Houk during the 1963 Series.

On November 15, 1963, Whitey Ford (center) was named the Yankees' player-pitching coach by manager Yogi Berra and general manager Ralph Houk.

Joe Pepitone, who hit 28 home runs and drove home 100 runs in 1964, is thrown out here in that year's World Series against the Cardinals. Current National League president Bill White took the throw.

(Above) Dick Groat, the Cardinals' shortstop, sneaks in behind Mickey Mantle for a pick-off attempt in the 1964 Series. In Game Four Groat successfully pulled the hidden-ball trick against Mantle, turning around the game and the Series in the Cardinals' favor.

Mel Stottlemyre pitched in a 5-2 loss to Bob Gibson in the fifth game of the 1964 Series. Rookie Stottlemyre won one and lost one in three starts.

Each of these three slugging outfielders (left to right) — Mickey Mantle, Tom Tresh, and Roger Maris — was on the down side of his career when this photo was taken in 1966.

But the World Series is the ultimate and I played in three of them. I've gotten a bad rap for the 1960 World Series, but there were reasons. In the 1957 World Series I pitched well in two mid-inning appearances, and overall, I pitched six scoreless innings. No one's given me credit for the job I did in the 1958 World Series, either. I got Ford out of that bases-loaded jam, and then I pitched an additional three and one-third innings of scoreless ball.

In 1960 I had pure bad luck. There were runners running and no one covering, and there were high hoppers on a cement infield. I said earlier that if balls went through the infield, I was in trouble. Howard Cosell mentioned every year for ten straight years that Casey made a mistake in not starting Whitey Ford in the opening game. But it was my best year. I was 15-9 to Whitey's 12-9. Yes, as it worked out, Whitey might have won three games, but anyone can second-guess. Casey and his coaching staff made the decision based upon the respective seasons we had. Even Whitey said, "I don't think Art had two consecutive bad starts during the whole season."

The best hit against me in my two starts was Dick Groat's double into the right-field corner. It bounced just inside the foul line. In my second start Smoky Burgess hit a broken-bat double. Then on a ground ball to Tony Kubek at shortstop, Burgess, who was a bad runner, went to third when he shouldn't have. The ball was hit in front of him. But Gil McDougald dropped Tony's throw. Then Bill Mazeroski hit a high hopper over Gil's head. Roberto Clemente did the same thing in Game One. The ground was like pavement.

There were no long balls. There were no walks. What happened, happened. My sinker was working. It just didn't work out. A lot of things didn't work out.

Tom Sturdivant

Tom Sturdivant was another pitcher whose meteoric start slowed to a snail's crawl. In his first four years with the Yankees, the Bombers won four consecutive pennants. In his first two full seasons he won sixteen games in back-to-back years. Then he injured his rotator cuff, and the rest of his career was a struggle. In his last seven seasons, he won a total of twenty-six games, less than four victories per season. His best season was 1957, when he was 16-6 with a league-leading .727 winning percentage and a 2.54 ERA. That year he pitched 202 innings. He never came remotely close to that number in his other nine seasons.

Sturdivant roomed with some good pitchers: Bob Turley, Ralph Terry, Whitey Ford, and Bob Friend. He also roomed with one non-pitcher, Rocky Colavito. His outstanding thrills were winning his first major-league game, winning his one World Series decision, playing on a world championship team, seeing Don Larsen pitch his perfect game, and pitching with the Yankees.

Tom has been in the trucking business for a long time. For seventeen years he was in the freight and truck leasing business, and for the last seven years, he has concentrated on freight. He is part-owner of R & R Trucking, Inc.

"I do national accounts," he says. "I drive between 65,000 and 75,000 miles a year. Generally, I won't fly, because I don't like jets. I'm in the steel business, and I know that no one knows about the wearing of steel."

When I first tried to contact Sturdivant in the summer of 1989, he was on a business junket to Ohio. I caught up with him in Akron and arranged the interview for the following Sunday. He lives in Oklahoma City, Oklahoma, with his wife, Elaine, three sons, and a daughter.

 I went to the Yankees in 1955, at the age of twenty-five. I got one start, and I got into thirty-three games. My record was only one-and-three, but I had a 3.16 ERA. Basically the Yankees' intention was to give me experience. It worked out well. That one start, I got beat by Vic Raschi, who was with Kansas City at the time. I remember Casey walking up and down the dugout, saying, "You've got to get to this guy early. You better get going. He's going to beat you. He's a pro, you know."

In 1956 I got into one less game — thirty-two — but seventeen of my games were starts. That wasn't the way it was in the beginning of the year. I was basically working out of the bullpen when I got on a roll. I won three consecutive games against Cleveland, Boston, and Chicago. Finally they gave me a start against Cleveland, and I won it. Then they put me in the lineup as a spot starter. One of the reasons was that Bob Turley had hurt his shoulder. Up until that point he was a power pitcher. Afterwards he could still throw as hard, but he couldn't throw hard for as long. Then he came up with that beautiful curve and had that great year in 1958. In 1956 I ended up with sixteen wins and a 3.30 ERA.

That year's World Series was a great one. We beat the Dodgers in seven memorable games. The Dodgers, you'll remember, won the first two games, then we won three straight. Whitey Ford beat Roger Craig in Game Three, 5-3. Enos Slaughter hit a three-run homer to turn the game around. In Game Four I defeated Carl Erskine, 6-2. And in Game Five Don Larsen pitched his perfect game against Sal Maglie, 2-0. We had momentum at that time but we lost it the next day. Clem Labine edged Turley in ten innings, 1-0. That's the day Enos misjudged Jackie Robinson's line drive. But Johnny Kucks pitched a great game in Game Seven, and we won, 9-0. Yogi Berra hit two two-run homers, Elston Howard hit a solo shot, and Bill Skowron hit a grand slam. They accounted for all of our runs.

I remember my game very well. I was winning 6-2 in the ninth inning, but I loaded the bases with no outs. The Old Man came out and said, "You've thrown 153 pitches. You usually throw 108 or 109. I'm going to give you one more hitter." I got him on a pop-up. Then Casey came out again. "I'm going to give you one more hitter." I got him out. On another pop-up, I think. Casey came out and said again, "I'm going to give you one more hitter." That's the truth. I got Junior Gilliam to fly out to Mickey Mantle in center, and the game was over. There were no more hitters to get.

You want to know something that not too many people know? In those last five games we got five complete games from five different pitchers. It had never been done before in the World Series. It's never been done since.

The following year I won sixteen games again. In 1956 I lost eight. In 1957 I dropped six. That's the year I won the league's winning percentage. Seven twenty-seven. I had an ERA of 2.54 that year. That was also my all-time low. But I didn't win the ERA title. Bobby Shantz beat me out on the last day of the season. It wasn't bad to lose to him, though. He was at one time a really great pitcher. If he hadn't gotten hurt, we can only guess how many games he might have won.

I was a better pitcher in 1957 than I was in 1956. I think it was confidence. Plus, I was the only pitcher who didn't go to the bullpen that year. You might say that everything went right. You might also say that I had a fantastic defense behind me. So many balls that I threw were ripped right back through the middle. I was sure they were going to center field. But when I turned around, I would see Gil McDougald playing the hitter just perfectly. He threw the runners out consistently. I guess the defense was playing where I was pitching.

There was another play that year that I'll never forget. Harvey Kuenn of the Tigers was the batter. In the first half of the game, I was pitching him inside. But late in the game they didn't want him to hit a cheap home run inside the foul pole, so they told me to pitch him outside, and that's what I did. Well, he hit a line drive toward the auxiliary scoreboard. It was where we wanted him to hit it. Hank Bauer couldn't reach the ball with his glove hand, though, so he dove and deflected the ball to Mickey who caught it after it bounced off his chest. The play saved a one-run victory. None of us had ever seen a play like that. Hank ran into the dugout and said without the trace of a smile, "Mick, after all that practice, we finally got a chance to use that play."

In the 1957 World Series I wasn't so fortunate. I started Game Four and was leading 1-0 until the bottom of the fourth inning, when Hank Aaron roughed me up for a three-run homer and Frank Torre touched me for a solo shot. We came back to take the lead, but the Braves scored three runs in the bottom of the tenth to win the game, 7-5. Remember, Eddie Mathews hit a two-run homer off Bob Grim. The wind was blowing hard, but Aaron hit the ball way back in the left-field seats. You could say he hit it harder than I threw it.

Everything turned sour in 1958. I ended the season with a three-six record. My trouble was a rotator cuff. It never worked itself out. Turley didn't help me any, either. He won five of his first six starts and went on to win twenty-one. He also won the Cy Young Award that year. Anyway, I never did really get in the swing that year, and it was someone else's turn.

The 1958 World Series was great — for the team — not for me. We fell behind the Braves, three games to one, but we came back to win three straight to take the world championship. It was awesome. And Turley was unbelievable. He won Game Five in a start. A 7-0 shutout over Lew Burdette. Then he saved Game Six in relief of Ryne Duren. The next day, in Game Seven, he pitched six and two-thirds innings of sensational relief. We won 6-2. I warmed up three times in the Series, but it was too cold. I didn't want to take the chance.

After the season the handwriting was on the wall. On May 26, 1959, I was traded to Kansas City with Johnny Kucks and Jerry Lumpe for Ralph Terry and Hector Lopez. But I was still disappointed. I had been a Yankee fan all my life, I had come up to the majors with the Yankees, and I had played in three consecutive World Series with them. They were a great team and they had a great bunch of guys. But I decided I would try to beat them every chance I got. Man, I tried, but I never did.

That torn rotator cuff has haunted me ever since 1958. The following year, I picked up a knuckleball and it worked out well for me, because my shoulder was never again strong. It still bothers me. Last year I went to a Fantasy Camp, and it locked up on me. A doctor looked at it and he said that the tear was too deep to fix. They wouldn't have been able to fix it then, either.

From 1959 to 1964 I bounced around quite a bit. I was with Kansas City twice, Washington, Pittsburgh, Detroit, and the Mets. I had a couple of good years with the Pirates. I was 5-2 in 1961 and 9-5 in 1962. I threw well with them, especially in the warm weather. I won in the middle of the season and lost in the beginning and at the close of it, when the weather was cold and damp. It was my best experience outside New York. Danny Murtaugh was a very fair manager. He gave me a chance to pitch and I responded well. Also, they had a heck of a club. Remember, they beat the Yankees in the 1960 World Series. And they had a good blend of veterans and young players. Maybe they felt they had done it once and they couldn't do it again.

Casey would get after me pretty strong. He knew that I was bullheaded, and he knew I pitched better when I was mad, so he stayed on my case. There were times when it paid off. You know, in the second half of 1957, I didn't lose one game that I started. In fact, Casey took me out when I was pitching a couple of shutouts. But I didn't mind. I knew we had Bob Grim and Shantz in the bullpen. You didn't mind turning a lead over to those guys. When I finished with the Mets in 1964, Casey was the manager there, too. He was still the same old Casey. Same psychology, same style, different horses. He and George Weiss set up a developmental program. They turned out pitchers like Tom Seaver and Al Jackson, who is a great friend of mine. Eventually they started winning, developed a pattern, and it has continued.

I missed baseball for a long time, but I don't now. The trucking and freight business has been very satisfying. I still enjoy taking my clients to the ballpark, though, especially in Cleveland. Doc Edwards is the manager of the Indians. He was my teammate with Kansas City. I like to talk with Herb Score, Cleveland's announcer, too. I'll never forget the night he got hit by Gil McDougald's line drive. How I wish we could take back that night and give back his sight. But he's handled it very well. He's never once mentioned it. Still, it's like it happened only yesterday. You know what he did when he got hit? He instinctively reached for the St. Jude medal he was wearing. I'll never forget it.

I hope the fans will remember that I had one good hitting year. I batted .313 and had twenty hits. Was it 1956? I'm proud of that season.

I've been pretty fortunate. I've had a lot of thrills. I saw Don Larsen pitch the only perfect World Series game. The day before, I pitched a complete-game win, my only World Series decision. Another day, in 1964 when I was with the Mets — it was Father's Day — I pitched four or five innings of scoreless ball. That was my last major-league game. It was also the day Jim Bunning of the Phillies pitched his perfect game.

Steve Hamilton

When Steve Hamilton left baseball in 1973, he didn't know what he wanted to do. He had a master's degree, so he returned to his alma mater, Morehead State in Kentucky, where he had been a basketball and baseball star, to teach and help the baseball coach.

During the next couple of years he bounced around quite a bit. He did some scouting, managed a rookie camp, sold insurance, and was Ralph Houk's pitching coach in Detroit. "I hated the insurance business," he says. "I was just not happy. I enjoyed working with Ralph, but I was away from home too much, so I left the Tigers after one season."

At the end of 1975, Steve's future stabilized. The president of Morehead State offered him the position of head baseball coach, and Steve accepted. "It was the best decision I've ever made," Hamilton says. "I love working with kids, not only on the playing field but also in the classroom and the corridors. Being around young people is invigorating. In fact, it makes you feel young, too."

Two years ago the president of the university asked Steve to move up to the post of athletic director. "I hated to give up baseball, but the athletic director's position posed a new challenge. I've simply expanded my base of operations. I'm still involved in sports, my lifelong love, and I'm still connected with youngsters, only this time on a broader scale."

Steve lives in Morehead, Kentucky, with his wife of thirty-four years, Shirley, and his four children, two sons and two daughters.

When I got the opportunity to

pitch for the Cleveland Indians in 1961, it was a dream come true. In those days they could keep twenty-eight players on the roster for the first thirty days of the season, then they had to cut down to twenty-five players. I was one of the three casualties. But I had a contingency contract that said I got $6,000 if I was there on Opening Day. Hoot Evers came downstairs from the front office on Opening Day and handed me a check for $6,000. I'd never seen so much money before. Then they asked me to pitch batting practice. No one even hit a loud foul off me. I was pumped up, because I never thought I would get to pitch in the big leagues.

The reason was, first, I thought I had limited ability and, second, the Indians brought their entire organization to spring training with them. When I was in Class "D" ball, we trained at Daytona, Florida. They had 350 players there. The odds seemed insurmountable. I gave myself four years to make the majors. One year I wrote a letter to President Gabe Paul and said I was going to quit at the end of the year if he didn't trade me. I had a master's degree and I intended to become a teacher. I wasn't going anywhere in the Indians' organization, so I said , "We'll both benefit if you trade me." Two weeks later he traded me. I'm grateful that he did and with the way it turned out. I've been very fortunate in life. I've been able to do everything I've wanted to. I even quit when the timing was right. A lot of players hang on until they're released and then can't cope with it for the rest of their lives.

Well, Paul traded me to Washington, and in 1962 I got into forty-one games with the Senators and had a 3-8 record. My Washington experience taught me that I could pitch in the major leagues. I didn't know if the team could play in the big leagues, though. We had some good players but overall we were bad. When I was traded to Washington, the Senators were in New York, and I was directed to report to Yankee Stadium. I took a flight to Newark Airport, then an eighteen-dollar taxi ride to the stadium. It was tough for me to get into the Stadium. They didn't believe I was a major-league player. I finally convinced them, and I dressed and went to the bench in the second inning. I said hello to manager Mickey Vernon, and he directed me to report to the bullpen. It was a strange experience. I didn't know anyone. I hadn't played with any of them in the minors. As it turned out, Gene Woodling, the old Yankee, hit a two-run homer to give us the lead, and Vernon signaled for me to come in and save the game. When I got to the mound, Kenny Retzer, the catcher, was there. I knew him. The rest of the Senators must have been saying, "Who the hell is he?" I forget who was the starter but, as it turned out, I saved his game. When I came into the clubhouse after the game, he gave me a big smooch. It was the weirdest experience I had ever had. I said to myself, "What have I gotten myself into?"

The next year I was traded to the Yankees. I had mixed emotions about that. There was a lot of excitement and a lot of doubt. Washington was a security blanket. New York was the world champs. I realized that if I didn't do well, I could be out of baseball. But the excitement was greater than the doubt. I got there more than a day early, and I had a good year with the Yankees in 1963. I was 5-1 out of the bullpen with five saves. My ERA was 2.94. My ERA was always good and I played on some poor teams. Overall it was 3.05. My forte was that I could get left-handers out.

One special game in 1963 stands out in my memory. I came in against the Orioles with two outs in the first inning and went all the way, striking out eleven — my career high — walking none, and getting two hits, one of which was a triple. To top it off, Dizzy Dean and Pee Wee Reese did the whole thing on the "Game of the Week." In that year's World Series I got into the ninth inning of the first game. That was the day that Sandy Koufax set a record when he struck out fifteen batters. I whiffed him in the ninth inning to add to the total two-team record. In that inning I was as nervous as I've ever been. I was just hoping that I could hit the catcher's glove rather than the screen with my pitches. Striking out Koufax and pitching one scoreless inning was a moral victory.

In 1964 we had a good team that struggled. Our biggest problem was that Tony Kubek was hurt. He came back from the service and hurt first his arm, then his back. The source of the injuries was a cracked vertebra in his back. He was such a competitor. He got it in a two-hand touch football game in the service. It was a deadly blow to us. He was our leader. I'm not trying to demean Phil Linz, who took Tony's place. I'm just saying that everyone knows he was not Tony Kubek. In 1964 I was 7-2. That sounds pretty good but I had those seven wins at the All-Star break. During one stretch, though, I pitched five games in three days, and I came down with tendonitis and missed virtually the whole second half of the season. Mel Stottlemyre, Pedro Ramos, and Roger Maris were the keys to 1964. Stottlemyre came up sometime in July and won nine games. He went on to start three games in the World Series. That's pretty amazing. Ramos came over to us in September and saved everything in sight. If he had been eligible for the World Series, we would have won it. And Maris turned it on in September. Just about every game we won, he had the game-winning hit. Yogi didn't make any great moves in September. In fact, it was the lack of moves that paid off. He pitched Stottlemyre every four days, he relied on Ramos out of the bullpen, and Maris made the difference on offense. Yogi played a set lineup every day. That was the key.

In the 1964 World Series I got into two games, the sixth and the seventh. In the sixth game I came in to get Bob Skinner, a lefty, but he singled up the middle. Then I got Curt Flood to hit into an inning-ending double play. In the seventh game I came in to strike out Lou Brock and Bill White, two lefties, but then Kenny Boyer took one of my sliders off the base of the bullpen wall. He was the MVP that year and he hit that ball a ton. Clete Boyer, his brother, was playing third for us. I looked over at third, where Kenny was standing, and I saw Clete with his glove in front of his face, laughing. He couldn't believe his brother had hit a ball so far. I laughed, too. Inside, I couldn't believe what was happening. Here we were, in the seventh game of the World Series, and two members of one club were laughing about an adverse event. But the game's supposed to be fun, right? Then Tim McCarver, a lefty, stepped into the box. I made him look bad on two consecutive pitches. What he did next surprised me. He crossed his eyes and blew out his cheeks. You know, his elevator wasn't always going to the top floor. But anyway we stood there laughing at each other. That just proves it — baseball is a funny game.

Boyer probably got the turning-point hit in the Series. It was in Game Four. We were winning 3-0 at the time, but the Cardinals loaded the bases and Boyer hit a grand-slam home run to give the Cardinals a 4-3 victory. He hit it off an Al Downing change-up, and it has gone down in history as a controversial pitch. Some people say that Downing should have stayed with his heat, especially because of the shadows that creep out toward the mound at Yankee Stadium in early October. But those shadows are a misconception. The batter can see the ball well. He just can't judge the speed. Boyer was a good fastball hitter. Curves and change-ups would throw his rhythm off, especially under the circumstances. I agree with Downing's choice of a pitch one hundred percent. Al just got the ball in a wrong location. He got the ball up. But if Bobby Richardson had made the play on the previous ground ball, we wouldn't even be talking about Al's choice of pitch. True, the ball took a funny hop but it was a playable ball.

If we had won the game, we would have been up three games to one. But we let the game get away from us, and the Series was tied at two games apiece. We let the fifth game get away from us, too. Yogi let Pete Mikkelsen pitch too long in that one. McCarver hit a three-run homer in the tenth inning to give the Cardinals a 5-2 win. I was warming up at the time. As I said before, I could always get left-handers out. That game really hurt. I should have been in that game. Ralph Houk, who was the general manager at the time, came up to me after the game and said, "Was your arm hurting?"

I said, "No, it was fine." I hate to second-guess Yogi, but he went with Pete too long. It was, I guess, another nail in Yogi's coffin.

In 1965 you could see that the dynasty was crumbling. The minor league system was deteriorating, and there were no left-handed arms in the system. I got my chance because Marshall Bridges, Bud Daley, and Luis Arroyo got hurt. CBS, when it took over the ownership of the Yankees, killed whatever was left in the minors. They cut back on the minor-league scouting and operational organization. And they made Mike Burke the president. He was a nice guy but he didn't know anything about baseball. CBS's acquisition of the Yankees was strictly a money deal. All they were interested in was ratings, but they plummeted after CBS took over. They even gave the club away. George Steinbrenner and his associates bought the club for $10 million. CBS didn't know anything about baseball.

The next couple of years were not fun. We had been the best. Now we were the worst. People didn't boo us anymore. When that happens, you know you're in trouble. Also, we had a lot of players coming and going. There was no continuity. Mickey had an arm operation, and he seemed to be coming back fine, but he didn't do the exercises that were prescribed for him, and he had a setback. I pitched well those years. I was 3-1 with a 1.39 ERA and 8-3 with a 3.00 ERA, but it was a hollow situation. Everyone suddenly was playing for himself, not the team.

We didn't make good moves upstairs, either. I got to bed on time and I didn't drink, so they used to room me with their first-round draft picks, guys like Archie Moore and Gil Blanco. The idea was to keep them out of trouble. But the year the Yankees picked Blanco, a first-round draft choice, the Orioles picked Jim Palmer, also a first-round draft choice. Palmer never left the Orioles. When Blanco left the Yankees, he never came back. When Boyer was traded to the Braves, I became the player representative. The front office treated me really well, as long as I didn't make waves. They permitted me to room alone. But when some sensitive issues came up, and I took a different stance with management, they changed. All of a sudden, I was rooming with Richardson.

A funny thing happened in 1969. Thurman Munson came up to the Yankees, and you could see that he was going to be great. I took him under my wing and he followed me around. Because I was the player rep, he asked me to help him with negotiations. He wanted me to help him make an extra hundred dollars a month. Years later, I found that ironic. My highest salary was $36,000 a year. He was making $1 million.

Well, Houk came back in 1966, and temporarily we hoped for a miracle. But the magic was gone. Later, I became his pitching coach in Detroit for one year, and I loved working with him. He wasn't an expert at handling x's and o's. That was no big deal with him. He was an expert at handling people. I learned a lot from him. He didn't hold a lot of meetings. When on occasion he did, he would say, "Who would you want, Mantle or . . . Maris or . . . Bobby or . . .?" Finally he would give up his position-by-position analysis, and he'd say, "Ah, shit, we've got no problem." He blew smoke your way and made you feel important. You always knew when you were coming in. He knew how to use his personnel. Hector Lopez, for example. Hector didn't have big batting averages, but he was a very important team player. Houk picked great coaches, too. For example, Johnny Sain. Sain, like Houk, was a great motivator. He communicated with you. Every suggestion he made, he made you feel was your idea. Sain got more publicity than Houk, but Ralph didn't mind. He gave all the credit to the players. Sain and Houk worked well together. Houk was a lot like Walter Alston. A good manager can't have a big ego.

The Folly Floater was my Rip Sewell change-up. It was like Seward's Folly, when he purchased Alaska. It was a folly that turned out well. My wife's an English teacher, so she's into alliteration and things like that. I had watched Luis Tiant exhibit all of his moves. I knew I needed another pitch, so I experimented with the Folly Floater in spring training one year. I found out that the batters couldn't hit it. I asked Houk if I could use it, and he wanted to say yes, but he thought that Lee McPhail would be upset if we did it during the regular season. But we didn't get off well, and one day Houk came up to me and said, "Do you want to try it?"

I didn't use it to embarrass hitters. Basically I used it when we were behind, against veterans, or guys who were having good years. The purpose of it was basically entertaining. It got so popular that players on the opposing teams used to say "Throw it to me." In all, I gave up only five singles with it. That was much better than my ratio with other pitches. My big fear was that someone would hit a home run against me. It never happened. One day Frank Howard came up against me. Momentarily I thought I would throw the floater, run around the mound, and then lie behind it. It would have been funny, but I said to myself, "No, that would be a hotdog move." Another day I used it against Tony Horton of the Indians with the bases loaded. There were 52,000 people in the stands. He popped the ball up to the infield. The fans loved it. Sam McDowell didn't.

He pitched a great game for the Indians, but I got all of the publicity the next day. He was pissed.

When I was traded from the Yankees to the White Sox in 1970, it was a bad situation. I didn't have a home in New York. If I had, I would have gone in with Curt Flood on the conspiracy anti-trust baseball suit. Houk told me that the Yankees weren't going to protect me in the expansion draft, and that the Mets wanted me. That was great because Jake Gibbs had a place, and I could have stayed with him and commuted to the ballpark. But I had to be waived. The way it normally works, no one claims you. But the White Sox did.

I said, "Why me?" The White Sox had lost 106 games the year before, and I was thirty-five years old. When I joined them, they were out of town, and they didn't even want me to join them. The next spring the White Sox dealt me to the Giants. The Cubs were in a pennant race with the Mets, and they didn't want the Mets to get me. I can't prove that, but the next spring the Cubs gave the White Sox a promising young player. Houk said to me when the White Sox claimed me, "I don't know what happened. But the third time you're claimed on waivers, you have to go." I didn't even know that I had previously been on waivers twice. You see, if the other teams claim you the first two times, they can take you off waivers and attempt to make a trade. That's the way they operate. But the third time, you're gone.

However, for a guy who had limited ability and never felt he'd make it to the major leagues, I certainly fulfilled a ten-year-old's dream. At that point in my life, my dream was to play at both Madison Square Garden and Yankee Stadium. I lived that dream. I played for two years with the Minneapolis Lakers in the National Basketball League, and I pitched with and against the Yankees for ten years.

Pedro Ramos

Pedro Ramos had only two winning seasons in fifteen major-league seasons. In fact, from 1958 to 1961, with the Washington Senators and the Minnesota Twins, he led the league in losses for four consecutive seasons. The only other pitcher to do that was Phil Niekro of the 1977-80 Atlanta Braves. But Pedro's managers continued to give him the ball every fourth day, because Ramos was a good pitcher. He just didn't have good infield support.

Ramos came to the Yankees in 1964, on September 5, just in time to give New York the pennant insurance they needed and five days too late to give them comparable World Series insurance. Pedro picked up one win without a loss and seven saves in the Yankees' stretch run in 1964. In all, he pitched twenty-two innings and didn't allow a base on balls. In order to be eligible for the World Series, however, a player must be on the parent club's roster by August 31. Many of the players that I've interviewed have said that Ramos would have made the difference for the Yankees in the 1964 World Series.

Pedro feels that he did pretty well for himself overall. He got to meet Fidel Castro and President Richard Nixon. "That's not too bad for a kid from Cuba who used to work as a water boy in a cigar field as a kid," he says. "Nixon was my friend. I used to invite him over for black beans. Other times he'd call and congratulate me for a good game or wish me luck in a coming game."

Life was a merry-go-round for Ramos then. He never thought of tomorrow. Only now does he think of the coming day. "There's nothing like the game of baseball," he says. "The game is what life's all about. The traveling, the fun, the people I met. Playing ball was my rainbow, my dream come true."

Since he left the majors in 1970, Pedro has worked in the cigar business, an insurance company, and a coiling company for air conditioners. Robert Haidy, the president of the coiling company, which is located in Princeton, New Jersey, once played in the Tigers' organization. Ramos also got in trouble with the law, serving a prison sentence for possession of drugs and a gun. But he says, "That's all behind me now. Everything's going to be fine. I hope to keep my nose clean."

Pedro has been married four times and has two children, a son and a daughter. When I spoke to him last summer, he was living in Miami, Florida, working as the pitching coach for Miami-Dade Community College, and looking forward to becoming involved in Florida's Senior League.

Baseball was a big influence on me as I was growing up. I loved the game so much that all I wanted to do was play. In 1953 I came from Cuba to the United States and played two years of minor-league ball. I was pretty good — good enough to get invited to spring training with the Washington Senators in 1955. I was supposed to report to Charlotte in Class A ball, but I did so well in spring training that I stayed with Washington. All along I had played winter ball in Cuba, and that made me a better pitcher. But I never dreamed that I would get to the major leagues so fast.

The 1955-60 Senators had some good hitters. They had guys like Mickey Vernon, Roy Sievers, Jim Lemon, Eddie Yost, and later, Bob Allison, Harmon Killebrew, Albie Pearson, and Jim Busby. But they had no defense. I led the American League in losses four years in a row, from 1958 to 1961 — the last year with Minnesota — but those teams never gave me the double play to get out of a jam. If you're on the field, you know what balls should be caught. In the papers the next day it looks different. But I know what happened. One day, when I was with New York, I was sitting out in the bullpen with Whitey Ford, and he said, "Pedro, if you had been with the Yankees for your whole career, you would have had a better record than me." Now who are you going to believe, the papers or Whitey Ford?

Once, when I was with Cleveland, Mickey Mantle and I almost had a footrace. I could run pretty well and I thought maybe I could beat him. One day he came up to me and said, "What do you say, Pedro, we race for $1,000?"

I said, "Mickey, you know I can't afford $1,000. Where would I get it?"

But I went to Gabe Paul, my boss, and told him about it. Paul said, "The front office will put up the money. But let's make it $2,000."

I was happy. I thought I had a chance. I knew it would be a close race.

So I told Mickey about Paul's offer.

But Mickey didn't seem too excited about the challenge. After thinking about it for a while he said, "It might not be a good idea for me. One, if I lose, I'll lose my reputation. Two, I might lose $2,000. And three, I might get hurt."

I didn't want Mickey to get hurt. He was my idol. But one day I did hit him with a pitch intentionally. I never tried to do that. I didn't want to hurt anyone. But Ralph Terry had knocked three of our players down. One of my teammates said, "Pedro, do something." So I hit Mickey. Afterwards I told him, "Mickey, I didn't try to hurt you. But I had to support my teammates. I hit you because you're the big guy." He understood. There was more mental toughness in the game then.

Birdie Tebbetts was my manager with Cleveland. One day I went to him and said, "Trade me. I don't want to play for you."

He said, "No one wants you."

"Well, then, let me buy my contract for what I make. I'll make my own deal."

"Oh, no, we couldn't do that."

Well, they made the deal. When I heard about it, it was like being hit in the head, like a dream come true. I joined the Yankees in Kansas City. Even now, when I return to Yankee Stadium for an Old Timers' Day game, I get a thrill. I love everything about the Yankees. As a kid in Cuba, I was a Yankee fan. I still am.

I joined the Yankees on September 5, 1964. The Yankees were five games out of first place at the time. But I felt seven feet tall. When I walked out onto the mound for the first time, I looked behind me and saw Richardson, Kubek, Boyer, Mantle, and Maris. Ellie Howard was in front of me. What a defense! I said to myself, "Nobody can beat me." Every game I pitched was tough, but every game I had great players behind me. I would say to myself, "You're not with the Senators now. You're with the Yankees." Overall I won my only decision, picked up seven saves, and didn't give up a walk in over twenty-two innings of pitching.

But I wasn't eligible for the World Series. I arrived five days late. You have to be on the roster before the first of September. I was devastated. The Yankees invited me to St. Louis to attend the away games, but I was so disappointed I couldn't go. I stayed in New York and watched them on television. Would we have won if I had been eligible? Well, Yogi thought I would have made the difference. I did, too.

I looked forward to starting the 1965 season with the Yankees. But all of a sudden the team began to deteriorate. The players got old together,

Mickey got hurt, and the pitchers no longer had the support they once did. But I had a pretty good year. I had a 5-5 record with nineteen saves. And saves were tougher to get then. Today I would have had a lot more. But actually I never cared much for relieving. With another team I would balk. With the Yankees I didn't mind. I would do anything to help the Yankees win. Still, I recorded fifty-five saves during my career.

My overall record could have been much better than 117-160. But you've got to remember that I played half my career in Washington, and they didn't have any defense. If I had played half of my career in New York, the numbers would have been reversed. Number one, I wouldn't have had to pitch against the Yankees. How many losses did they give me? I think my losses would have been closer to ninety-five and my wins would have been closer to two hundred. It's the difference between riding first class and coach.

My biggest thrills? Just getting to the major leagues was the first. Coming to the Yankees was second. And twice hitting two home runs in a game was third. Hey, I could hit. Did you know that I hit fifteen career home runs? And Washington wasn't an easy park. It was tough. But I could put the ball in the upper deck, lefty or righty. One of the times I hit two home runs in a game was with the Indians. We hit four in one inning that day. Larry Brown, Woodie Held, Tito Francona, and me. That's a record.

I hit some long ones. Gave up some long ones, too. There was nothing cheap about me. I always challenged the hitters. I didn't like to walk anyone. That's what I tell my pitchers at Miami-Dade Community College. If you throw strikes, you have a chance to get hit sometimes. But if you don't throw strikes, you don't have any chance to win.

I made a pitch too good to Joe Pepitone in this year's Old Timers' Day game at Yankee Stadium. He hit it for a three-run homer. I told him afterwards, "Next time, I'll put one behind your ear and blow your wig off." But don't get me wrong. I love Pepi.

I still like to put on the uniform. I play softball with the Miami Masters. We play in national tournaments. I'm their best designated hitter. I hit third or fourth. I'm still a switch-hitter and I still hit long home runs. I'm the Mickey Mantle of my league!

Hal Reniff

Hal Reniff was born in Warren, Ohio, in 1938. Twenty-three years later he was pitching with the Yankees, and he did pretty well: in twenty-five appearances he won both of his decisions, he saved two games, and he posted a 2.58 ERA.

Reniff almost always posted good ERAs. In addition to his 2.58 in 1961, he was 2.62 in 1963, 3.12 in 1964, 3.80 in 1965, and 3.21 in 1966 with the Yankees. And those last two clubs were bad teams. Overall his ERA was 3.27 in seven seasons.

Hal's repertoire included a running fastball, an occasional change, and a hard-breaking curve. It served him well. He pitched in 276 major-league games, none of them starts, and posted twenty-one wins and forty-five saves. His best season was 1963, when he was 4-3 with eighteen saves and a 2.58 ERA. He was a workhorse, too. From 1963 to 1967 he appeared in an average of forty-eight games a year. His low number was forty-one in 1964. Reniff finds that inexplicable, since he was coming off his best season.

His roommates with the Yankees were Ralph Terry and Roger Maris. "I just saw Ralph on the Senior Pro Golf Tour the other day," he says. "He looked pretty good. I watch him whenever he's on television."

Maris, he believes, got a bad rap from the media. "He was a professional ballplayer," Reniff says. "He did what he had to do. Sure, he was no Babe Ruth. No one else was, either. But he did something in one year that Ruth couldn't do. Neither could anyone else. He was a ballplayer's ballplayer."

Hal has held several different jobs since 1972, when he retired from baseball. For the last four years he has been an inspector for General Dynamics.

He and his wife of twenty-five years, Ann, have a son and a daughter, and live in California.

I wasn't in awe of the Yankees when I came up to the parent club in 1961. The big thing then is that I got to the majors. The Yankees of that era were great, but I didn't think of who they were or what they had done until later.

When I think of my rookie season, I think of Roger Maris and Mickey Mantle, and I know that as a team we hit a record 240 home runs. But at the time I had more pressing concerns. I wanted to personally do well and make the club. What I remember most about 1961 is that I was not scored on in my first twelve games. People remember all kinds of things about 1961, but I bet that no one else you talk to will remember that. Overall, I pitched in twenty-five games, won two, lost none, saved two, and had a 2.58 ERA. I felt good about that.

I didn't get into the World Series in 1961. I came close, though. One pitch. It was in the last game, when we defeated the Cincinnati Reds for the fourth time in five games. We won big, 13-5, I believe. Ralph Terry started for us but he didn't have it that day. Bud Daley and I were warming up in the bullpen, and he went in ahead of me. He went well for a few innings and then he got into trouble. Johnny Edwards was up in a crucial spot, and he ran the count to three-two. One more ball and Bud was out and I was in. Well, Bud threw a pitch up around Edwards' eyes, and Johnny swung at it and missed. Bud regrouped and finished up for the win. I didn't mind. I was a member of a world championship club in my rookie year. I was on cloud nine.

In 1962 I went into the service for six months before the start of the season, and I came out with a sore arm. I had a bad tendon, so I took treatments for it, and I went back to Richmond. It was a wasted season.

The following year, I became the Yankees' dominant closer. I appeared in forty-eight games, won four of seven decisions, saved a team-high eighteen contests, and posted a 2.62 ERA. It was the highlight of my career. I felt that I had finally gotten a chance to do something. In 1961 I was behind Luis Arroyo, who had a phenomenal year. If everything had gone right for me in 1962, I could have had the same shot as I did in 1963. On Opening Day of 1962, Arroyo hurt his arm. But you've got to get through the rough things for yourself.

There was a pretty good pennant race in 1963 until around Labor Day. Up to that point, the Angels had surprised everyone, but they faded in early

September. On Labor Day, I believe, the Tigers were only a game and a half behind us. But then they played four games against us, three against the Orioles, and four against the Red Sox, and proceeded to drop ten of eleven games while we reeled off fourteen consecutive victories. In that year's World Series I appeared in three of the four games and didn't give up an earned run, but the Dodgers won in four straight games anyway. They had an awesome pitching staff.

The following year was the big disappointment of my baseball career. I had earned the role of the number-one man out of the bullpen. I should have had a chance to lose it. But Yogi Berra took the job away from me and handed it to Pete Mikkelsen. I didn't blame Pete. He was trying to do the same job that I was. But he didn't earn it, the way I did.

I had a short holdout problem that spring. When I arrived, I was suddenly a mop-up pitcher. Who knows, maybe Yogi as a catcher preferred sinkerball pitchers. He came to me with some excuses, but I always had good retorts.

He said, "I want a closer who can keep the ball in the park."

I said, "Don't give me excuses. Give me answers." I gave up only thirteen home-run pitches in my six and one-half years with the Yankees. Of course, each year I was susceptible to something going wrong. I might not have started off right, or I might have been injured. That's part of the job. But Yogi gave me a bad shake. It was very disappointing.

But somehow we pulled it out that year. In September we lost four straight games to the White Sox, and we fell five and one-half games behind Baltimore and five games behind Chicago. When you're trailing two teams by that much at that stage, you shouldn't win it. I have to give Yogi credit there. He did some juggling at the end.

During the season Mikkelsen, Daley, and Bill Stafford experienced some arm problems, so I got more work in the second half of the season. Overall, I appeared in forty-one games, won six of ten decisions, and saved nine contests. But evidently it was just good enough to get me one-third of an inning in that year's World Series against the Cardinals. I pitched to a couple of hitters and he came and got me. I wasn't disappointed. I figured if someone else can do the job, fine. I didn't feel dejected or rejected. The moves in the World Series are the manager's business. I wasn't upset about the World Series. I was upset about the season. I felt that Yogi shafted me all year long.

From 1965 to 1967 there was too much transition. Clete Boyer moved to Atlanta, Ellie Howard moved to Boston, Tony Kubek and Bobby Richardson retired and were replaced by Ruben Amaro and Horace Clarke.

Amaro had one and one-half steps to his right and one step to his left. Yogi had won the pennant in 1964 but even he was gone in 1965.

So when I was traded to the Mets in 1967, I was happy. The only place that I would have preferred was the Angels in California. I was dead with the Yankees. Stagnated. We were no longer a winning club. We were just going through the motions. It was a new adventure for that once-proud organization. I felt rejuvenated by the trade, and that's the way I pitched for about twenty games. Then my arm went dead and it didn't come back for two years, when I was with Syracuse of the International League.

But I had a lot of thrills. My biggest thrill was just being in the majors. You spend a few years in the minors, and you see guys in front of you, beside you, and behind you who don't make it. There's a lot of self-doubt in the minors. Everyone experiences it. You say to yourself, *Will it ever happen to me?* When it does, it's the greatest feeling and thrill that you can experience.

Later on, you realize other things, like who you played with and what they did. Like four consecutive pennants, and what Maris and Mantle accomplished in 1961. In the beginning everyone was rooting for Babe Ruth. The fans didn't want anyone to break his record. Then, when it was inevitable, they started rooting for Mickey because they felt he was the most deserving player. Based upon track records, they were right. But Roger had fifty homers in August. That's an incredible feat. Then when the people realized that Roger was going to break Ruth's record, they dragged out the asterisk. It was never mentioned when there was no threat.

It's great when you set a record while everyone's rooting for you, but it's remarkable to do it while everyone's rooting against you. Maybe the fans thought Mickey was more deserving of the accolade. But you only deserve it if you do it. Roger did it.

Buddy Daley

Leo "Buddy" Daley was born on October 7, 1932, in Orange, California, and lives today with his wife of thirty-six years, Dorothy, in Lander, Wyoming. They have four children, two sons and two daughters, and four grandchildren.

Daley had his best seasons in 1959 and 1960, the two years before he was traded to the Yankees. He won sixteen games in each of those back-to-back years. In New York he won a total of eighteen games in four seasons. Of course, he was on the shelf with an arm injury for virtually all of the 1963 season and appeared in only thirteen games in 1964. Still, in World Series play, in 1961 and 1962, he got into three games, picking up one win and not allowing an earned run.

Buddy had three roommates with the Yankees: Stan Williams, Phil Linz, and Jim Coates. "I roomed with Coates for only a week," he says. "He slept with his eyes open. I thought he was dead. I had to get away from him."

After Daley got out of baseball, he lived in California and sold packaging. Fourteen years ago he moved to Lander, and began selling lawn sprinklers. Always an avid golfer, he was approached by the board of directors of his local golf club two years ago and asked if he would like to be the greenskeeper for their club.

"I had never been a greenskeeper before, so I didn't know," Daley says. "But I've always liked being around golf, so I said, 'Yes.' Sprinklers were my strength. Grass I didn't know. But it's worked out well. I like it."

I had never seen a big-league game, or been in a big-league park, before the Indians brought me up at the end of the 1955 season. Well, I got to Cleveland's Municipal Stadium about eight o'clock in the evening, just at the start of the game, but instead of reporting to the clubhouse I went up and sat in the stands. The park, as you remember, held eighty thousand fans. That night there were about thirty thousand in the stands. I was awed by the sight.

In 1954 the Indians won an American League record 111 games and beat out the Yankees by eight games. That broke the Yankees' streak of five consecutive world championships. The Indians were still good in 1955. We were leading by four games with eleven to play, but we lost nine of our last eleven. Detroit swept us four straight. I pitched the final game of the season, when we were out of it, and got tagged with the loss.

The 1955-56 Indians didn't win but they had great players. They had Wertz, Avila, Strickland, and Rosen in the infield, and Smith, Doby, Kiner, Woodling, and Pope in the outfield. Hegan was behind the plate. And how about that awesome pitching staff: Wynn, Lemon, Garcia, Score, Feller, Houtteman, Narleski, Mossi, and Newhouser. But in 1956 they had a lot of injuries and the players started getting old together.

In 1957 I was just 2-8, so in spring training of 1958 the Indians dealt me to Baltimore, but on opening day the Orioles dealt me to Kansas City for Arnie Portocarrero, so I never pitched for Baltimore. I came into my own with the Athletics. In 1958 I was 3-2, then won sixteen games in each of the following two seasons. Johnny Sain, who became our pitching coach, made the difference for me. He made a bet with manager Harry Craft in spring training in 1959 that I would win more games than any other pitcher on the staff. Sain knew that I needed to work a lot, and he pushed Craft to use me. Basically he and I just talked about pitching situations. Not pitches or how to grip the ball. He told me that I should never get beaten by a catcher's call. He told me, "You're the guy who gets credited with the loss, not the catcher. It's foolish not to get beat with your own pitch. I pitched to twenty catchers in my big-league career. It would have been foolish of me to turn over my bread and butter to twenty different people, wouldn't it?" I agreed totally. I always went with my best pitch in a tight situation.

I got my first start on May 11 and pitched six or seven innings of shutout ball on a Thursday night. On Sunday I started at Yankee Stadium and had a 1-0 lead going in to the ninth, but they scored two runs to win it. The next day we beat Boston 16-0. That's the way it sometimes went with Kansas City. But from that point on I was on a roll, and I ended up winning sixteen games, six more than any other pitcher on the staff.

The following year, 1960, I won sixteen games again. I lost the same number. But I suffered a lot of tough defeats that year. At the All-Star break I was 12-4. In the second half of the season, I reversed those numbers: 4-12. I remember the first game after the All-Star Game, Bob Elliott, the manager, said to me, "Do you want to pitch tonight or tomorrow?"

I said, "Tonight." I got beat 1-0. The next game we scored twelve runs. That's the way it went.

But my biggest thrill came in that year's All-Star Game. Al Lopez was the manager that year. The White Sox had won the pennant in 1959. In 1960 there were two games, on a Monday and a Tuesday. I had pitched on Sunday so Lopez gave me a choice. "Do you want to pitch the last inning in Kansas City or start in New York?"

I said, "Let me pitch in Kansas City." I'll never forget that game. The moment I opened the bullpen fence in center field, the crowd rose to its feet and didn't stop applauding until I reached the mound. I struck out two batters and got the other on a fly ball to the outfield. I was pumped up. It was like the ovation that Nolan Ryan got last year when he returned to Anaheim to pitch against the Angels.

That was the year that Charlie Finley bought the club and hired Frank Lane as his general manager. As soon as he did, I put my home in Kansas City up for sale. Lane had traded me once before, from the Indians to the Orioles. One night before the trading deadline, we were in Minnesota and Lou Klimchock picked up the phone to make a call and hooked into a conversation between Roy Hamey of the Yankees and Lane. He shouted to me, "Hey, Buddy, you've just been traded to the Yankees. For Art Ditmar and Deron Johnson."

Later in the evening Finley called me and said, "Buddy, if we were to trade you, where would be your first two choices?"

I said, "The Yankees or the Angels." I lived in California at the time.

"Well, pack your bags. I've traded you to the Yankees." But I already had them packed. I was ready to go. I knew. And I was happy.

When I went over to the Yankees, I lost four or five in a row. I was trying too hard. So I went up to Ralph Houk and said, "Maybe you better put me in the bullpen."

But he said, "Nah, the law of averages are on your side." And they were. But from that point on he started to use me as a spot starter and a reliever. I helped the club more that way. In August and September I was awesome. At one point I pitched thirty-five consecutive scoreless innings. Two of those games in September stand out in my mind. In a big weekend series against the Tigers, on a Friday night, Whitey Ford hurt his leg in the third inning. The game was scoreless at the time. I relieved Whitey and pitched shutout ball through the ninth inning. But the game was still scoreless. Ralph pinch hit Johnny Blanchard for me. We won it in the tenth, 1-0, with Luis Arroyo getting the win. I also won the clincher against Baltimore. I always pitched well against the Orioles. So although I started slowly with the Yankees in 1961, I came on like gangbusters.

I started thirty-nine and thirty-seven games in my two full years with Kansas City. I never did that with the Yankees. In fact, in 1962 I started only six times. And I never won as many games with the Yankees as I did with the Athletics. But that didn't bother me. It would have in Kansas City. There was a different attitude with the Yankees. In Kansas City you pitched for yourself. In New York you pitched for the team. I know that in 1961 and 1962 I made a positive contribution to the Yankees. I'm happy about that.

The Yankees of 1961 were awesome. They must have been one of the three best teams of all time. My son recently told me that *The Sporting News* didn't even pick them as one of the top ten teams of all time. I can't believe that. They had six players who hit more than twenty home runs that year. Three catchers did it. Berra, Howard, and Blanchard. Skowron at first hit twenty-eight. Mickey hit fifty-four. And Roger hit an all-time-high sixty-one. Overall, they hit an all-time-high 240. No one's broken it yet. And they had a heck of a pitching staff. Ford, Terry, Stafford, Sheldon, Coates, and Arroyo, who won fifteen and saved twenty-nine out of the bullpen. It was a fantastic club. If we stayed within a run going into the seventh, eighth, or ninth, we knew that we were going to score some runs and win the game. With those Yankee teams, you knew that if you could stay even going into September, you would win it. That's what happened in 1961. We won eleven straight games. The Tigers went on to lose seven of eleven. They didn't have our bench. We had guys like Blanchard, Lopez, Cerv, DeMaestri, and Gardner. One of those guys could replace a starter for two or three days, and we lost nothing. Our depth was unbelievable.

No one doubted we would win that year's World Series against Cincinnati. And we had Mantle and Berra out with injuries. Maris hit just .105. Yet we beat the Reds in five games. I got a win in that Series, in the final game. Actually, two days before, I came in and got one guy out. Then Blanchard pinch hit a homer to tie the game. Arroyo relieved me and got the win when Roger hit a game-winning homer in the ninth. I wasn't a bit nervous that day. But in the final game I was very nervous when I came in to relieve Terry in the third. My knees were shaking so hard I thought the umpire might call a balk. But after I got the first man out, I settled down. I guess it was the pressure of knowing I was coming in to nail down the decisive game. The score was 5-3 at the time. We went on to win 13-5. Blanchard and Lopez played in place of Berra and Mantle. Blanchard hit a two-run homer and Lopez hit a three-run shot. Hector drove home five runs that day. I ended up giving up two unearned runs. In eight innings of World Series pitching in 1961 and 1962, I didn't give up an earned run. But it's no big deal to me. The bottom line was helping the team win.

The thing I remember most about the 1961 World Series was our scouting report on them. We were told to take advantage of their out-fielders: Wally Post, Vada Pinson, and Frank Robinson. The report said to take big turns on the bases, that their outfielders never hit the cut-off men, and that they made bad throws. The report turned out to be so true. It was right on the money, and we capitalized on it.

The reason I spent more time in the bullpen in 1962 was that Ford, Terry, and Stafford were a solid nucleus. And Bouton came up that year. Also, Arroyo had arm problems and Marshall Bridges was good but erratic in the pen. I did a better job out there for the club than I could have as a starter.

In 1963 I was told that I was to be the number-one short man. On Opening Day Whitey got into a bases-loaded jam with one out in the ninth. I came in and got the side out. But two days later, warming up in Washington, I noticed that my arm was swollen. The doctor checked me out and said, "You've got bone chips. Do you want to have the operation done now or after the season?"

Well, I rested for a few days and then tried to play catch. But it swelled up again so I said, "Do it now."

I pitched only that one inning all year. The next year I went to camp early and had my best spring training. I had no arm problems at all. My arm felt perfect. On Opening Day Yogi said I was going to be a spot starter and a reliever. He started me the second game, and I was winning 2-1 in the seventh when the game was interrupted by a 45-minute rain delay. I went back out and won 2-1. But then I didn't pitch for ten days. That's the way it went: I would pitch just once a week. In spring training I had been pitching an inning or two every two or three days. By mid-season my arm started to bother me. I didn't get enough work. I liked Yogi as a person but I blame him completely for that. I wasn't the only one he messed up. Stan Williams and a couple of other guys came down with arm problems, too. Yogi was such a good catcher that I thought he'd know pitchers better. He didn't.

We picked up Pedro Ramos from Cleveland in September for a player-to-be-named-later. I was that player. During the World Series I was traded to Cleveland. But they wanted to cut my salary 25 percent. I thought that was too much. So I held out for a few weeks. When I signed, I tried to rush my arm, it acted up, and they released me. Because I couldn't pitch, the Yankees sent the Indians Terry in my place.

I was happy with the Yankees. They were the best thing that ever happened to me. But when I was traded and released, I was disgusted. I got out of baseball and I've only seen a couple of games since. I don't follow the game closely. If I had known how the pension was going to take off, I would have stayed in it. I could have been a good pitching coach. Remember, I was a starter, a spot starter, and a reliever. I could have helped pitchers with my experience. Sain recommended me to a few clubs, but I didn't pursue it.

I didn't have the greatest stuff in the world, but I was a bear-down guy. Frank House, my catcher with Kansas City, said, "Buddy, you do more with less than any other pitcher I've ever seen."

That's the way I'd liked to be remembered.

Bill Stafford

At the age of twenty-one, Bill Stafford was a stand-out starting pitcher on the 1961 Yankees. At the age of twenty-eight, he was washed up with the 1967 Kansas City A's. It's a repetitive story with Yankee pitchers from this era. It happened to Johnny Kucks. It happened to Rollie Sheldon.

Going into the 1963 season, Stafford was young and in the best shape of his life. But on Opening Day in Kansas City, a day on which the temperature was hovering around twenty-five degrees, he irreparably hurt his arm and it was never the same again.

It makes one wonder. The previous season, Luis Arroyo had ruined his arm on Opening Day, too. The temperature was about thirty-five degrees in Detroit, but the Tigers had a crowd of around forty thousand people, and the game went on. On Opening Day, in 1974, one of the two years that the Yankees played at Shea Stadium, Mel Stottlemyre hooked up with Gaylord Perry of the Indians. It was so cold that even the coffee wasn't warm. There was a temperature reading on the tower of a building beyond center field. Once during the day, the numbers on the neon lights changed from thirty-four degrees to thirty-five degrees, and the crowd roared its approval. Before the season was over, Stottlemyre's exceptional major-league baseball career was ended by a torn rotator cuff.

I've often wondered whether there was any connection. I've also wondered if the warm days of spring training in the South properly prepare pitchers for the frigid first weeks of the North during the regular baseball season.

When I spoke to Bill in mid-July of 1989, it was perfect baseball weather. He told me that his father, William, a former semi-pro baseball player, had been the strongest influence on his baseball career. He built a mound for Bill in

144

their backyard. Bill and Sherry, his wife of eighteen years, have two children, a son and a daughter, and he has worked in a lot of fields. Presently he's in sales promotion in Michigan.

When we finished our conversation, he asked to see if his old roommate, Clete Boyer, the manager of the Yankees' farm team in Ft. Lauderdale, ". . . needs a fifty-year-old sore-armed pitcher to help his club in the stretch run."

I was a hard-luck pitcher. You don't have to take my word for it. Look at my record. There are certain pitchers who just don't get any runs behind them. I was one of those pitchers.

Before I came up to the Yankees in 1960, I was 11-7 with Richmond. Yet I should have been much better. I had allowed just ten bases on balls in 144 innings, and I was leading the league in ERA. When I was in the Eastern League, I led the league in ERA, too.

I didn't come up to the Yankees until the middle of August, yet I pitched in eleven games. The Yankees were in a pennant race, and remember, I was only twenty-one years old at the time. I remember my first start in Boston. I went seven good innings, but we didn't win until the tenth, 3-2. I also remember the third batter that I faced, Ted Williams. He hit a ball back to the mound, and I threw to Bobby Richardson for a force play. I was in a lot of no-decision games in September, but I just didn't get any runs. Casey must have thought that I pitched well, though, because he used me twice in the World Series against the Pirates. I pitched a total of six innings and allowed just one run for an ERA of 1.50. In fact, Casey came to me the night before Game Seven and said, "Get a good night's rest. You're going to start tomorrow." Well, he changed his mind. You know that he liked to go with veterans in big games. But some of the coaches were opposed to the switch, as they told me later. Instead he started Bob Turley, who was in his fifth World Series, but he lasted only one inning. Then I pitched one shutout inning. Bobby Shantz, Jim Coates, and Ralph Terry also pitched. We lost, 10-9, on Bill Mazeroski's sudden-death home run.

My best year was 1961, my first full year in the majors. I was 14-9 with a 2.68 ERA. But it could have been much better. My ERA was the second lowest in the American and National leagues. I came close to having the lowest mark. Dick Donovan of the White Sox ultimately won the honor. Going into the last game of the season, he was two below the number of innings that was required. He needed 162 and he had only 160. The White Sox started him and when he pitched scoreless ball in the first two innings, they took him out. I pitched the last game, too. It was historic: Roger Maris hit his 61st home run that day. I beat Tracy Stallard of Baltimore, 1-0.

That year six of my nine losses were by one run. In three consecutive games I pitched twenty-seven innings of one-run ball, but my record for that period was no wins and one loss. I also came out of six games in which I had leads of two runs or more, and I didn't get one of those decisions. Luis Arroyo was in the bullpen that year. I've read that he saved more than half of Whitey Ford's twenty-five wins that year. Well, he relieved for me, too, and he got all of my wins. He would blow the lead and then hang tough and pick up the victory. But don't get me wrong, Luis is a good guy, and he was a very good pitcher. I'm just trying to point out the way it went for me. There's no doubt in my mind that with a little luck I could have won twenty-five games that year. In Game Three of the 1961 World Series, against the Reds, I left the game in the seventh inning when we were losing, 2-1. Arroyo came in and held them. In the meantime, Johnny Blanchard hit a pinch-hit home run in the eighth inning to tie the game, and Roger Maris hit a game-winning blast in the ninth.

The year 1962 was more satisfying in some respects. We didn't hit 240 home runs, as we had in 1961, but we worked hard, hung together, and came back to win our second consecutive world championship. From the team standpoint, we felt pretty good. From a personal standpoint, though, I was disappointed. I didn't get off well, and I was on the disabled list for a couple of weeks. But I finished well, so I thought I could have won seventeen or eighteen.

In the third game of that year's World Series, I picked up a 3-2 win. I pitched a four-hitter. Actually it should have been a three-hitter. With two outs in the bottom of the ninth inning, at Yankee Stadium, I had a shutout, but Bob Bailey hit a two-run homer. He golfed it right inside the right-field foul pole, 296 feet from home plate. I would have gotten the start in either the sixth or the seventh game, too, but in Game Three I got hit on the shin with a line drive, and it swelled afterward, so I lost my start.

At that point I was on top of the world. I was just twenty-three years old, yet I had had three good years in a row, and I had been in three straight World Series. I thought that with my experience, my team behind me, and my expected change of luck, I would surely win twenty games in 1963. I decided that off-season to work harder than I ever had before. I took three weeks off so that my shin would heal, then went on a concentrated conditioning program. I worked as hard as a rookie. Five hours a day on the Nautilus, the weights, the sauna, and the road. I went to spring training in the best shape of my life. Then I pitched forty innings — that's a lot for spring training — and gave up just one run. There was no way, I thought, that I wouldn't win twenty games.

But the best laid plans . . .! In my first start of the season, in Kansas City, the temperature was about twenty-five degrees. On the bench, between innings, I wore an electric jacket throughout the entire game. Late in the game, I was winning 2-0. I had two strikes on Bill Bryan, and Ellie Howard called for a slider. But I thought I could blow the ball by him, so I shook Ellie off. I reached back to fire and that was that. I heard a snap in my shoulder. Ralph Houk came out to the mound and took me out of the game. They wanted me to rest for a few weeks, but I was too stubborn to take the time off, because I had worked so hard to prepare myself for the season. As a result, I had my worst year ever: four and eight. They gave me radiation treatments. Johnny Sain had taken them. So had Eddie Lopat, Whitey Ford, and Ralph Terry. But you can't take too much because radiation breaks down calcium. It was probably a rotator-cuff tear. But they said they would have to cut all the tissue to find out. They also said there was a fifty-fifty chance that, if they did, I would lose the use of my arm. It was too risky.

My managers were Casey, Houk, Berra, and Keane. I got along fine with Casey, but I could never understand what he was saying. At first I was scared to death of him. Houk was great. He was the best manager I ever saw. He knew how to handle each individual. You always knew where you stood with him. Yogi was good, too. I had dressed right next to him, so there were no problems there. Keane was good, but no match for the others.

Yogi put me in the bullpen in 1964. It was tough on the arm so it was an adjustment. I wanted to start but my arm wasn't right. Still I was 5-0 with four saves. I said to myself, "If I can do this with a bad arm, just imagine what I could have done when I was right."

I didn't want to leave the Yankees, but in 1966 I was sent to Syracuse for a while. I was pitching well and my arm felt great. One day the Yankees told me that they were calling me up. But I was to pitch that night against Buffalo, before rejoining the big club the next day in Detroit. What I didn't know, though, was that Eddie Lopat of Kansas City was in the stands that night. The next day, when I got to Detroit, I was told to report upstairs. Houk said to me, "Well, I've got good news and bad news. Look at my pitching schedule. I've got you penciled in for the next eight to ten starts. That shows what I think of your recovery. But here's the bad news. We need a catcher and a pitcher. We think Kansas City has what we need. So we made a deal with them. We were hoping it would be Gil Blanco and Roger Repoz for Fred Talbot and Bill Bryan. But they want another player. Lopat won't make the deal without you in it." I was shocked. I flew to

Detroit thinking that I was going to start for the Yankees, and I was detoured to Kansas City.

What a switch. I went from first place to last, from champs to clowns. My Kansas City experience was crazy. They had a lot of characters and a lot of chaos. Sometimes some of their players would nail all of our hats to the poles. When I'd walk down to the bullpen, some of the guys would have six hot dogs and six cokes with them. Charlie Finley used a taxi to drive the relief pitchers to the mound. Sometimes he used a fire truck. One day they asked me if I would ride the mule in. I said, "That's it. I quit." But it didn't come to that. In 1967 I appeared in fourteen games and had an ERA of 1.69. In my last thirteen innings in the big leagues, I allowed four hits, struck out ten, and gave up just one run. Then I didn't pitch for the rest of the season. Two months. That was it.

At the age of twenty-eight, I was through, left with just memories. I've got some good ones. I played on five pennant-winning teams my first five years in the majors. I played on two world title teams. I was on the same pitching staff as Whitey Ford, the best pitcher I ever saw. I played with good guys and some of the best players who ever wore a major-league uniform. I pitched a complete-game World Series victory. Actually I could have done better. Against Cincy I got the third-game win. I was going to come back again in Game Six, but we ended it in five. Against the Giants I probably would have pitched Game Six or Game Seven, but I hurt my shin when I got hit with that line drive. But overall I did pretty well. My ERA in four World Series games is 2.08.

One of my greatest thrills was walking into the Yankee clubhouse for the first time. I saw all those stars standing around, then I looked at the name tags over their dressing stalls. Maris, Richardson, Kubek, Ford, Skowron, Boyer, Terry, Berra, and Mantle. I was a New York boy. They were all my idols. And then I saw the name tag over my locker. Bill Stafford. I couldn't believe I was there. And then when it was over, I couldn't believe I wasn't.

I wish I hadn't gotten hurt. I could have won a lot of major-league games. How many? With those Yankees and my experience, two hundred, I'd say.

Eddie Robinson

Eddie Robinson has lived a unique baseball life. He had a thirteen-year career and ended up with a .268 lifetime batting average and 172 career home runs. For four consecutive years he hit more than twenty home runs in each season, and for three consecutive seasons he drove home more than 100 runs in each season. In addition, he played in two World Series for two different teams.

His post-playing career also has been unique. First he was the head of player development for the Baltimore Orioles. Then he was the assistant general manager under Paul Richards in Houston. He was also the farm director and the head of player development in Houston for five years. Following a two-year stint as the farm director of the Kansas City Athletics, he hooked up with Richards again, and became the farm director of the Atlanta Braves until 1972. From 1972-76 he served as the general manager of the Braves. Then he returned to Texas — he was born in Paris, Texas, and lives in Fort Worth — to become the general manager of the Rangers for seven years. Following a three-year term as a vice-president/consultant with the Yankees, he went into business for himself.

Today he serves as a major-league scouting consultant for the Phillies, the Astros, and the Twins. "There's a lot of traveling," he says, "but our three boys are grown and my wife Bette and I like to travel. I'm the only one doing it and it's working out well."

Eddie, who is seventy, is not interested in retiring. "I enjoy going to the park," he says. "I've enjoyed the associations and the friends I've made. It's a good life. You're writing a book, I'm writing a book. You send me yours and I'll send you mine."

It's a deal, Eddie.

149

I remember how excited I was when I first came to the major leagues with the Indians in 1942. I was twenty-one and in awe of the major leagues. There were only sixteen teams in those days, so there were only four hundred jobs. The competition was intense. And I had come from Texas, which was far away at that time. Yet in just three years, two years in Class D and one year in Class A, I was there.

Then in my second full year, 1948, I experienced the highlight of my major-league career: I played on a world championship club. The Indians weren't supposed to win that year. The Yankees and the Red Sox were the pre-season favorites. Yet we beat the Yankees, defeated the Red Sox in a one-game playoff for the pennant, then bested the Braves in six games in the World Series. What a sensational infield we had! I was at first, Joe Gordon was at second, Lou Boudreau was at short, and Kenny Keltner was at third. We averaged 108 RBIs. Keltner had 119; Boudreau, 106; Gordon, 124; and I had 83. Larry Doby and Dale Mitchell in the outfield each hit better than .300. Jim Hegan was a great defensive catcher and handler of pitchers. And what a pitching staff that was! Gene Bearden and Bob Lemon each won twenty, while Bob Feller copped nineteen. In the playoff game Keltner and Boudreau each had great days. Lou, I believe, had four extra-base hits that day, two homers and two doubles.

I remember that playoff game against the Red Sox very well. We could have cinched the pennant outright if we had beaten the Tigers on the last day of the season. But Hal Newhouser beat us that day. After that loss on Sunday, Boudreau, the manager, held a meeting in the clubhouse. He said, "I'm leaning with Bearden to pitch the playoff game. I think he's been our best pitcher recently. But this meeting is open. You've got a vote in this, too. Does anyone have anything to say?"

We said, "You've got us this far. You can take us all the way." Well, we had to ride the train all night for the game in Boston, and we went right to the park to play. The pressure was tremendous. The anticipation of the game was awesome, and the letdown after it was incredible. It was a big load off our shoulders.

I had two pretty good years in Cleveland, but in 1949 they sent me to Washington, and that's where I learned how to hit. In the minor leagues I had been a fastball hitter. But in the majors I found out that the pitchers could spot the curve on the black part of the plate. It took me two years to cope with that fact. But Joe Kuhel and Clyde Milan, two coaches with the Senators, worked with me — not on my batting but on my mental approach at the plate. That made the difference. I spent only a year and a little bit of

1950 with Washington, but what I learned there carried over to Chicago, Philadelphia, and New York. Actually my White Sox days were my best. I loved playing for Paul Richards. He was by far the best manager I played for. He turned around a second-division club. We finished fourth in 1951 and third in 1952. In 1951 I hit twenty-nine home runs and drove home 117 runs. The number of homers was a club record for about twenty years. Boy, I could hit in Comiskey Park.

But in 1953 I was traded to Philadelphia, and that was an absolute disaster. The Philadelphia fans were the worst in the world. Everyone will tell you that. Look at what they did to Del Ennis, and he was a .284 lifetime hitter with 288 career home runs. When I was there, they abused Gus Zernial in the same way. He was a left fielder, too. One day he fell while chasing a fly ball and broke his collarbone. We all stood around big Gus, empathizing with him. Lying on the ground in pain, he looked up at us and said, "Don't feel sorry for me. I feel sorry for you. For six weeks I'm not going to have to listen to them boo me. They'll find someone else to take it out on." He was right. They did.

By contrast, my trade to the Yankees before the 1954 season was wonderful, just great! I was so happy to leave my Philadelphia brothers and get out of the City of Brotherly Love. And the Yankees were loaded with talent. I'm just sorry that I didn't get more of a chance to play with them. I was coming off three consecutive one hundred RBI seasons, and I had hit more than twenty home runs for four straight years. The Yankees had just lost Johnny Mize, who'd retired in 1954 after leading the league in pinch-hits for three consecutive years. But they had Joe Collins, and Bill Skowron came out of the blue to have a great year. I was the oldest of the three so I got the least playing time. I guess Casey figured that I was the right guy to replace Mize off the bench. He never told me what my role was. But he pinch hit me forty-nine times in 1954. That was the league high. And I got fifteen safe pinch-hits. That was the league high, too. So I guess I was able to figure out my role without being told. On the bench I would study the pitchers. I knew what they were going to throw. When it was almost time to pinch hit, I would go into the runway and loosen up. And I got along fine with Casey. I thought he was a good manager. He didn't present theory or instruction, he just tried to keep some of the players angry at him. I never got angry. But each of us came through, in our own way.

We didn't play well enough in 1954 to win the pennant, but we played well enough to win 103 games. That was the most a Stengel team had ever won. The five years before I came over to New York, the Yankees won less than one hundred games each year, but they won five pennants and five world championships. The year I came, we won one hundred and three games, but we finished second, eight games behind the Indians. They were unbeatable, although I believe we split the Series with them. But give them credit. That year they were destiny's team.

In 1955, though, we beat them by three games. It was a good pennant race. We won some big games against them in September. But that was the year the Dodgers beat us in the World Series in seven games. Johnny Podres and Sandy Amoros were awesome in the final game. I didn't have too much post-season luck in my two years with the Yankees. I was sort of in between their October success stories. But I did all right in my only chances with them in the World Series. In 1955 I was two for three in the Fall Classic. One of my two hits was a pinch hit. In 1948, with Cleveland, I was six for twenty, so overall, I'm a .348 hitter in World Series play. I'm pretty proud of that. I'm also proud of my production with the Yankees. In 1955 I had thirty-six base hits and forty-two RBIs. There aren't any players around today doing that. Also in 1955, check the production that Casey got out of his first basemen: Skowron hit twelve homers, Collins hit thirteen, and I hit sixteen. That adds up to forty-one round-trippers at one position. I hit the most and I got only 173 at bats. That's one home run for every eleven times I went to the plate. Between the three of us we drove home 146 runs. Did I say that the Yankees were loaded with talent?

But on June 14, 1956, I was sent to Kansas City in a four-player deal.

It was all downhill from there. I went from a team that was four games in first to a club that was six games in the cellar. It was devastating. I almost went nuts the rest of the year. I wish I could have finished my career with the Yankees. Being with the Yankees was my second biggest thrill in baseball. They were a bunch of great guys. Every team has great guys. You have to have that type of personal quality to get to the big leagues and stay. But they were special. It's a good feeling to know that they wanted me on those teams. I was part of a dynasty.

My biggest thrill was something I did *against* the Yankees, when I was with the world-champion Indians of 1948. We were playing the Yankees in a doubleheader before 85,000 people on a Sunday in Cleveland. In the first game we were behind by a big score. But I hit a home run in the fifth inning, and Boudreau pinch-hit a double in the ninth inning to tie the game. Then in the tenth inning I hit my second home run of the game to win it. In the second game Bob Porterfield was beating us 1-0 when I hit my third home run of the day to tie the score. We went on to win the doubleheader. I've had better days in the big leagues, but under the circumstances that's got to stand out as my biggest thrill.

The only times that the Yankees didn't win the pennant between 1947 and 1958 were 1948 and 1954. I was with Cleveland in 1948, and I was with the Yankees in 1954, when the Indians won it again. The Indian-Yankee connection. I was on both ends of it.

Dale Long

When Dale Long left the major leagues in 1963, he left bitter. He was a coach for the Yankees, when, after the World Series, he read in the newspaper that he had been released. No one had bothered to tell him. He was thirty-seven and out of a job. He realizes now that he should have gotten in touch with Johnny Johnson, who was the head of operations for the Yankees' minor leagues. But that's hindsight.

Instead, he became an insurance man, a salesman, and an ironworker. Ten years ago his wife of forty-two years, Dorothy, had an aneurism, and he began to look at baseball again. This time he did get in touch with Johnson, who was then in charge of baseball's minor leagues. Johnson said, "Work with me," then spent a year finding the right position and getting clearance from then-Commissioner Bowie Kuhn, because the major leagues subsidize the minors.

In March of 1983, Dale was finally back in baseball. He thinks that's great. He also thinks that the minor leagues are being rejuvenated. "Until recently," he says, "there was too much emphasis on college baseball. Baseball players need exposure to the minor leagues."

Two field representatives evaluate operations in the minors, Don Lee in the West and Dale in the East. Among other things, they check the lights, the safety factors, the cleanliness of the parks, the distances between bases, and the distances between the mound and the plate on the regular field and in the bullpen. They also serve as good-will ambassadors for baseball.

At present, Dale is working on a book. "It's not historical," he says. "It's instructional. It's the type of book that a father can give to his son as a present. It's going to be my present to baseball."

The Longs have two sons and live in Palm Coast, Florida.

Don Mattingly tied a record of mine. In 1956 I hit a home run in each of eight consecutive games, and a few years ago Don did the same thing. Actually I enjoyed his run. It got me a lot of attention. I'm sixty-three. Ancient history. But today's kids relate to Mattingly. They say to me, "You did the same thing he did?" It helps. Don's going to get a lot of other records before he's through. I'm glad I share that one with him.

I came up to the major leagues with the Pirates in 1951, at the age of twenty-five. It was just for a cup of coffee, because after ten games the Pirates sent me to the Browns for the waiver price. After the season I was sent back to the minors, where I stayed for three more seasons. Ralph Kiner constantly tells me, "Branch Rickey kept you in the minors for an extra four or five years." The reason was that Rickey experimented with me as a left-handed catcher. I was the first left-handed catcher in the majors in over fifty years, so I was a phenomenon at the time. I didn't want to catch. I was a first baseman. But what could I say: "Let me play out my option"? You couldn't do that in those days. Rickey would have sent me so far from home that they would have had to pipe daylight in. One year Kiner hit forty-nine home runs and, come contract time, told Rickey, "I hit forty-nine homers. I need a raise."

Rickey said, "Where did we finish last year?"

"Last."

"We could have finished there without you." What could Ralph say? What could I say? Besides, I wanted to stay in the major leagues. I would have done anything they asked.

I said that the Pirates sold me to the Browns after ten games in 1951. It was one of those look-see deals that was signed with a handshake. They said, "If you like him, sign him." Bill Veeck, the owner of the Browns, evidently liked me. He signed me. But it was a tough adjustment in St. Louis. The right-field corner was real short, but I was a straight-away hitter. I hit 420-foot outs to center. In 1952 the Browns sent me to San Francisco of the Pacific Coast League. I wanted to stay in the majors but the Browns were three teams at the same time: one coming, one going, and one playing.

With the Seals in San Francisco, I played for Lefty O'Doul. He was a great batting coach. The thing that made him different than others was he worked on your strength, not your weakness. He was pretty successful with a lot of players, including Joe DiMaggio and Gene Woodling. On the other hand, I played for Rogers Hornsby. He couldn't instruct like O'Doul. Ted Williams tried to correct my swing, too. But I told him, "Your medicine is my poison." The thing some coaches and managers don't understand is that no two people are alike. I remember Gil McDougald at Beaumont. Hornsby was his manager, and when Rogers first looked at Gil's unorthodox stance, he said, "No one can hit with that stance." But Hornsby got a wire from New York. It said, "Don't change him. Play him." Fortunately, someone there knew something about individuals.

After three more years in the minors, including the 1953 season, when I was the MVP with the Hollywood Stars in the Pacific Coast League, I got back to the major leagues. I was just happy to be back, and I did well. I batted .291, hit sixteen home runs, and drove home seventy-two runs. I also tied Willie Mays for the league lead in triples. Thirteen. I felt pretty good about that. I had to *hit* them. He could *run* them.

In 1956 I set that record, the one Mattingly tied. I started out well that year. I remember we were traveling north from spring training with the Tigers. At the time Joe Gordon was the first-base coach with Detroit. He had the reputation of being a good batting instructor. One day he said to me, "Look at Al Kaline and Harvey Kuenn on our club. See how they get out front and roll their wrists. They've got perfect swings." I thought so, too. I started to copy their style and I got hot. On Opening Day I hit two home runs against Johnny Antonelli of the Giants. He was no slouch. He won twenty games that year. I stayed on a roll and sometime in May I hit one in each of eight consecutive games. That put me in the record book. Actually it didn't cause much of a commotion until I reached five. Suddenly everyone was paying attention. Six was the magic number. Willie Mays, Johnny Mize, and Lou Gehrig had done that. When I was going for the record, we were in Philadelphia at the time. The photographers had me posing before the game with seven bats and seven balls. I said, "Suppose I don't hit one?"

They said, "We'll throw the film away."

The day I hit my record seventh, Stu Miller was pitching against us. I couldn't hit him with a canoe paddle. He had all that off-speed stuff. He was tough to time. Mickey Mantle had a tough time with him, too, until the day he hit his five-hundredth career homer off him. Anyway, my teammates got Miller out of there, and I was lucky enough to set the record. I remember my eighth, too. We were supposed to play a doubleheader in Philadelphia on a Sunday, but we were rained out so we went back to Forbes Field to play the Dodgers on the following Monday. I hit my eighth against Carl Erskine. All of a sudden, all hell broke loose. Not only had I set the record, but I'd also broken the one I set. Dave Garroway and Ray Scott called me at four o'clock the next morning to appear on the "Today Show." I went on around seven-thirty. It was the morning of a day game, so I didn't bother going home. I stopped at a restaurant, ate breakfast, and reported directly to the ballpark. Don Newcombe pitched against us that afternoon. I hit one about 430 feet against him, but you've got to remember that the center field fence at Forbes Field was 457. Duke Snider went back and made an easy catch. That was my best shot to hit a homer in nine straight games. If I had pulled it, it would have been an easy home run, but that was the story of my baseball life.

Right before the trading deadline, on June 14, I believe, I had hit seventeen home runs, and I was red hot. Then something happened to me that never happened before or since. On the same day I fouled two balls off the same ankle. I was really in pain. I remember Bobby Bragan, our manager, said to the team, "Our big guy's out. He's hurt real bad. There goes our long-ball threat. We're going to have to scratch for runs now."

What the hell are you going to do? I said, "Hell, I'll play." They didn't believe in the disabled list in those days. Today a player with that injury would be out for ninety days. Well, I played and went one-for-fifty, or something like that. I ended up the season batting .263, with twenty-seven home runs and ninety-one RBIs. But I can guarantee you those numbers would have been a lot higher if I had not gotten hurt or at least had treated my injury.

There have been a couple of left-handed catchers since my time. Mike Squres did it and this kid Benny Distefano does it now. Most of my catching took place during spring training. Actually I caught only one and two-thirds innings of regular major-league baseball. But I got a lot of mileage out of it. I used a first baseman's glove behind the plate, you know. Cooperstown wants that glove. I've been thinking lately that I might give it to them.

Most people think that a left-hander is too unorthodox to catch in the big leagues, but I'm not so sure. I think one could do all right, especially if he began as a catcher. Most of the hitters in the major leagues are right-handed hitters, so it's easier to keep runners close at first. Bill Dickey once told me, "The only problem you'd have is with a runner stealing third with a right-hander's curve breaking low and away."

I said, "That would be no problem. I'd throw him out at second before he got to third." My main problem was I threw a slider to the fielder who was covering. It would break down and away from him.

Rickey used to tell me, "You've got to get on top of your throws." He was always talking about revolutions, velocity, and trajectory. I didn't understand a word he said.

In 1958 I was moved to the Windy City, and I enjoyed my two years with the Cubs. At the beginning it was tough to adjust to all day games, but when I got used to it, it was fun. It was nice to be at home at night and eat a meal with my children. Wrigley Field was a pleasant place to play, and Mr. (Phil) Wrigley was one of the finest gentlemen I ever saw. He would say, "I may not know too much about baseball, but I know a lot about business. Listen to me and I can help you." He helped a lot of players. In 1958 we had five of us hit twenty or more home runs: Bobby Thomson, Lee Walls, Walt Moryn, Ernie Banks, and me. Ernie hit a league-leading forty-seven. He won the MVP Award in both 1958 and 1959. But we finished fourth in 1958 and fifth in 1959. It comes down to pitching, I guess. Glen Hobbie led the club with ten wins in 1958 and sixteen in 1959.

The following year I was moved to San Francisco, but it was a lousy park and I didn't do well. I batted just .167 in thirty-seven games. Then I got a reprieve and turned those numbers around. On August 22 the Giants sold me to the Yankees. I was ecstatic. In a little more than a month with the Yankees, I played in almost as many games as I had in San Francisco, and I batted .366 for a pennant-winning team. The prospect of joining the Yankees was so exciting that I reported to them a day earlier than I was due. Besides, I was joining my first manager, Casey Stengel. He had been my skipper when I'd broken into organized ball with the Milwaukee Brewers in 1944. Basically I was a pinch-hitter, but I got a big kick out of playing for Casey again. After I reported to the Yankees, I was there for three or four days before I was needed. Suddenly Casey said, "Where's that new fellow?" I looked around. No one moved. "Me?" I said. "Yes, you. This guy throws garbage. You know why we got you." He sent me up to the plate with the idea that I would get a hit, and I did. It was a super club. Everyone knew his job and did it. There were no recriminations about insufficient playing time. Our job was to produce when we were called on, and usually we did.

On a great team like that one, you can bust each other without getting on each other's nerves. I remember one day when Whitey Ford was pitching and I let a ground ball go right through my legs for an error. It gave the other team a 1-0 lead. Whitey came into the dugout and said to me, "Don't screw with my money." I didn't say anything. No pitcher had ever said that to me before. Well, eventually I hit a three-run homer, and we won, 3-1. When I finished running the bases, I came into the dugout, walked up to Ford, and said, "Let's see if you can hold the lead. I don't want anyone screwing with *my* money." He laughed. So did I. The bottom line was winning.

Another time I remember was when Moose Skowron's dad died. Moose went home to Chicago for a week. I took his place and had a whale of a week. We won nine of ten games, I think. Moose came back and I returned to the bench, but when he walked into the clubhouse, he came right up to me and said, "Thanks for having a hell of a week. I appreciate it." How many guys today would do something like that? They'd be afraid you were trying to steal their jobs. But he knew it was his turn again. He said, "I'm going to hit a homer for my dad tonight."

I said, "Go ahead, I'm rooting for you." He did. The Yankees of those days had guys like that.

In the 1960 World Series I pinch hit three times and got one hit. The first two times I hit the ball well, but right up the shaft. My last time up, in the final game in Pittsburgh, I hit a sinking drive to right that fell for a base hit. I should have hit that pitch nine miles. I just missed it. If I had hit it right, the state of Pennsylvania couldn't have held it. Then I was singled to third, and Casey put Gil McDougald in to run for me, so I didn't even get the chance to score in a World Series. But I don't feel bad. In the same Series Casey sent me up to bat for Clete Boyer — in the second inning! I'm going to see Clete next week. He reminds me of it all the time.

I got tied up in expansion in 1961. Every team had to put seven players in the pool. The expansion teams could claim any one of them for $75,000. The Yankees lost all seven players they put up. I went to Washington, and we finished last while the Yankees were hitting a record 240 home runs. The year before, we hit 195. I thought that was extraordinary. I hit our last one, on the last day of the season. But those 240 home runs left our mark in the dust.

On July 11, 1962, I was traded back to New York for Dor Lock. There was a lot of pressure on the Yankees to repeat in 1962. The previous year, they had won everything. But we did defend our world title, and we were justifiably proud. I was pretty proud of my contribution to our stretch run. With the Yankees I batted .298 in forty-one games. In the World Series I was one-for-five. That was a dramatic World Series. It went seven games. But that wasn't the half of it. There was a six-day rain delay before the weather cleared. Then the Series went down to the last pitch — Ralph Terry against Willie McCovey. Willie hit it hard but, thank God, Bobby Richardson was there to make the catch.

I played for both Casey and Houk, and honestly there wasn't too much difference between the two of them. They were two good baseball people. Of course, they had the horses. But bad managers can lose with all the horses. Casey and Houk knew how to bring a good team home first.

In 1963 I didn't get many at bats. In the latter part of August, they came to me and said, "We have a chance to get Tom Metcalf, a pitcher, for the stretch drive. Would you be interested in becoming a coach for the rest of the season?"

I said, "Yes." I was thirty-seven or thirty-eight, and it was a chance to stay in the game, and that's what I wanted to do. Earlier in the season, Houk had come to me and said, "We got rid of Skowron because we want to give Joe Pepitone a full shot at first base." But Pepitone was no Skowron. They asked me to work with him. I said I would. On the field it was easy, but off the field, there was no way I could keep up with him.

The Yankees kept me as a coach through the World Series. Then one day I read in the newspaper that they had released me. I was without a job, and I left the game very bitter. That's all over now. I'm back in the game working with young players, and I feel rejuvenated.

Baseball's been my life and I've enjoyed the whole trip. I played with three pennant winners, and I met a lot of great guys in and out of baseball. Three of those people were presidents: Eisenhower, Kennedy, and Nixon. One Opening Day, President Kennedy and I talked for about five minutes about Massachusetts and the things we had in common. When I played in Hollywood, I met a lot of stars. They wanted to be baseball players and I wanted to be an actor. We got along just great.

Rollie Sheldon

Rollie Sheldon was born in Putnam, Connecticut, in 1936. He grew up rooting for the Red Sox, so he was doomed to seasons of frustration. "I never could understand why the Red Sox didn't win more often," Rollie says. "They had so much talent. I still don't understand."

In 1961 Sheldon joined the Yankees at the age of twenty-four and had his best major-league season. It's a recurring theme for young Yankee pitchers of this era. He was 11-5 with a 3.60 ERA and two shutouts The only other time he posted wins in double figures was 1965, when he recorded a 10-8 mark with the Kansas City Athletics. That was quite an accomplishment. Kansas City finished tenth that year. The following year, the Athletics traded him to Boston, where he finished his major-league career with a 1-6 mark with the Red Sox. It was ironic. As a boy, he couldn't figure out why the Red Sox couldn't win. As a man, he couldn't figure out why he couldn't win with the Red Sox. After spring training tryouts with the Reds (1967) and the Pilots (1969), he retired in 1970. Overall, his record was 38-36 with a 4.08 ERA and four shutouts.

Rollie, who lives in Lees Summit, Missouri, works for All-State Insurance. A claims representative and staff claims analyst, he has been with them for nineteen years and will retire in a couple of years. He and his second wife, Shirley, have been married for three years. He has two daughters and two stepsons.

"Everyone's writing books today," he says. "It's hard to go back twenty-five years. But it was fun. I enjoyed the trip."

The man who had the most influence on my baseball career was J.O. Christian. He was the baseball coach at the University of Connecticut, and he was well known in the Yankee Conference at that time. I had transferred from Texas A&M, and he nursed me along because I was ineligible. He allowed me to practice, throw batting practice, and travel with the team.

A funny thing happened when I was at the University of Connecticut. Harry Hesse, the scout, took an interest, and one day he started filling out a card on me. He asked me how old I was. I said twenty-three, but for some reason he wrote twenty on the card. Another day we talked about bonus money, and he made a couple of telephone calls. We were in my house, and suddenly I realized that he thought I was only twenty. I thought the misconception might blow the whole deal. I left the room and whispered to my parents, "Please sign," and they did.

One year later, at the age of twenty-four, I was a member of the New York Yankees. It was fantastic. Early in 1961 a couple of sportswriters came down from Connecticut and said, "Something's wrong. He's older than twenty."

Bob Fischel of the Yankees came into the dugout one day and said, "They say you're older than we've got you listed." I told him what had happened and why there was the discrepancy between the ages twenty-four and twenty-one. It might have helped me in the long run. I really didn't have that much pitching experience. They might have thought I had more maturity than I did. The year before, Casey wouldn't have kept me. But Ralph Houk believed that the people with the best baseball talent made the team. Thank God!

In spring training in 1961, I got knocked around once, but everything else was positive. I remember one day I was pitching in Sarasota against the White Sox. I struck out Roy Sievers twice and Floyd Robinson once. I believe I made the club that day.

My first two outings in 1961 were good ones, but I was the losing pitcher in both games. I lost to Hal Woodeshick of the Senators, 2-1, and Steve Barber of the Orioles, 3-2. Ralph Houk brought me along slow in the beginning. Basically he pitched me against the expansion clubs and the second-division outfits. All of a sudden I pitched a couple of shutouts and ran up six consecutive victories. The stars on the club began to accept me, and I felt like a contributing member of the team. I know that I got some breaks. I felt like a pledge in a fraternity. It was a tough experience. I was paying my dues. But gradually I sensed that my teammates were saying, "This guy might be for real." I was on the same club with these great stars, in the same clubhouse with them. It was like a dream come true.

Johnny Sain was a great pitching coach with some unusual theories.

Other coaches believed that pitchers should do a lot of running on their off-days. Sain believed in running to a degree, but he would say, "You can't run the ball across home plate."

One night he wanted me to throw on the sidelines the night before a game. I said, "I'm pitching tomorrow."

He said, "Yes, but if you don't throw tonight, you might go back to the hotel thinking that you won't be able to pitch tomorrow night." He was an inspirational teacher and a master of psychology.

At the end of the 1961 season, we had the pennant clinched, and Ralph was preparing us for the World Series. I came into both of the last two games I pitched in the seventh inning with the score tied, and I won. I remember that Hector Lopez won one with a single through the middle. It was the difference between finishing 9-7 and 11-5. I finished 11-5 with a 3.60 ERA.

In 1962 I slid to 7-8. The difference was that I didn't come up with an extra pitch. I had a fastball, a hard-breaking curve, and a change. But I didn't pick up a fourth pitch. The hitters knew me better and I didn't pitch as well in 1962 as I did in 1961.

I didn't get into the 1961-62 World Series. Teams had a ten-man staff when they got down to nitty-gritty time before the Series. The manager had decided on his three starters, his two long men, and his two short men. That meant three were odd men out unless some games went extra innings. Actually in 1961 I warmed up in Cincinnati one day, but I didn't get into the game.

Things were worse in 1963. I had a terrible spring training, and I was sent to Richmond of the International League. It was the first time in my life that I had not made the team. I sulked and didn't turn myself around until the following year. In spring training in 1964, I didn't make the club again, but this time I had a better attitude, and I went back to the minors with a more mature approach. I came up to the big club in June, won five of seven decisions, and saved a couple of games for Mel Stottlemyre down the stretch.

In that year's World Series I pitched in two games. I don't remember too much about Game One — I do know that the Cardinals didn't score against me — but I recall Game Seven vividly. We were losing 3-0 in the bottom of the fifth inning. Stottlemyre had started against Bob Gibson. Yogi had Al Downing and me warming up. He opted to go with Downing in the bottom of the fifth. Lou Brock hit his first pitch up on the roof. Ken Boyer singled and Bill White doubled. St. Louis had one run in, runners on second and third, and no one out. That's when Yogi brought me in. I got Dick Groat to hit the ball off the end of the bat to Bobby Richardson, but one run scored because the ball was hit so slow. Then I got Tim McCarver to fly to short right. Mickey Mantle was out there because Roger Maris was hurt. Mickey's throw was twenty feet off the plate, and the Cardinals scored another run.

On May 3, 1965, Johnny Blanchard and I were traded to Kansas City for Doc Edwards. I was astonished by the trade. Blanchard had had some fantastic years with the Yankees. The deal didn't make sense. Elston Howard was on the shelf with a bum shoulder. Bob Schmidt, the other catcher, could hit an occasional home run if you threw a diet of fastballs right down the middle. But if you threw him a curve, he was dead meat. Plus, he was a right-handed hitter. They dealt Blanchard, a lefty, for Edwards, another righty. Johnny was broken-hearted. He went home for a couple of days before he reported to the A's. For me, it was a great opportunity. In New York I was a little fish in a big pond. I pitched my best ball in Kansas City. Overall I was 10-8. But I was even better than that. I won seven of my last eight decisions. That was for a tenth-place club. I thought I would be there for the next five or six years. But Haywood Sullivan, our manager, took a cushion job with the Red Sox, and Al Dark came in and made major changes. He traded away the nucleus of our pitching staff: Fred Talbot, Ralph Terry, John O'Donoghue, and me. I was traded to Boston. I had pitched there once in a while. The Green Monster never bothered me when I was on the visiting club, but when I was pitching there for a living, it was a nightmare. Hitters like Tony Oliva and Boog Powell would inside-out the ball against the wall, and batters that I jammed on the fists would reach the wall. I didn't get along with pitching coach Sal Maglie, either. He tried to change my style and I didn't like it. The result was I was 1-6 with the Red Sox and traded to the Reds after the season.

In spring training in 1967, there were eighteen pitchers with big-league experience in camp. I pitched well enough to make the club, but I didn't. Vada Pinson came up to me before camp broke and said to me, "You should be going north with us." I thought so, too. But I wasn't. I was through at twenty-nine.

Still, I had some thrills. Being a part of the everyday hoopla of the press in 1961 was exciting. The writers were always interviewing Maris and Mantle. Being able to contribute to one of the greatest clubs in the history of baseball also was exciting. I was a celebrity in my hometown when I returned after the season.

I had a great manager, too! Ralph Houk. He would call meetings that were very meaningful. Yogi, on the other hand, couldn't communicate.

Other players you interview will tell you that. You never knew where you stood with him. When he called a meeting, he would get right to the point, and it would be over before it started. Ralph, by way of contrast, would tell us, "You're the best damn players in the world. There's no way anyone can beat you." He was a tremendous motivator.

You always knew where you stood with Ralph. He was open and honest. If he had something to say to you, he would call you in. He didn't criticize you in the press the way they do today. If you were the tenth pitcher on his staff, he would tell you why. I liked him and evidently he liked me, too. I haven't read his book yet but I intend to. I know that in it he said, "If you ever wanted a son, you would want him to be like Rollie Sheldon. If you were searching for the ideal son, he'd be it."

Mickey Mantle

Mickey Mantle was born in Spavinaw, Oklahoma, on October 20, 1931, and lives in Dallas, Texas, with Merlyn, his wife of more than thirty-five years. They have four sons.

Mantle has been involved in various business ventures since he retired from baseball in 1968. For a while he owned a Dallas bowling alley. Then he and a group of investors founded "Mickey Mantle Country Cookin'." The first store opened in San Antonio, Texas, and the chain eventually expanded to thirteen franchises before he extricated himself from a potential fiasco. He has been a first-base coach with the Yankees and a batting instructor for them in spring training. In addition, he's teamed with Curt Gowdy and Tony Kubek on NBC's "Saturday Game of the Week" and served as a public-relations representative for Reserve Life Insurance Company of Dallas and the Claridge Hotel in Atlantic City, New Jersey. He and Willie Mays, who worked as a public-relations representative for Bally's Park Place across the street, were suspended from baseball for being associated with gambling casinos. They were reinstated in 1985.

I have tried for five years to arrange an interview with Mickey Mantle. All of my attempts have failed. Letters to his house in Dallas have been returned with the words "Refused to Accept" stamped on them. Letters and at least twenty phone calls to his business agent have not been answered or returned. An attempt by the business manager of Mickey Mantle's Restaurant in New York City to arrange an interview was turned down.

Naturally, I'm disappointed. But I draw consolation from the fact that almost every other player from this era did grant me an interview. Future baseball historians will be grateful to them.

One of the players that I interviewed put everything into perspective. "Have you ever read one of his books?" he said. "You can write it better than he can tell it. He was never impressed with anything he did on the ball field. You were, we were, and the fans were. You write it, we'll tell it, and the fans will love it."

When you think of Mickey Mantle, you think of home runs, long ones. Here, then, are some of the Mick's longest home runs, as witnessed by the teammates who marveled at them.

What can one say that hasn't already been said? A bit more, I think.

Mickey Mantle had a phenomenal rookie spring training in 1951. No one tells about it better than Gil McDougald.

"It was an exceptional spring, because Mickey Mantle joined the Yankees that year, and he had one of those springs that Babe Ruth must have dreamed about. Everywhere we went, they'd point to a spot where so-and-so hit one, and he'd proceed to hit one farther. You might remember that the Yankees and Giants switched camps that year. We went to Phoenix, Arizona, and they came to Florida for the first and, I think, the only year. We barnstormed up the West Coast, playing in all the towns of the Pacific Coast League — San Francisco, Oakland, Los Angeles. They're all in the major leagues now. In Los Angeles Mickey hit a couple of homers in one game. One of them was hard to believe. It was one of those two-iron shots he'd hit to center field. The center fielder broke in quickly and cut over, but the ball just took off and kept going. It landed at least forty to fifty feet behind the center-field fence.

"I remember another day we were at USC. The University had a field house beyond the fence. He hit a ball right over the field house. Really, I've never seen anyone move a ball like that. Then we went up to San Francisco, where I was born, and we played at Seals Stadium, where only ten or twelve balls had been hit over the right-field wall until that time, because there was a perpetual wind blowing in from right. Well, that night Mick first went up right-handed, and he hit one across Guererro Street so fast that you wouldn't believe it. The people were shocked. All the years that I played in that park, I didn't see left-handers hit balls over that wall. Then I see a right-hander, who was only nineteen, rifle one over it. Then he got up left-handed and hit one out in left center. But that was the way that spring went for Mickey Mantle. He got $20 million dollars worth of publicity in two months. He overshadowed everyone else, including Joe DiMaggio, who was reaching the end of the line."

Mickey got his first major-league hit, a single, off Bill Wight of the White Sox on April 17, 1951, and he got his first home run off Randy Gumpert of the White Sox on May 1, 1951. It was a long one at Comiskey Park. The writers said it traveled about 450 feet. But the hits and home runs were few and far between. The pitchers passed the "book" on Mantle around the league: "Pitch him high and tight and he's just another strikeout victim." Mickey went into a prolonged slump and it affected his fielding. One night, with Eddie Lopat pitching, he let a fly ball drop at his feet. Lopat grabbed him between innings and snarled, "If you don't want to play, get the hell out of here, because we want to win, and you're screwing with our money." The day after Allie Reynolds pitched his first no-hitter of 1951, Mantle was sent down to Kansas City to build up his confidence. He continued to struggle, however, until his father visited him and gave him the pep talk he needed. Over his last forty games in the minors, he batted .361, hit eleven home runs, and drove home fifty runs. The Yankees brought him back from Kansas City around the end of August, and he batted .267 with thirteen home runs and sixty-five RBIs.

Joe DiMaggio retired after the 1951 season, and the writers wondered who would become the "big man" on the Yankees in 1952. One day at Yankee Stadium, Joe Collins and Mickey vied for that distinction. Collins, who was batting in front of Mantle, hit a 450-foot shot into the third deck in right field. When he crossed home plate, he said to Mantle, "Go chase that." Well, Mickey hit one just as high and much farther, halfway up the right-center field bleachers. When he returned to the dugout, he walked down to the water cooler, where Collins was sitting, and said to Joe, "How'd you like that shot, Joe?"

"Aw, shit," Collins said.

Early in 1953 Mickey Mantle hit what has been recorded as the longest home run in the history of professional baseball. Red Patterson, the Yankees' publicity director, was in the Washington press box at the time. He was so impressed with the length of the blow that he set out to find the ball and measure the distance it had traveled. He discovered that it had cleared the field at the 391-foot mark, hit a beer sign on the football scoreboard, cleared the stadium and the street outside, and landed in a backyard four houses up the street. He measured it out to 565 feet.

Yankee players of that era still marvel at the distance that the ball traveled. Bob Kuzava, who was sitting in the bullpen when it happened, told me, "I watched the ball go right by me in the bullpen. I was sitting with Ralph Houk and Charlie Silvera. The wind was blowing out and he gave it a blast. We couldn't believe the shot he hit. I never saw a ball hit so far. You could have cut it up into fifteen singles."

Irv Noren, who played beside Mantle in the outfield for five years, recalled that night for me. "I was in the outfield with him before the game," he said. "The wind was blowing out a little. He'd just hit two shots in batting practice. I said, 'Mick, you can hit one over the back wall tonight.' It was a coincidence that I said it and he did it.

"Another day he hit one clear up in the center-field bleachers off Alex Kellner. I saw the pictures in the papers the next day, and he was on his back knee when he hit it. That's how strong he was.

"When Reggie Jackson was playing, they compared him to Mantle. I was a coach with Oakland for four years when Reggie was there. He didn't compare. No one else today does, either."

Gene Woodling still remembers the 565-foot home run, too, but he doesn't think it was Mantle's longest. "He hit one farther later that year at Sportsman's Park in St. Louis. But he got so much publicity from the shot he had hit at Griffith Stadium that they couldn't surpass it. No one, including Babe Ruth, hit them consistently as far as Mantle did. Mickey was unbelievable. I don't think he ever realized the talent he had. He was just a small-town boy who came to New York to swing a bat."

Mantle did not benefit too much from the "short porch" in right field at Yankee Stadium. Most of his home runs at the Stadium were hit to the far reaches of the park. Less than half of his career home runs — 266, to be exact — were hit at Yankee Stadium. He hit 270 on the road. "Death Valley," Yankee Stadium's deep center field, gobbled up a number of Mickey's long blows. But even that didn't intimidate him. On May 13, 1955, in a game against the Tigers, he hit three towering shots into the center-field bleachers — two left-handed and one right-handed.

Noren was there. He told me, "Every day you played with Mantle, you thought he would hit one farther than the day before. What he did that day was incredible for anyone else. Each homer cleared the 461-foot sign. But it was just another day for Mickey. I'm sure he fully expected to hit one farther the next day, too."

On May 31, 1956, he came within one foot of becoming the first player to clear the roof at Yankee Stadium with a fair ball. "Yes, he almost hit one of my throws out of Yankee Stadium," Pedro Ramos told me. "I thought the ball was going to Connecticut. When he first hit it, I thought it was just a high fly ball. But it kept carrying. I knew the ball was deep but I didn't think it was that deep. Mickey says he hit ten home runs off me. Let me tell you, a few of them went over 500 feet."

Mantle has always maintained that the only way someone could hit the ball out of the Yankee Stadium of his day was to hook one over the Yankee bullpen. A ball hit in that spot would not have to contend with the three decks in right field or the steep ascent of the bleachers in right center. The distance to the right-field bullpen was 407 feet. The length of the bullpen was eighty feet, and the retaining wall in that spot was only ten feet high. It would have taken the perfect shot to clear the wall in that twelve-foot area. No one ever hit it.

Mickey hit some tapemeasure shots in World Series play, too. One of them was a grand-slam home run off Russ Meyer in the third inning of the fifth game in 1953. Batting left-handed, he hit a towering home run into the upper deck in left-center at Ebbets Field. In the 1960 World Series, at Forbes Field in Pittsburgh, he hit two mammoth shots in Game Two. Both of them cleared the 440-foot sign in deep right-center field. One of them was measured at 478 feet. And in the 1964 Fall Classic, in the ninth inning of Game Two, he hit a game-winning blast against Barney Schultz of the Cardinals deep into the upper deck in right field.

Mantle believes that the hardest ball he ever hit came against Bill Fischer of the Kansas City A's on May 22, 1963. It hit the façade atop the third deck in right field and came within a few feet of clearing the roof. Jimmy Dykes, a Hall of Famer, was the third-base coach for the A's that night. He had played against Babe Ruth in the late 1920s and early 1930s. After the game he was asked to compare Mantle's blast with some of Ruth's best. "Gentlemen," he told the press, "we have just witnessed the hardest ball that has ever been hit with a baseball bat. I've been in this game for forty years, and, believe me, I have never seen a ball hit that hard before tonight. No one else I've ever seen could hit a ball that hard, not even Ruth."

One can only wonder where a ball that he hit in a game against the White Sox at Yankee Stadium in 1964 would have landed if he had "hit it right." Ray Herbert was the pitcher for Chicago, and Mantle got under one of his fastballs and hit a towering fly ball to deep center field. Mantle was so mad at himself because he thought he had missed his pitch that he broke his bat at home plate before he started to run. But the ball got up over the roof of the Stadium and into the wind currents that hover above the field. Gene Stephens, the center fielder, kept drifting and drifting with the ball, but he ran out of room at the 461-foot sign in center. The ball landed one-third of the way up in the center-field bleachers. It was measured at 502 feet. A red-faced Mantle crossed home plate. He probably still has nightmares about "missing" that pitch. Who knows, if he had hit it right, he might have become the first player to hit a fair ball out of Yankee Stadium — in the deepest recesses of the park, no less.

Which one of them was the longest ball he ever hit? Experts have estimated that the blast he hit against Fischer would have traveled 620 feet if the façade had not impeded its path. But McDougald probably has the best answer to that question. "Mickey probably doesn't even know," he said. "He hit so many that any one you bring up probably didn't impress him at all."

Yogi Berra

Lawrence Peter "Yogi" Berra was born in St. Louis, Missouri, on May 12, 1925. He grew up on "The Hill" and rooted for the St. Louis Cardinals. His hero was Joe Medwick, who played left field for the Cardinals, won the Triple Crown in 1937, and was inducted into the Hall of Fame in 1968. Yogi and his wife, Carmen, have been married for more than forty years and have three sons.

When I wrote to Yogi, Carmen replied. She said, "If you know Yogi, as I'm certain you do, you know he hates to gives interviews. He doesn't like to talk about himself. Do you want to hear about our six grandkids? But give your views. Those were very productive and happy years for Yogi. Let's hear about them. Love, Carmen Berra." Yogi was a central part of the Yankees from 1955 through 1964, and with the help of many of his former teammates I have been able to tell his story.

If you look in The Baseball Encyclopedia, *you will see that Yogi Berra owns most of the records for catchers during the regular season and in World Series play. If you look at his business dossier, you will see that he's been pretty busy in that respect, too. At one time he and Phil Rizzuto owned a bowling alley in Montclair, New Jersey, where Carmen and Yogi reside in the off-season. He also has served as an executive for Yoo-Hoo, a chocolate-flavored soft drink. In addition, he attends card shows, does commercials, reviews movies on television, and has coauthored several autobiographies.*

He has remained close to the game he loves. He managed the Yankees to a pennant in 1964. A good part of the following chapter deals with that dramatic, traumatic, and transitional period in New York Yankee history. Then he managed the New York Mets for four years, including the pennant-

winning season of 1973. For a long time he served as a coach for the Yankees before once again assuming the managerial reins of the Bombers in 1984 and remaining in that position sixteen games into the 1985 season. For the past few years he's been a coach with the Houston Astros.

Despite a few disappointments as a major-league manager, Yogi has come a long way in life. When he was a kid in St. Louis, he was the paper boy for Joe Medwick. When Yogi was breaking in and Joe was bowing out in the late 1940s, Medwick was asked by the Yankees in spring training to refine Berra's skills as an outfielder. In 1972 Yogi Berra was inducted into Baseball's Hall of Fame — a mere four years after his childhood hero.

Charlie Keller, the former slugging outfielder with the New York Yankees, once said, "Yogi Berra won't talk about himself. You're going to need all the help you can get." Fortunately, his former teammates aren't so reticent.

Yogi was genuinely liked by his Yankee teammates, especially the players from the "old days." Frank Shea, for example, told me a few years ago, "I broke in with him. Some guys you just have to like. Yogi was one of them. He was a good hitter, a good bad-ball hitter. He did everything according to Hoyle. He obeyed all the rules and regulations. I remember I went with him over to New Jersey when he picked out his first house. He roomed with me at the time.

" 'He said to me, 'Should I buy it?'

"I said, 'Yeah.'

"We came back to the Stadium, and he was telling everyone about the house. He said, 'It's a big house. All it's got in it is rooms'."

Allie Reynolds, one of the Yankees' "Big Three" pitching greats, made an insightful comment about his former teammate. "We Indians have a saying: 'White eyes monitor time; the Indian enjoys it.' Yogi was an Indian. He enjoyed playing the game. Like Joe Page, he didn't know how hard it was. He never got too high or too low over a game. He had the perfect disposition for a player or a friend, but not a manager."

Joe Ostrowski, a pitcher with the 1950-52 Yankees, placed another diamond in Yogi's World Series rings when I spoke with him up in West Wyoming, Pennsylvania. "He was 'dumb as a fox'," he said. "When I pitched, I never shook him off. I don't think he has an enemy in the world. He didn't speak much with anyone. But he didn't speak against anyone, either."

When Yogi came up to the majors in the last week of the 1946 season, he was already a natural hitter. In fact, in that last week of the 1946 season, he hit two home runs in twenty-two at bats and batted .364. Billy Johnson, the resident third baseman of that era, remembers the first time he saw Yogi hit. "He was the best argument against platoon baseball," says Johnson. "Shortly after he came up to the Yankees, we went into St. Louis, and the manager, Johnny Neun, asked him to hit some balls in batting practice. 'Let's see what you have,' he said.

" 'Where do you want me to hit the balls?' Yogi asked.

" 'You see that lower screen out there in right?'

" 'Yeah.'

" 'That's where I want you to hit the balls.'

"Yogi proceeded to hit four or five balls off the screen. The last pitch he hit was about six inches off the ground.

" 'Where was that last pitch?' Neun asked.

" 'Right down the middle,' Yogi said.

"Yogi was just a good bad-ball hitter," Johnson concluded. "If you're a good hitter, you can hit any pitching, lefty or righty."

Bill Dickey, the Hall of Fame catcher, thought that Yogi could have hit .360 if he had concentrated more at the plate. The problem with Yogi, he said, was that he only bore down when there were men on base or the game was on the line. Keller said that Berra was the best .285 hitter in the history of baseball. Gil McDougald, the Yankees' Rookie of the Year in 1951, put it this way. "Many people ask me, 'Who's the best hitter you ever saw?'

" 'It all depends,' I say. 'Are you talking about batting average, home runs, or who you would like to see up there with the game on the line in the ninth inning?' If they mean with the game in the balance, I say, 'Give me Yogi any time'."

But Yogi was not a natural defensive player when he arrived on the major-league scene in 1946. It took a lot of instruction, determination, and hard work to convert him into one of the greatest catchers ever to play the game. Spud Chandler, who won 109 games and posted a winning percentage of .717, the highest for any pitcher with one hundred wins, was the first moundsman to pitch to Yogi in the major leagues. "He was not a good catcher and he knew it," Chandler said. "In fact, he was uptight about it. But the following year, he improved a great deal, and then George Weiss brought Bill Dickey in, and eventually Yogi became a great catcher. I couldn't believe his progress. Bill gets most of the credit for the conversion, but Yogi had to be doing a lot of homework on his own, too."

Charlie Silvera, a back-up catcher to Yogi from 1949-56, told me that Dickey noticed right away Yogi's good arm and quick feet. Everything

Dickey taught him, Silvera said, evolved from those two attributes. Johnny Sain told me that Yogi was downright smart. "One day in a World Series game (in 1953) he threw out two consecutive runners at third base. The Dodgers had first and second with no one out. On those plays there was no way that the pitcher could have fielded those balls and made those outs. Both bunts should have been base hits. But Yogi threw the runner out at third both times. He could get out from behind the plate quicker than any catcher I ever saw. And I pitched to twenty different catchers in my career. He threw well, too. He had an unorthodox throw to second. But he helped his pitcher a lot. The son of a gun could do it all."

Al Downing, who once struck out the side on nine pitches, came up to the Yankees in 1961 at the age of twenty. Yogi was thirty-six at the time, but to Al's young eyes, he seemed fifty. The first time that Al pitched to Yogi, his catcher told him to let him field all bunts and topped balls around the plate. Al couldn't believe what he had been told and mentioned it to his friend and roommate, Elston Howard. Ellie laughed and said, "He may look slow back there but he's as quick as a cat. Let Yogi do anything he wants."

One play in 1949 changed Yogi's image as a defensive player. The Red Sox had the bases loaded with one out at the Stadium. Al Zarilla lined a one-hop single to Cliff Mapes in right field. Mapes charged the ball and threw home, thinking that he had a play on Ted Williams, who was on second base. But Johnny Pesky, the runner on third, got confused and didn't run until it was too late. Perhaps Pesky thought Mapes was going to catch the ball. Joe Paparella, the plate umpire, was confused, too. He called Pesky safe, because Yogi caught the ball like a first baseman, leaning up the third-base line, and didn't tag Johnny. The 63,000 fans in the stands were confused, also. Yogi was perhaps the only person in the park who knew that Pesky was out.

"He's out, Joe," he said to Paparella. "Force out."

"By God, you're right, he is out," Paparella said.

After the game Dickey told the writers, "I've been telling you all season that Yogi's the best catcher in the American League. Maybe now you'll begin to believe me."

From that point on, there were no more jokes about Yogi's catching. There was only praise. Only two more harrowing moments behind the plate come to mind over the rest of Yogi's career. One was a passed ball in the ninth inning of Game Three of the 1952 World Series. It allowed two Dodger runners to score, and they made the difference in the 5-3 game. The other was in Allie Reynolds' second no-hitter of 1951. Reynolds remembers the sequence of events well: "The second no-hitter I pitched that year, the one that clinched a tie for the pennant, had a dramatic ending. We had a big lead over the Red Sox, and Ted Williams was the batter. How would you like to get Ted Williams for the last out of a no-hitter? Well, as it turned out, I had to get him twice. The first time, he hit a towering pop fly, foul, toward the Yankee dugout. Yogi circled and circled under the ball. Then he finally lunged for it, and dropped it. I could have caught the ball easily. I could have caught it, too, if it had popped my way. But it bounced the wrong way off Yogi's glove. In Yogi's defense the ball was nine miles high, and there's a tricky wind above the Stadium.

"I said to him, 'Did I cut you, Yogi?'

"He said, 'No.'

" 'Okay, let's try it again.'

"On the next pitch Williams popped the ball in the same direction. Yogi had trouble with the ball again, but this time he dived and caught it. I didn't worry about Williams at the time. I was winning big. All winter long, though, I worried about that first pop."

Yogi said simply, "I prayed all the while that second pop was coming down. I was never so scared in my life. Afterwards I thanked God for the second chance."

Yogi has been chastised by some critics who contend that he didn't call the pitchers' pitches. They claim that Casey Stengel called them from the bench. Reynolds told me that he was concerned about that, too. The "Chief" pointed out that Yogi had only one and a half years of experience before he came up to the Yankees, and, in his opinion, didn't have an exceptional arm. He got concerned that Yogi was worried about calling pitches and throwing runners out, so he asked his catcher if Casey or his coaches were calling the signals from the bench. When Berra told him they weren't, Allie said that he would call his own game, and Yogi was relieved. Reynolds said that he told Casey and Jim Turner, the pitching coach, what he was doing, and Eddie Lopat began to do it, too. Allie wasn't sure if Vic Raschi did, also.

The point has become a topic of debate. Phil Rizzuto said that if it had happened, he would have been able to tell from his position at shortstop. He insists it didn't happen. Ralph Houk, the third-string catcher at the time, said that he wanted Yogi's job and watched his every move, so if it had happened, he would have known. Whitey Ford pooh-poohed it, saying that if he shook Yogi off too many times, his catcher would let him know about it. But the probability is that veteran pitchers Reynolds, Lopat, and Raschi, knowing that Berra was inexperienced behind the plate, took an additional pressure off his mind. Maybe Sain did, too. It would have been stupid of him to turn his "bread and butter" over to twenty different catchers. He called his own pitches. Sain was the pitching coach of the 1961-63 Yankees. Some of his pitchers, who have been interviewed for this book, had heard the same story from Sain, who said that they'd be foolish if they didn't call their own game. In time, Reynolds, Lopat, Raschi, and Sain moved on and were replaced by younger pitchers who had more confidence in Berra's defensive skills. And rightly so, because Yogi had emerged as perhaps the best catcher in the American League — though Jim Hegan advocates would argue the point.

There was one day when a pitcher shook him off with his permission. Berra, of course, called the signals in the only perfect game in World Series history. He got good defensive support from his teammates, too. Gil McDougald made a good play, Andy Carey made another, and Mickey Mantle made an exceptional one. Don Larsen had a great fastball and pinpoint control that day. He showed that to Dale Mitchell, the last hitter of the game. They went fastball, slider, fastball, fastball, curve. Before the last pitch Don shook Yogi off twice. That was set up in advance. They had Dale guessing. He was looking fastball and Don gave him a curve for a called strike. Dale averaged only eleven strikeouts a year in his entire career, and they got him to look at a third strike. Don deserves a great deal of credit, but so does Yogi. He thought along with his pitcher all day.

Berra had a lot of success in World Series play. He played in the most games and had the most at bats, hits, and doubles. In addition, he finished as the runner-up in runs and RBIs and third in bases on balls and home runs. Two of his twelve home runs came against Don Newcombe in Game Seven of the 1956 Fall Classic. Yogi had good success against Newcombe. Altogether, he hit three home runs off Don in that World Series. Newcombe, on the other hand, had poor luck in Fall Classic play, though he was a very good pitcher. In 1956, for example, he won 27 games.

Yogi Berra has been depicted as a humorous man. He insists, though, that no one who ever played the game of baseball was ever more serious than he was. Still, he has been credited with countless classic one-line jokes, and former Yankees have been adroit in turning some one-liners his way. Billy Martin, for example, said, "If Yogi dug a hole at second base, he'd strike oil." Charlie Silvera says, "Yankee Stadium may be the house that Ruth built, but my house in San Mateo is the house that Yogi built."

There is some credence to the contention that Yogi was a Teflon player but a non-Teflon manager. Gerry Coleman, who played second base with the 1949-53 world champion New York Yankees, told me the following story about Berra. "Three days before the 1950 season ended, Joe DiMaggio was hitting .301. It was a tense time for him. Everyone, especially the press, was wondering if he could keep his average above .300. Well, that afternoon, Joe hit a screaming line drive at Eddie Joost, the Athletics' shortstop. The ball handcuffed Joost but he made the play. After we made out, Joe went mumbling out to center. In the pre-inning warmups, Yogi overthrew me and the ball hit Joe in the heel. Already in a bad mood, he snapped at me, 'You little banty rooster, can't you catch the ball?' Then he whipped the ball back at me, and it hit me in the knee. Both of us were limping around. In the meantime, Yogi, who had started the whole thing, was standing at home plate with his hands on his hips, wondering what our problem was."

Yogi didn't have the same good fortune as a manager, though. In 1964 he took over a team that had won four straight pennants and led them to a fifth; in the World Series, despite the virtual absence of Whitey Ford and the actual absence of Tony Kubek, he pushed the Cardinals to seven games in a Fall Classic that the Yankees could have won. His team had won ninety-nine games, a number that the Bombers wouldn't duplicate until 1977, when Billy Martin's charges won one hundred.

The morning after the final series loss, Yogi was fired by co-owners Dan Topping and Del Webb.

Why?

There are several different theories, none substantiated.

Phil Linz, who got involved with Yogi with the famous harmonica incident in 1964, became one of the manager's staunchest supporters. "Don't let anyone fool you," he said, "Yogi got fired during the season. The reason was he wasn't good with the press. That's ironic, isn't it? All those years they made up those funny stories about him, which weren't true, and in the end they got him canned because he wasn't good copy."

Billy Martin, who loved Yogi as a friend, said, "He was the greatest coach in the world. He knows so much. But he couldn't be a good manager, because he wasn't mean enough." Allie Reynolds says the same thing.

Coleman, who does the play-by-play for the San Diego Padres these days, says, "Yogi made only one mistake as a manager. I made the same one. He thought the players wanted to win as badly as he did."

Al Downing agrees. "Yes," he says, "I do think some of the players took advantage of him, because he was a friend and former teammate. The press said that he was too dumb to manage. But I contest that. Some managers over-manage to try to impress you. Any time he came out to the mound to talk to me, he was practical and made a lot of sense. I was always impressed with his knowledge, and I always thought he got a bum deal."

Mel Stottlemyre, who as a rookie pitched three games in the 1964 World Series, also thinks his dismissal was unfair. "If we had had Whitey, we would have won it. We didn't have Tony Kubek, either. If we had had Tony, we would have won it. Pedro Ramos was ineligible. If we had had Pedro, we would have won it. Would they have fired him if he had won the World Series? It's hard to say. We didn't think they would fire him after he won the pennant and carried the Cardinals to seven games."

Richardson sums up most of his teammates' feelings. "He befriended me when I was a young player. I never forgot that. It was a pleasure to play with him and under him. I never understood why he got fired, even though a lot of other people — who didn't know, either — have told me why."

Yogi rejects the theory that either he was too lenient with his former teammates or they took advantage of him. He says simply that, if it were the other way around, he wouldn't lay down on a former teammate. He doesn't agree with those who say he was incapable of leading, either. He points to the fact that in his rookie year as a manager he led the Yankees to ninety-nine wins with an aging squad short-circuited by injuries. "The bottom line is if we had had Whitey Ford, we would have won the Series," he says.

Yogi says that Whitey hurt his arm in the first game of the 1964 World Series. Historical accounts support that position. But Jim Bouton says Whitey hurt his arm *before* the Series. In either case, there's an interesting ironic twist. Casey Stengel got fired after the 1960 World Series because he *didn't* start Whitey in Game One, and Yogi may have been fired after the 1964 World Series because he *did* start Whitey in the first game. In 1960, if Whitey had pitched three times, he might have won three games. In 1964, if Bouton had pitched three times, he might have won three games. That's conjecture, but no more so in 1964 than it was in 1960.

Yogi doesn't permit himself to be bitter, but when he talks these days of the Yankees, he tends to talk most often about the "old Yankees," when they were one happy family playing the only way they knew — all out.

He draws some consolation from the following factual account, though. Del Webb, the co-owner of the Yankees in 1964, had the same physician that Yogi did. Shortly before Webb died, he asked the doctor if he saw Yogi often. The doctor admitted that they saw each other as frequently as they could.

Webb then said, "Tell Yogi I made an error."

Elston Howard

Elston Howard was born on February 23, 1929, in St. Louis, Missouri, and died in New York City in 1980.

A touch of irony surrounds Howard and Roger Maris, the subjects of memorial tributes in this book. Both died on the same date, December 14, Ellie in 1980 and Roger in 1985. Both were fifty-one years old when they died, and both had their uniform numbers retired on the same day in 1984 at Yankee Stadium.

One of the greatest events of Howard's youth was hearing on the radio that Jackie Robinson had signed a contract to play with the Brooklyn Dodgers. Knowing that his dream of playing in the big leagues had a chance of becoming a reality, he turned down several college football and basketball scholarships to play in the old Negro Leagues with the Kansas City Blues.

In 1955, when he became the first black player to join the New York Yankees' parent club, that dream came true. He was twenty-six years old at the time, and thirty-one years old by the time he caught 100 games (111 actually) in a major-league season. That was 1961, the year he also had his best all-around major-league season. He batted .348, hit twenty-one home runs, and drove home seventy-seven runs.

Ellie loved his pitchers and understood them well. They loved him for it. One of them, Whitey Ford, benefited from the fact that Howard got right on top of the batter. That allowed Whitey to pick up a lot of low strikes on his sinkerball and curve. Ellie called Whitey "The Chairman of the Board." It's no wonder that Howard's pitchers loved him — he was one of the best catchers, and one of the best men, this game has ever seen.

Ellie wanted to manage the Yankees one day. He thought that dream might be fulfilled, too. But the closest he got was first-base coach for the Bombers. He was disappointed but not bitter.

He and his wife, Arlene, founded the Elston Howard Printing Company in Teaneck, New Jersey, and she still runs the company. They have one son and one daughter, Cheryl, who has appeared in Broadway and Atlantic City musicals.

Not enough has been written about this wonderful man. I hope the following tribute helps to make up for that oversight.

All of the players I've questioned about Elston Howard have been unanimous in the following endorsement. "He was one of the finest gentlemen I've ever met."

They cite his ability to handle pressure, his competitive nature, his sense of humor, his game preparation, and his versatility. They also point to his patience, his ability to call a game, his propensity to come up with big plays, his knack for almost always being one step ahead of the opposition, his ability to teach young and old alike, and his deft handling of pitchers — and others.

Here, then, is how his fellow Yankees remember Elston Howard.

Billy Hunter, now the athletic director at Towson State College, remembers battling Howard for a job. "You'll remember that in 1955 he had just become the first black player called up to the Yankees. Well, later in the season, Casey had to send a player down to the farm system. Ellie and I were the only players with options left. But if they sent him down, they would have been crucified. They could well afford to send me to Denver. As it turned out, the move was academic. I was just an average player. He went on to become great."

Norm Siebern, who was replaced in left field by Howard in Game Five of the 1958 World Series, remembers Ellie's early days with the Yankees, too. "I first met him in 1953 at the 'Acceleration School' in Lake Wales. We were down there two weeks before the veterans reported, working on fundamentals and execution. And also to get to know each other. It was a good idea. Ellie was just out of the service. Bill Virdon was there, too. In those days the Yankees were being harshly criticized for being slow to bring a black player up to the parent organization. The Yankees claimed that they were waiting for the right man. In retrospect, you'd have to say that they couldn't have done better. He had great morals, personality, and character. He was just an outstanding individual."

In Game Five of the 1958 World Series, Casey Stengel inserted Howard in left field, hoping that his bat could turn the Yankee fortunes around. The

Yankees had fallen behind the Milwaukee Braves, three games to one. The preceding year the Braves had defeated the Yankees in seven games. No team had defeated the Yankees in back-to-back World Series since the 1921-22 New York Giants. There was a lot of pride at stake. Another reason that Stengel went to Howard was that Siebern had lost two fly balls in the sun in Game Four, contributing heavily to a 3-0 loss and leaving the Bombers one game away from extinction. Well, Howard contributed with his bat and his glove, making a defensive play that has been recognized as the turning point in that year's Fall Classic. Gil McDougald had hit a solo home run in the bottom of the third inning to account for the only run of a game that was going to the top half of the sixth. Billy Bruton led off the frame with a single, and then Red Schoendienst followed with a slicing fly ball to left field. Howard raced in, dived, and made a sensational one-hand grab of an apparent base hit. Bruton, who had rounded second on the play, was an easy double-play victim at first. Eddie Mathews followed with a base hit that would have scored two runs and possibly buried the Yankees if Howard had not made the play in left field.

The Yankees were rejuvenated. They scored six runs in the bottom half and eventually coasted to a 7-0 victory. They proceeded to win Game Six, 4-3, and Game Seven, 6-2, becoming just the second team in World Series history to come back and win a Fall Classic they had trailed in games, three-one. Elston Howard, by the way, got the game-winning single in Game Seven.

Howard came up to the major leagues as an outfielder. In his first four seasons in the big leagues, he caught only ninety-one games. He went on to become one of the Yankees' most versatile players, filling in at catcher, left field, right field, and first base. But after the Series in 1958, he did most of the catching for the Bombers. His final statistics show that in his career he caught 1,138 games, played the outfield in 265 contests, and filled in at first base 85 times. The truth is, he had to bide his time until Yogi Berra's skills behind the plate began to erode.

Hal Reniff, a relief pitcher for the Yankees in the 1960s, recalls just how good Howard's receiving skills were. "Unless you pitched to him, you wouldn't know how good he was, how agile behind the plate. He wasn't in the same mold as Bill Dickey or Roy Campanella or Johnny Bench, and for a long time he played in Yogi's shadow, but in the early 1960s he came into his own. We kept throwing pitches away and he kept coming up with them. In addition, he threw runners out and won games with his bat. He'll never make the Hall of Fame, but he's in mine."

Buddy Daley, a spot starter and reliever with the early 1960 Yankees, says that Howard was the second best catcher he pitched to. "Jim Hegan in Cleveland was the best," he says, "Ellie was a close second. What I especially liked was that he thought along with you. He was in sync with you. By contrast, you'd shake Yogi off, and he'd always come back to what *he* wanted you to throw."

Bobby Shantz and Ryne Duren thought that Howard was the best catcher they ever saw.

Shantz, a one-time Most Valuable Player, says, "He got more strikes for his pitcher than any other catcher I ever saw. He had an outstanding corner. When the ball hit his glove, it didn't move. His glove stayed right there. Most catchers give a little. They fade with the pitch. Not him, though. The umpires can tell the difference between the great ones and the not-so-greats. They gave him the call. He was a pitcher's best friend."

Duren, who was a flame-throwing relief pitcher for the Yankees in the late 1950s and early 1960s, concurs. He says that Howard was the best catcher he ever threw to, and Yogi was the worst. He says that Ellie blocked everything in the dirt, his glove didn't move, and he was a great hitter with a great arm. Yogi's glove would always move, he says, he was a poor target, and he didn't have Elston's arm.

"One day I said to Howard, 'Ellie, you're so much better than Yogi. Suppose you catch me. Let's go tell the Old Man.'

" 'You're right, Ryne,' he said, 'but who's going to tell the Old Man?'

" 'I will.'

"Well, I told Casey and the Old Man said, 'I know all that. But who's going to tell Mr. Berra?'

" 'I'll tell him.'

"I went to Yogi and suggested the switch. I reminded him that his hand always puffed up when I pitched, and I told him that another reason I preferred Ellie was that he could throw better than him.

" 'I don't give a damn,' Yogi said. 'Make the switch. I don't like to catch you, either.' How about that! Who ran that club anyway? We had to get his permission to make the switch."

One of the keys with Howard was instruction. Al Downing and Johnny Blanchard spoke of that part of Ellie's makeup. Downing, who roomed with Howard, was in awe of his backstop and mentor. He says, "He was the finest human being I ever met. It was a pleasure to room with him. We talked about a lot of things. He always got right to the point. I remember one of our conversations. He said, 'You have the ultimate confidence in me. You never shake me off. But you should call your own pitches and take control of your game. One day I won't be here and you're going to want to be in command. You better start preparing for that day.' So I started shaking him off. It's a good thing. In 1967 he was traded to the Red Sox. But he prepared me for his departure.''

In Game Four of the 1964 World Series, a shake-off hurt the Yankees. Ken Boyer was the Cardinal batter with the bases loaded. Howard called for a fastball but Downing shook him off. He wanted to throw a straight change. Boyer hit the pitch for a grand-slam home run, and it turned the Series around in favor of St. Louis. Downing says he would still throw the same pitch. It was his best pitch to a right-handed batter. Besides, Boyer was a dead fastball hitter.

Blanchard, also a catcher, agrees with Downing's decision. He says that both of them were working toward the same end, and two heads on the ball field are quite often better than one. "Either way is correct if you're out-thinking the hitter," Blanchard told me. "Downing's choice of a pitch was correct. It was his location that was wrong." Blanchard, like Downing, thinks that Ellie was as fine a human being as he's ever met. The two of them would talk about catching by the hours.

"He would teach me how to block pitches, how to set up hitters, and how to pitch 'Punch and Judys.' Fastball, fast breaking curve, no change. He would tell me, 'Work on weaknesses but stay away from patterns.' You know, he wanted to manage in the majors. If he did, both he and his wife Arlene wanted me to be one of his coaches.''

He was a keen competitor. "He could be very serious when the situation warranted it," Dale Long says. But he was also perceptive enough to know the strengths and weaknesses of his pitchers. With Rollie Sheldon, a young pitcher fighting control problems, he exhibited great patience, encouraging the right-hander whenever he could. "C'mon, kid, you can do it," he would say. "You've got the tools. All you need to do is bear down. C'mon now, just hit my glove." With Tom Sturdivant, who had bulldog tenacity on the mound, Ellie would get tough. "I thought you had a good snake. Well, where is it? I want to see it. Let's see if you can hit my glove with it." Howard's competitive nature helped propel the Yankees to nine pennants and the Red Sox to one. He got some big hits in the World Series: a home run in Game Seven of 1956, the game-winning hit in Game Seven in 1958, a home run in a 2-0 Whitey Ford shutout in 1961, and a game-winning hit for the Red Sox in Game Five of 1967. Ellie was well past his prime when Boston picked him up in 1967. He batted just .196 for New York and .147 for the Red Sox that year. In the World Series he hit just .111, but one of his two hits won a game. Boston didn't get him for his hitting, though. The Red Sox got him for his leadership abilities and his ability to handle a pitching staff, and he didn't disappoint them. He carried the corps to seven games in the Fall Classic. If he had been the Elston Howard of old with the bat, the Red Sox probably would have won rather than lost that Fall Classic.

The thing Steve Hamilton remembers about Howard's competitive nature is that, although he was a bear-down guy, he didn't let it consume him. If he was oh-for-six in a game, for example, he wouldn't feel sorry for himself and retreat to a lonely corner of the bench. Instead he would sit next to his game pitcher and think ahead. "He was a total team player," Hamilton, a relief pitcher from the 1960s, told me. "When they talk about true Yankees, they should put his name right at the top of the list."

Hamilton says that Howard was good in the clubhouse, too. He was always loose and you could tease with him. He liked to laugh. "Remember those long drives he used to hit to Death Valley in left-center field? Every year he could have led the league in triples, but he would always try for that inside-the-park home run. I don't think he ever made it. He would always run completely out of gas between third and home. One day I said to him, 'Ellie, blacks are supposed to be able to run and dance. I hope you can dance.' He just laughed.

"Another day I didn't have a thing and Ralph Houk came out to the mound. 'What's he got, Ellie?' he said.

"Ellie said, 'He's all right, Skip.'

"I said, 'Shut up, Ellie, I don't have a thing. They're raking me. I want to get out of here.' Houk laughed that day."

Dale Long recalls a bit of repartee with Howard, too. "Remember the Harlem riots? Well, sometimes I used to go down through Harlem and Central Park to the city. I said to Ellie, 'How're things there?'

" 'I wouldn't go there,' he said.

" 'Good, I won't either.' "

Howard was a consummate leader. His pitchers had tremendous confidence in him. Luis Arroyo, who had a phenomenal year out of the bullpen in 1961, cites one of the many reasons for that faith. In Arroyo's first game with the Yankees, in the middle of the 1960 season, Casey called Arroyo in to face Roy Sievers. "Ellie was one of my best friends," Arroyo says. "We had played winter ball in San Juan. But I didn't know anything about Sievers. I had been in the National League for my whole career, so I said to Casey, 'How do you pitch this guy?'

"Casey said, 'I don't know. You're the pitcher.'

"When he went back to the dugout, Ellie laughed and said, 'Don't pay any attention to him. That's just his way. Sievers is a high-ball hitter. Just follow my pattern. We'll set him up.' I did and I saved the game.

"Casey was waiting for me when I walked to the dugout. He said, 'You pitched him the way I told you.' That's just the way he was. Ellie winked at me."

Overall, Elston Howard batted .274, hit 167 home runs, and drove home 762 runs in his fourteen-year career. The numbers would have been much bigger in a park more suitable to his left-center to right-center field power. Still, he hit .348 with twenty-one home runs and seventy-seven RBIs in 1961. From 1961 to 1963 he hit more than twenty home runs each season. And in 1963 his career was crowned when he was named the American League's Most Valuable Player. He had a good year in 1964, too, but in 1965 he developed a sore arm, and he was never the same player again.

Pedro Ramos still shakes his head in wonder about a sequence of developments in a key game with the White Sox in September of 1964. "It was the ninth inning and we had a one-run lead," he says, "But Luis Aparicio led off the inning with a single, and we were afraid that he was going to steal. Ellie called a pitchout, but Aparicio didn't run. I'm behind on the count, one-and-oh. Ellie called another pitchout, but Aparicio didn't go. Now I'm behind on the count, two-and-oh. Ellie called a third pitchout. Aparicio went and Ellie threw him out. Now I'm behind on the count, three-and-oh. But they can't bunt or hit-and-run. I got out of the inning and saved the game. I'll never forget that play. He was something special."

That was Ellie Howard. Something special.

Roger Maris

Roger Maris was born in Hibbing, Minnesota, on September 10, 1934, and died in Houston, Texas, on December 14, 1985.

Ironically, he was not happy to be traded to the Yankees from the Athletics before the 1960 season. Kansas City was a good hitter's park and he was happy with the city. They appreciated him. Yankee Stadium was a good hitter's park for a left-handed pull hitter like Maris, too. Casey Stengel thought that Roger would be a natural long-ball hitter in the comfortable confines of the "short porch" in right field, and he was right. Roger put big numbers on the board from 1960-64 and the Yankees did, too: they won five consecutive pennants and two world championships. Not too many players, in addition to Maris, have played on five consecutive pennant winners. No one, besides Roger, has hit as many as 61 home runs in a season. Roger Maris should have been happy in New York. But he wasn't. They were always comparing him to someone else. Babe Ruth and Mickey Mantle, for example. They never permitted him to be just himself.

When the Yankees traded Maris to the Cardinals after the 1966 season, Roger was happy to leave New York. In St. Louis, in 1967 and 1968, he didn't have typical Roger Maris production years. He hit .261 with nine home runs in 1967 and batted .255 with five round-trippers in 1968. But the Cardinals acquired him because they knew he was a winner, and he helped them win back-to-back pennants in those years. Out of gratitude to Maris, who agreed to play one last year for the Cardinals in 1968, owner Gussie Busch awarded him a beer distributorship in Gainesville, Florida, where he lived with his wife Pat and their six children, four sons and two daughters. The Yankees, on the other hand, didn't even give him a bonus when he hit the record sixty-one home runs in 1961.

187

Maris was bitter. At one point he hadn't returned to New York City in ten years. But George Steinbrenner helped to soften the pain in Roger's final years, convincing him to return to the Stadium on April 12, 1978, for the traditional raising of the world championship flag on Opening Day; on July 21, 1984, to have his uniform number retired; and in April of 1985 to receive the Lou Gehrig Pride of the Yankees Award.

Roger Maris' plaque in Yankee Stadium reads as follows:

ROGER EUGENE MARIS AGAINST ALL ODDS IN 1961 HE BECAME THE ONLY PLAYER TO
HIT MORE THAN 60 HOME RUNS IN A SINGLE SEASON IN BELATED RECOGNITION OF ONE
OF BASEBALL'S GREATEST ACHIEVEMENTS EVER HIS 61 IN '61 THE YANKEES SALUTE HIM
AS A GREAT PLAYER AND AUTHOR OF ONE OF THE MOST REMARKABLE CHAPTERS IN THE
HISTORY OF MAJOR LEAGUE BASEBALL
ERECTED BY NEW YORK YANKEES JULY 21, 1984.

I never got the chance to interview Roger Maris. This is my personal memorial tribute to him. I hope it offers some fresh insight into the character of a proud man.

On December 23, 1985, the high and the low of the baseball world squeezed into St. Patrick's Cathedral in New York City to say good-bye to Roger Maris. Two days before, many of those in attendance had said their initial farewell in Fargo, North Dakota, where Roger was buried beneath a foot of snow in a scenic spot overlooking a hill in Holy Cross Cemetery.

Former President Richard Nixon, one of those in attendance at St. Patrick's Cathedral, spoke briefly. In the early 1960s he had spent evenings with Whitey Ford and Billy Martin and Roger Maris at Toots Shor's Restaurant in New York. He alluded to those halcyon times. He also pointed out the similarities between himself and Maris then, citing their unfair treatment by the press and their alleged cold exterior. Then he concluded by saying, "One must often wait until the evening to see how splendid the day was." It was a lucid, laconic tribute to the life — and death — of Roger Maris.

He broke into the major leagues with the Cleveland Indians in 1957, and he showed early promise as a home run hitter. That year he batted .235, hit fourteen home runs, and drove home fifty-one runs. Roger's major-league power stats surprised Buddy Daley, who was a teammate of Maris in Indianapolis, Cleveland, Kansas City, and New York. "He wasn't a power hitter in the minor leagues," Daley says. "I remember one night in Louisville we had the bases loaded with two outs in the ninth inning. What did he do? He drag-bunted the winning run home." In retrospect, that story bears out what all of the Yankees in this book have told me. He was a complete player. He could hit, hit with power, drive home runs, field, throw strongly and accurately, run, take the extra base, go from first to third, take out the pivot man at second base — and bunt.

"The press may have put a bum rap on him," says his former roommate, Hal Reniff, "but I'm sure you haven't run across one of his former teammates rapping him. He could do it all."

The one thing he didn't do was hit for average. That bothered him, because he always felt that he could hit .300. The fact that he played the game so hard perhaps prevented him from doing so. He was beset by a host of nagging injuries. In 1957, his rookie season, he hurt his wrist running into a wall, he pulled a hamstring, and he was laid up for a couple of weeks when he pulled a rib muscle. Manager Kerby Farrell, who was worried about his team's and his own fortune, put him back in the lineup before he returned to health, and his batting average of .280 dipped to .235. At that point the Cleveland journalists began questioning in print whether Maris was ready for the majors. Roger was upset by the stories because he knew that, if he were healthy, he could hit major-league pitching.

Frank Lane, Cleveland's general manager, wanted him to play in the Dominican Republic during the winter season, but Roger didn't think $1,000 a month was enough, so he went home and got a job with a local radio station. By the time Lane had raised the figure to $1,500 a month, Maris was ensconced in his new employment. "Besides," he said, "I don't feel like playing winter ball in the Dominican Republic, and I don't think I need the extra work." Lane decided he didn't need a rebellious rookie, branded him as a troublemaker, and traded him to Kansas City before the trading deadline in 1958.

Roger had two productive years in Kansas City. In 1958 he batted .240, slugged twenty-eight home runs, and drove home eighty runs. In 1959 his batting average went up, but his production went down. He batted .273, hit sixteen home runs, and drove home seventy-three runs. But there's justification for his decrease in home runs. On May 22, 1959, Maris was rushed to the Kansas City General Hospital for an emergency appendectomy. Weak and tired, he resumed playing three weeks after surgery, and in two dismal stretches he went four for sixty in one and eleven for ninety in another.

Bob Cerv, who played with Maris in New York from 1960-62, was also a teammate of Roger's with the 1958-59 Athletics. "Roger could have been a solid .300 hitter if there was a man on second base every time he came to the plate," he says. "His eyes lit up when there were runners on base. He seemed to care about getting base hits when they counted most. 'That's what they pay off on,' he would say."

Ralph Terry, who also played with Maris in Kansas City and New York, offered the following insight into Roger's Kansas City personality, one that would remain with him for the rest of his life. "He and I got along really well. In fact, the two of us got along with everyone on the Kansas City club. The only difference was I could laugh things off. Roger couldn't. If he trusted you and you crossed him, you wouldn't get a second chance. I'd laugh about it, and forget it. Roger didn't. He was too serious about some things."

Roger's home-run swing was serious, too. He would stand at the plate with his feet spread eighteen inches apart, his helmet pulled down over his eyebrows, his bat held up high over his left ear, his right shoulder tucked in against his cheek, and pull the ball hard to the right side, with his top hand releasing from the bat, and his head arching to follow the flight of the ball toward the right-field stands. His picture-perfect swing attracted a lot of attention. One of his distant admirers was Casey Stengel. Over dinner one night he told general manager George Weiss, "Get Maris. He'll be a natural at Yankee Stadium."

The Yankees were in a state of transition. After winning pennants from 1955-58, they finished third in 1959, just four games over .500. On December 11, 1959, the Yankees sent Hank Bauer, Norm Siebern, Don Larsen, and Marv Throneberry to Kansas City for Maris, Joe DeMaestri and Kent Hadley. With one brilliant maneuver, they changed their future. From 1960-65, with Maris batting either third or fourth, they won five consecutive pennants.

But Maris, unlike the many transplants from Kansas City to New York, was not ecstatic with the trade. "I'm not happy at all," he told the sportswriters after arriving in spring training. "I liked Kansas City. I thought I would spend the rest of my career there."

Roger put three phenomenal years back-to-back, though. In 1960 he batted .283, hit thirty-nine home runs, and drove home a league-leading 112 runs. The following year, in 1961, he batted .269, hit a record sixty-one home runs, and had a league-leading 142 RBIs. The numbers fell off somewhat in 1962, but they were still more than respectable. He batted .256, hit thirty-three home runs, and drove home an even 100 runs.

Roger Maris had done what Casey Stengel knew he would: reversed the Yankees' fortunes. His impact was immediate, not only on the team's performance, but also on the players themselves. "He was a great guy," Johnny Blanchard says, "and highly underrated in almost every facet of the game. He felt bad about the unfavorable press he got. They tried to build up a rivalry between Mickey and him. Mickey, sensing the writers' intent, would say, 'I hate you, Roger,' in front of some reporter in the clubhouse, the writer would run off to embellish the 'rivalry,' and Mickey, Roger, and Bob Cerv would go back to their hotel room and laugh about it. There was no jealousy. There was competition, though. They were both competitors from here to there. And they both wanted to win. Winning's what it's all about. Whether it's games, pennants, World Series — or home run championships."

Roger Maris said the same thing himself, in the last year of his life. He noted that he had won the MVP Award in both 1960 and 1961, but Mickey had edged him out for the home run title in 1960, 40-39, when he hit two home runs in the last week of the season off Chuck Stobbs. "I wanted to win that home run duel in 1961," he said. And he did, but the pressure affected him profoundly. For a while his face broke out in a rash, then his hair began to fall out. Both allergies were caused by nerves. As his pursuit of Babe Ruth's hallowed record grew more intense, he was besieged by a horde of fifty or more writers after each game. He didn't like the ritual but he accepted it as part of the price of being a professional ballplayer. He answered every reporter's question, often perfunctorily and without emotion, but tried to keep his responses as terse as he could. Sometimes he would become exasperated with the silliness of a question, though. It was only natural.

Luis Arroyo remembers a moment late in the 1961 season when Maris had fifty-nine home runs. "A reporter asked him, 'Do you think you deserve to break Ruth's record'?" he recalls. "I thought Roger was going to punch him. He was a wonderful guy and a great family man. I was winning and saving all of those games in 1961. Whitey and Mickey would invite me out after the games. Roger, too. But he'd say, 'Nah, I think I'll go home and see my family'."

In the final week of the 1961 season, another writer asked him, "Which would you prefer: to hit sixty-one home runs or to bat .300?"

Maris was nonplussed. "Which would you prefer to do?" he said.

"Hit .300."

"Well, to each his own."

One of Roger's emotional outlets during the 1961 season was eating. Among his teammates, his appetite was legendary. Blanchard recalls, "He'd eat a bucketful of crabs, let out a burp, and then say, 'Let's get a steak.' That's why he didn't drink that much. He was too busy eating."

Dale Long, another Maris roommate, tells a different story about Roger's fondness for food. "He was a country boy from the Dakotas, and I was a city boy from Massachusetts. Every Monday we had off after a doubleheader, I would go home to Massachusetts. I had a friend up there who would pick corn in the morning and give me a couple of bushels at noon to take back to the players. One day he ate twenty-eight ears of corn. He put them in a pound of butter, salted them, and ate them. We couldn't believe it."

No one could believe what Maris accomplished in 1961, either. Never a good starter, he started slowly in 1961. He didn't hit his first home run until April 26, and he didn't hit his seventh until May 21. At the time, he was concerned. He was also worried about his batting average, which was hovering around the .240 mark. That's when co-owner Dan Topping sat him down and said, "Stop worrying about your batting average. We would prefer to see you hit a lot of home runs and drive home 100 runs than bat .300." That relieved Roger. It was exactly how he had always seen his role. From that point, there was no stopping him. Roger's major problem the rest of the season was his inability to be diplomatic. He was not good at small talk or talking about himself. If he said he wasn't interested in Ruth's record, people didn't believe him. If he said he was bearing down on it, they thought he was treading on hallowed ground. One day toward the end of the season, he hit a home run in Detroit, and the ball bounced back on the playing field. Al Kaline, the right fielder, threw the ball into the Yankee dugout. After the game one of the players suggested that it was a nice gesture on Kaline's part.

Maris said, "I don't know, I would have done the same thing."

Pitcher Steve Hamilton made a pointed observation about Maris. "He and Bobby Richardson were the best clutch players we had," he says. "His teammates knew how good he was. But he didn't handle the press well. He would say something which was nontraditional, like 'I'm not going to run into that wall out there and get hurt,' and then he would go out there and do exactly what he said he wouldn't. He didn't handle the fans well, either. Most of the time he didn't mean what he said. He never 'laid down' a day in his life. I just wish he had been better at public relations."

Two other factors conspired against Maris in 1961. First, he and Mickey Mantle challenged Ruth almost to the wire. But Mantle, worn down by a virus, took himself out of the race in September, when he had fifty-three home runs. Later he returned and hit his fifty-fourth home run, but he had to check out of the lineup once again, this time with an abscessed hip that would plague him through the World Series. Mantle had been booed vociferously by the fans before Maris arrived in New York. But when it seemed inevitable that one of the two would break Ruth's record, the fans unanimously decided that Mantle was the more deserving. Then, Commissioner Ford Frick, an old buddy of Ruth's, declared that if the record wasn't broken in 154 games, the length of the season when the Babe set the mark, an asterisk would go into the books next to the new record holder's name. Frick reasoned that Maris and Mantle had an unfair advantage on Ruth, since their schedule ran to 162 games.

Reniff offers an insight into the Maris-Mantle debate. "Based on Mantle's track record, perhaps he did deserve to break Ruth's record," he says. "But anything you deserve, you have to earn. Instead of detracting from Roger's phenomenal accomplishment, I think we all should applaud him. It's hard enough to break a record when everyone's rooting for you. It's just about impossible when everyone's rooting against you. And Roger did it."

About Frick's ruling, Roger simply said, "A season's a season." He didn't feel any more kindly to Topping's response to his season. "You know what he gave me for those 61 homers? Not a cent. Not a gift. The attendance was 1.7 million, the highest it had been in ten years, and he gave me nothing."

In ensuing years, whenever Maris was asked how tough 1961 was on him, he would say, "1961 was okay. It was a picnic compared to 1962." Roger didn't get off well with the press in 1962. He didn't like some of the uncomplimentary things that had been said about him during the winter. During spring training Maris refused to pose for a picture with Hall-of-Famer Rogers Hornsby, who had said disparaging things about him during his record-run in 1961. Hornsby said defensively, "He's a busher. He couldn't carry my bat." Oscar Fraley, a columnist for United Press, asked Maris for his account of the dispute. When Roger refused to give it, Fraley wrote a scathing attack of him and his record. It ran all over the country in his syndicated column. Then Maris didn't show up for an interview with Jimmy Cannon, one of the most respected sports columnists in the country. Cannon, again in a syndicated column, satirized Roger and his record. From that time on, Maris never fully trusted any reporter.

As a player, Roger had a good season in 1962. But in 1963 he suffered a back injury, a problem with his elbow, and several muscle pulls. He got only 312 at bats, and he made the most of them: he hit twenty-three home runs. In 1964 he had his last super season. He batted .281, hit twenty-six home runs, and drove home seventy-one runs. Many of the players in this book contend that Roger and Pedro Ramos were the reasons the Yankees won in 1964. In the last month, they say, Roger delivered just about every game-winning hit the Yankees made. Yogi Berra, his manager, said, "Mickey was hurt that year. I needed a center fielder, so I went to him and asked him if he would make the switch. He said it was no big deal. He did it and he played great. I really appreciate what he did for the club."

On June 28, 1965, Maris suffered an injury that negated his effectiveness in his last two seasons with the Yankees. In a slide at home plate he broke a bone that wasn't discovered on x-rays taken by the Yankees' doctors. He suffered excruciating pain, but was accused of being a malingerer because the x-rays showed no damage. Finally, in desperation, he went to his own doctor, and the broken bone showed up on the new x-rays.

In 1985 Maris said, "The Yankees didn't treat me right. They should have told the press I was hurt. Instead they listed me as day-to-day, giving the impression I was faking an injury. They didn't send me to the right doctor. They were only interested in the gate. They wanted me to get back in the lineup." Knowing that his days in New York were over, Roger was ready to quit baseball, but when he was traded to the St. Louis Cardinals after the 1966 season, he made the switch, enjoyed the new atmosphere, made many new friends, played in two successive World Series, and retired on a happy note. Augie Busch, the owner of the Cardinals, asked Roger in 1968 to play one more year and promised to take care of Maris after the season. The St. Louis owner lived up to his word, granting Maris a Gainesville, Florida, beer distributorship that gave the family financial stability. When he retired, Roger said, "I'm tired of baseball. I'll be busy with my job, and I'll be able to come home to my family every night. I won't miss the game."

It took the evening of Roger's life to highlight the splendor of the earlier days. Bobby Richardson, in a stirring eulogy at Maris' funeral, spelled out the message of Roger's life for those who were too blind to see it.

"Some of Roger's problems started with the press," he said. "They might keep Roger out of baseball's Hall of Fame. But he's in God's Hall of Fame right now. In life, one's deeds are soon forgotten. But in God's Hall of Fame, they live for eternity."

In March of 1989, Richardson talked to me in his office at Liberty University in Lynchburg, Virginia. Of Roger Maris he said, "I think what they did to Maris was sad. He came over from Kansas City in 1960 and had a super season. He won the MVP Award. He won it again in 1961. But he was never truly appreciated by the press, the fans, or his teammates.

"I marveled at his feat. And I thought the way it ended — on the last day of the season — was excellent. The baseball world had put so much pressure on him all along. Roger, in true poetic-justice fashion, carried the baseball world right to the very end before he broke the game's most cherished record. I applauded Roger Maris then. I applaud him now."

APPENDIX

Luis Arroyo

		W	L	PCT	ERA	G	GS	CG	IP	H	BB	SO	ShO	SV
1955 STL	N	11	8	.579	4.19	35	24	9	159	162	63	68	1	0
1956 PIT	N	3	3	.500	4.71	18	2	1	28.2	36	12	17	0	0
1957		3	11	.214	4.68	54	10	0	130.2	151	31	101	0	1
1959 CIN	N	1	0	1.000	3.95	10	0	0	13.2	17	11	8	0	0
1960 NY	A	5	1	.833	2.88	29	0	0	40.2	30	22	29	0	7
1961		15	5	.750	2.19	65	0	0	119	83	49	87	0	29
1962		1	3	.250	4.81	27	0	0	33.2	33	17	21	0	7
1963		1	1	.500	13.50	6	0	0	6	12	3	5	0	0
8 yrs.		40	32	.556	3.93	244	36	10	531.1	524	208	336	1	44

WORLD SERIES														
1960 NY	A	0	0	—	13.50	1	0	0	.2	2	0	1	0	0
1961		1	0	1.000	2.25	2	0	0	4	4	2	3	0	0
2 yrs.		1	0	1.000	3.86	3	0	0	4.2	6	2	4	0	0

Yogi Berra

		G	AB	H	2B	3B	HR	R	RBI	BB	SO	SB	BA
1946	NY A	7	22	8	1	0	2	3	4	1	1	0	.364
1947		83	293	82	15	3	11	41	54	13	12	0	.280
1948		125	469	143	24	10	14	70	98	25	24	3	.305
1949		116	415	115	20	2	20	59	91	22	25	2	.277
1950		151	597	192	30	6	28	116	124	55	12	4	.322
1951		141	547	161	19	4	27	92	88	44	20	5	.294
1952		142	534	146	17	1	30	97	98	66	24	2	.273
1953		137	503	149	23	5	27	80	108	50	32	0	.296
1954		151	584	179	28	6	22	88	125	56	29	0	.307
1955		147	541	147	20	3	27	84	108	60	20	1	.272
1956		140	521	155	29	2	30	93	105	65	29	3	.298
1957		134	482	121	14	2	24	74	82	57	25	1	.251
1958		122	433	115	17	3	22	60	90	35	35	3	.266
1959		131	472	134	25	1	19	64	69	43	38	1	.284
1960		120	359	99	14	1	15	46	62	38	23	2	.276
1961		119	395	107	11	0	22	62	61	35	28	2	.271
1962		86	232	52	8	0	10	25	35	24	18	0	.224
1963		64	147	43	6	0	8	20	28	15	17	1	.293
1965	NY N	4	9	2	0	0	0	1	0	0	3	0	.222
19 yrs.		2120	7555	2150	321	49	358	1175	1430	704	415	30	.285

WORLD SERIES

1947	NY A	6	19	3	0	0	1	2	2	1	2	0	.158
1949		4	16	1	0	0	0	2	1	1	3	0	.063
1950		4	15	3	0	0	1	2	2	2	1	0	.200
1951		6	23	6	1	0	0	4	0	2	1	0	.261
1952		7	28	6	1	0	2	2	3	2	4	0	.214
1953		6	21	9	1	0	1	3	4	3	3	0	.429
1955		7	24	10	1	0	1	5	2	3	1	0	.417
1956		7	25	9	2	0	3	5	10	4	1	0	.360
1957		7	25	8	1	0	1	5	2	4	0	0	.320
1958		7	27	6	3	0	0	3	2	1	0	0	.222
1960		7	22	7	0	0	1	6	8	2	0	0	.318
1961		4	11	3	0	0	1	2	3	5	1	0	.273
1962		2	2	0	0	0	0	0	0	2	0	0	.000
1963		1	1	0	0	0	0	0	0	0	0	0	.000
14 yrs.		75	259	71	10	0	12	41	39	32	17	0	.274

Johnny Blanchard

		G	AB	H	2B	3B	HR	R	RBI	BB	SO	SB	BA
1955	NY A	1	3	0	0	0	0	0	0	1	0	0	.000
1959		49	59	10	1	0	2	6	4	7	12	0	.169
1960		53	99	24	3	1	4	8	14	6	17	0	.242
1961		93	243	74	10	1	21	38	54	27	28	1	.305
1962		93	246	57	7	0	13	33	39	28	32	0	.232
1963		76	218	49	4	0	16	22	45	26	30	0	.225
1964		77	161	41	8	0	7	18	28	24	24	1	.255
1965	3 teams	NY	A (12G — .147)		KC	A (52G — .200)		MIL	N (10G — .100)				
	total	74	164	30	3	0	4	12	16	17	20	0	.183
8 yrs.		516	1193	285	36	2	67	137	200	136	163	2	.239
WORLD SERIES													
1960	NY A	5	11	5	2	0	0	2	2	0	0	0	.455
1961		4	10	4	1	0	2	4	3	2	0	0	.400
1962		1	1	0	0	0	0	0	0	0	1	0	.000
1963		1	3	0	0	0	0	0	0	0	0	0	.000
1964		4	4	1	1	0	0	0	0	0	1	0	.250
5 yrs.		15	29	10	4	0	2	6	5	2	2	0	.345

Jim Bouton

		W	L	PCT	ERA	G	GS	CG	IP	H	BB	SO	ShO	SV
1962	NY A	7	7	.500	3.99	36	16	3	133	124	59	71	1	2
1963		21	7	.750	2.53	40	30	12	249.1	191	87	148	6	1
1964		18	13	.581	3.02	38	37	11	271.1	227	60	125	4	0
1965		4	15	.211	4.82	30	25	2	151.1	158	60	97	0	0
1966		3	8	.273	2.69	24	19	3	120.1	117	38	65	0	1
1967		1	0	1.000	4.67	17	1	0	44.1	47	18	31	0	0
1968		1	1	.500	3.68	12	3	1	44	49	9	24	0	0
1969	2 teams	SEA	A	(57G 2-1)		HOU	N	(16G 0-2)						
	total	2	3	.400	3.95	73	2	1	123	109	50	100	0	2
1970	HOU N	4	6	.400	5.42	29	6	1	73	84	33	49	0	0
1978	ATL N	1	3	.250	4.97	5	5	0	29	25	21	10	0	0
10 yrs.		62	63	.496	3.57	304	144	34	1238.2	1131	435	720	11	6
WORLD SERIES														
1963	NY A	0	1	.000	1.29	1	1	0	7	4	5	4	0	0
1964		2	0	1.000	1.56	2	2	1	17.1	15	5	7	0	0
2 yrs.		2	1	.667	1.48	3	3	1	24.1	19	10	11	0	0

Andy Carey

		G	AB	H	2B	3B	HR	R	RBI	BB	SO	SB	BA
1952	NY A	16	40	6	0	0	0	6	1	3	10	0	.150
1953		51	81	26	5	0	4	14	8	9	12	2	.321
1954		122	411	124	14	6	8	60	65	43	38	5	.302
1955		135	510	131	19	11	7	73	47	44	51	3	.257
1956		132	422	100	18	2	7	54	50	45	53	9	.237
1957		85	247	63	6	5	6	30	33	15	42	2	.255
1958		102	315	90	19	4	12	39	45	34	43	1	.286
1959		41	101	26	1	0	3	11	9	7	17	1	.257
1960	2 teams	NY	A	(4G — .333)		KC	A	(102G — .233)					
	total	106	346	81	14	4	12	31	54	26	53	0	.234
1961	2 teams	KC	A	(39G — .244)		CHI	A	(56G — .266)					
	total	95	266	68	18	5	3	41	25	26	47	0	.256
1962	LA N	53	111	26	5	1	2	12	13	16	23	0	.234
11 yrs.		938	2850	741	119	38	64	371	350	268	389	23	.260
WORLD SERIES													
1955	NY A	2	2	1	0	1	0	0	1	0	0	0	.500
1956		7	19	3	0	0	0	2	0	1	6	0	.158
1957		2	7	2	1	0	0	0	1	1	0	0	.286
1958		5	12	1	0	0	0	1	0	0	3	0	.083
4 yrs.		16	40	7	1	1	0	3	2	2	9	0	.175

Buddy Daley

		W	L	PCT	ERA	G	GS	CG	IP	H	BB	SO	ShO	SV
1955	CLE A	0	1	.000	6.43	2	1	0	7	10	1	2	0	0
1956		1	0	1.000	6.20	14	0	0	20.1	21	14	13	0	0
1957		2	8	.200	4.43	34	10	1	87.1	99	40	54	0	2
1958	KC A	3	2	.600	3.31	26	5	1	70.2	67	19	39	0	0
1959		16	13	.552	3.16	39	29	12	216.1	212	62	125	2	1
1960		16	16	.500	4.56	37	35	13	231	234	96	126	1	0
1961	2 teams	KC	A	(16G 4-8)	NY	A	(23G 8-9)							
	total	12	17	.414	4.28	39	27	9	193.1	211	73	119	0	1
1962	NY A	7	5	.583	3.59	43	6	0	105.1	105	21	55	0	4
1963		0	0	—	0.00	1	0	0	1	2	0	0	0	1
1964		3	2	.600	4.63	13	3	0	35	37	25	16	0	1
10 yrs.		60	64	.484	4.03	248	116	36	967.1	998	351	549	3	10

WORLD SERIES

		W	L	PCT	ERA	G	GS	CG	IP	H	BB	SO	ShO	SV
1961	NY A	1	0	1.000	0.00	2	0	0	7	5	0	3	0	0
1962		0	0	—	0.00	1	0	0	1	1	1	0	0	0
2 yrs.		1	0	1.000	0.00	3	0	0	8	6	1	3	0	0

Art Ditmar

		W	L	PCT	ERA	G	GS	CG	IP	H	BB	SO	ShO	SV
1954	PHI A	1	4	.200	6.41	14	5	0	39.1	50	36	14	0	0
1955	KC A	12	12	.500	5.03	35	22	7	175.1	180	86	79	1	1
1956		12	22	.353	4.42	44	34	14	254.1	254	108	126	2	1
1957	NY A	8	3	.727	3.25	46	11	0	127.1	128	35	64	0	6
1958		9	8	.529	3.42	38	13	4	139.2	124	38	52	0	4
1959		13	9	.591	2.90	38	25	7	202	156	52	96	1	1
1960		15	9	.625	3.06	34	28	8	200	195	56	65	1	0
1961	2 teams	NY	A	(12G 2-3)	KC	A	(20G 0-5)							
	total	2	8	.200	5.15	32	13	1	108.1	119	37	43	0	1
1962	KC A	0	2	.000	6.65	6	5	0	21.2	31	13	13	0	0
9 yrs.		72	77	.483	3.98	287	156	41	1268	1237	461	552	5	14

WORLD SERIES

		W	L	PCT	ERA	G	GS	CG	IP	H	BB	SO	ShO	SV
1957	NY A	0	0	—	0.00	2	0	0	6	2	0	2	0	0
1958		0	0	—	0.00	1	0	0	3.2	2	0	2	0	0
1960		0	2	.000	21.60	2	2	0	1.2	6	1	0	0	0
3 yrs.		0	2	.000	3.18	5	2	0	11.1	10	1	4	0	0

Al Downing

		W	L	PCT	ERA	G	GS	CG	IP	H	BB	SO	ShO	SV
1961	NY A	0	1	.000	8.00	5	1	0	9	7	12	12	0	0
1962		0	0	—	0.00	1	0	0	1	0	0	1	0	0
1963		13	5	.722	2.56	24	22	10	175.2	114	80	171	4	0
1964		13	8	.619	3.47	37	35	11	244	201	120	217	1	2
1965		12	14	.462	3.40	35	32	8	212	185	105	179	2	0
1966		10	11	.476	3.56	30	30	1	200	178	79	152	0	0
1967		14	10	.583	2.63	31	28	10	201.2	158	61	171	4	0
1968		3	3	.500	3.52	15	12	1	61.1	54	20	40	0	0
1969		7	5	.583	3.38	30	15	5	130.2	117	49	85	1	0
1970	2 teams		OAK	A (10G 3-3)		MIL	A	(17G 2-10)						
	total	5	13	.278	3.52	27	22	2	135.1	118	81	79	0	0
1971	LA N	20	9	.690	2.68	37	36	12	262	245	84	136	5	0
1972		9	9	.500	2.98	31	30	7	202.2	196	67	117	4	0
1973		9	9	.500	3.31	30	28	5	193	155	68	124	2	0
1974		5	6	.455	3.67	21	16	1	98	94	45	63	1	0
1975		2	1	.667	2.88	22	6	0	75	59	28	39	0	1
1976		1	2	.333	3.86	17	3	0	46.2	43	18	30	0	0
1977		0	1	.000	6.75	12	1	0	20	22	16	23	0	0
17 yrs.		123	107	.535	3.22	405	317	73	2268	1946	933	1639	24	3

LEAGUE CHAMPIONSHIP SERIES

		W	L	PCT	ERA	G	GS	CG	IP	H	BB	SO	ShO	SV
1974	LA N	0	0	—	0.00	1	0	0	4	1	1	0	0	0

WORLD SERIES

		W	L	PCT	ERA	G	GS	CG	IP	H	BB	SO	ShO	SV
1963	NY A	0	1	.000	5.40	1	1	0	5	7	1	6	0	0
1964		0	1	.000	8.22	3	1	0	7.2	9	2	5	0	0
1974	LA N	0	1	.000	2.45	1	1	0	3.2	4	4	3	0	0
3 yrs.		0	3	.000	6.06	5	3	0	16.1	20	7	14	0	0

Ryne Duren

		W	L	PCT	ERA	G	GS	CG	IP	H	BB	SO	ShO	SV
1954	BAL A	0	0	—	9.00	1	0	0	2	3	1	2	0	0
1957	KC A	0	3	.000	5.27	14	6	0	42.2	37	30	37	0	1
1958	NY A	6	4	.600	2.02	44	1	0	75.2	40	43	87	0	20
1959		3	6	.333	1.88	41	0	0	76.2	49	43	96	0	14
1960		3	4	.429	4.96	42	1	0	49	27	49	67	0	9
1961	2 teams		NY	A (4G 0-1)		LA	A	(40G 6-12)						
	total	6	13	.316	5.19	44	14	1	104	89	79	115	1	2
1962	LA A	2	9	.182	4.42	42	3	0	71.1	53	57	74	0	8
1963	PHI N	6	2	.750	3.30	33	7	1	87.1	65	52	84	0	2

1964	2 teams	PHI	N	(2G 0-0)		CIN	N	(26G 0-2)						
	total	0	2	.000	3.09	28	0	0	46.2	46	16	44	0	1
1965	2 teams	PHI	N	(6G 0-0)		WAS	A	(16G 1-1)						
	total	1	1	.500	5.56	22	0	0	34	34	22	24	0	0
10 yrs.		27	44	.380	3.83	311	32	2	589.1	443	392	630	1	57

WORLD SERIES

1958	NY A	1	1	.500	1.93	3	0	0	9.1	7	6	14	0	1
1960		0	0	—	2.25	2	0	0	4	2	1	5	0	0
2 yrs.		1	1	.500	2.03	5	0	0	13.1	9	7	19	0	1

Whitey Ford

		W	L	PCT	ERA	G	GS	CG	IP	H	BB	SO	ShO	S
1950	NY A	9	1	.900	2.81	20	12	7	112	87	52	59	2	1
1953		18	6	.750	3.00	32	30	11	207	187	110	110	3	0
1954		16	8	.667	2.82	34	28	11	210.2	170	101	125	3	1
1955		18	7	.720	2.63	39	33	18	253.2	188	113	137	5	2
1956		19	6	.760	2.47	31	30	18	225.2	187	84	141	2	1
1957		11	5	.688	2.57	24	17	5	129.1	114	53	84	0	0
1958		14	7	.667	2.01	30	29	15	219.1	174	62	145	7	1
1959		16	10	.615	3.04	35	29	9	204	194	89	114	2	1
1960		12	9	.571	3.08	33	29	8	192.2	168	65	85	4	0
1961		25	4	.862	3.21	39	39	11	283	242	92	209	3	0
1962		17	8	.680	2.90	38	37	7	257.2	243	69	160	0	0
1963		24	7	.774	2.74	38	37	13	269.1	240	56	189	3	1
1964		17	6	.739	2.13	39	36	12	244.2	212	57	172	8	1
1965		16	13	.552	3.24	37	36	9	244.1	241	50	162	2	1
1966		2	5	.286	2.47	22	9	0	73	79	24	43	0	0
1967		2	4	.333	1.64	7	7	2	44	40	9	21	1	0
16 yrs.		236	106	.690	2.75	498	438	156	3170.1	2766	1086	1956	45	10

WORLD SERIES

		W	L	PCT	ERA	G	GS	CG	IP	H	BB	SO	ShO	S
1950	NY A	1	0	1.000	0.00	1	1	0	8.2	7	1	7	0	0
1953		0	1	.000	4.50	2	2	0	8	9	2	7	0	0
1955		2	0	1.000	2.12	2	2	1	17	13	8	10	0	0
1956		1	1	.500	5.25	2	2	1	12	14	2	8	0	0
1957		1	1	.500	1.13	2	2	1	16	11	5	7	0	0
1958		0	1	.000	4.11	3	3	0	15.1	19	5	16	0	0
1960		2	0	1.000	0.00	2	2	2	18	11	2	8	2	0
1961		2	0	1.000	0.00	2	2	1	14	6	1	7	1	0
1962		1	1	.500	4.12	3	3	1	19.2	24	4	12	0	0
1963		0	2	.000	4.50	2	2	0	12	10	3	8	0	0
1964		0	1	.000	8.44	1	1	0	5.1	8	1	4	0	0
11 yrs.		10	8	.556	2.71	22	22	7	146	132	34	94	3	0

Steve Hamilton

			W	L	PCT	ERA	G	GS	CG	IP	H	BB	SO	ShO	S
1961	CLE	A	0	0	—	2.70	2	0	0	3.1	2	3	4	0	0
1962	WAS	A	3	8	.273	3.77	41	10	1	107.1	103	39	83	0	2
1963	2 teams		WAS	A	(3G 0 1)	NY	A	(34G 5-1)							
	total		5	2	.714	2.94	37	0	0	64.1	54	26	64	0	5
1964	NY	A	7	2	.778	3.28	30	3	1	60.1	55	15	49	0	3
1965			3	1	.750	1.39	46	1	0	58.1	47	16	51	0	5
1966			8	3	.727	3.00	44	3	1	90	69	22	57	1	3
1967			2	4	.333	3.48	44	0	0	62	57	23	55	0	4
1968			2	2	.500	2.13	40	0	0	50.2	37	13	42	0	11
1969			3	4	.429	3.32	38	0	0	57	39	21	39	0	2
1970	2 teams		NY	A	(35G 4-3)	CHI	A	(3G 0-0)							
	total		4	3	.571	2.98	38	0	0	48.1	40	17	36	0	3
1971	SF	N	2	2	.500	3.00	39	0	0	45	29	11	38	0	4
1972	CHI	N	1	0	1.000	4.76	22	0	0	17	24	8	13	0	0
12 yrs.			40	31	.563	3.05	421	17	3	663.2	556	214	531	1	42

LEAGUE CHAMPIONSHIP SERIES

			W	L	PCT	ERA	G	GS	CG	IP	H	BB	SO	ShO	S
1971	SF	N	0	0	—	9.00	1	0	0	1	1	0	3	0	0

WORLD SERIES

			W	L	PCT	ERA	G	GS	CG	IP	H	BB	SO	ShO	S
1963	NY	A	0	0	—	0.00	1	0	0	1	0	0	1	0	0
1964			0	0	—	4.50	2	0	0	2	3	0	2	0	1
2 yrs.			0	0	—	3.00	3	0	0	3	3	0	3	0	1

Elston Howard

			G	AB	H	2B	3B	HR	R	RBI	BB	SO	SB	BA
1955	NY	A	97	279	81	8	7	10	33	43	20	36	0	.290
1956			98	290	76	8	3	5	35	34	21	30	0	.262
1957			110	356	90	13	4	8	33	44	16	43	2	.253
1958			103	376	118	19	5	11	45	66	22	60	1	.314
1959			125	443	121	24	6	18	59	73	20	57	0	.273
1960			107	323	79	11	3	6	29	39	28	43	3	.245
1961			129	446	155	17	5	21	64	77	28	65	0	.348
1962			136	494	138	23	5	21	63	91	31	76	1	.279
1963			135	487	140	21	6	28	75	85	35	68	0	.287
1964			150	550	172	27	3	15	63	84	48	73	1	.313
1965			110	391	91	15	1	9	38	45	24	65	0	.233
1966			126	410	105	19	2	6	38	35	37	65	0	.256
1967	2 teams		NY	A	(66G — .196)		BOS	A	(42G — .147)					
	total	108	315	56	9	0	4	22	28	21	60	0	.178
1968	BOS	A	71	203	49	4	0	5	22	18	22	45	1	.241
14 yrs.			1605	5363	1471	218	50	167	619	762	373	786	9	.274

WORLD SERIES

1955	NY	A	7	26	5	0	0	1	3	3	1	8	0	.192
1956			1	5	2	1	0	1	1	1	0	0	0	.400
1957			6	11	3	0	0	1	2	3	1	3	0	.273
1958			6	18	4	0	0	0	4	2	1	4	1	.222
1960			5	13	6	1	1	1	4	4	1	4	0	.462
1961			5	20	5	3	0	1	5	1	2	3	0	.250
1962			6	21	3	1	0	0	1	1	1	4	0	.143
1963			4	15	5	0	0	0	0	1	0	3	0	.333
1964			7	24	7	1	0	0	5	2	4	6	0	.292
1967	BOS	A	7	18	2	0	0	0	0	1	1	2	0	.111
10 yrs.			54	171	42	7	1	5	25	19	12	37	1	.246

Billy Hunter

			G	AB	H	2B	3B	HR	R	RBI	BB	SO	SB	BA
1953	STL	A	154	567	124	18	1	1	50	37	24	45	3	.219
1954	BAL	A	125	411	100	9	5	2	28	27	21	38	5	.243
1955	NY	A	98	255	58	7	1	3	14	20	15	18	9	.227
1956			39	75	21	3	4	0	8	11	2	4	0	.280
1957	KC	A	116	319	61	10	4	8	39	29	27	43	1	.191
1958	2 teams	KC	A (22G — .155)			CLE	A (76G — .195)							
	total		98	248	46	11	3	2	27	20	22	44	5	.185
6 yrs.			630	1875	410	58	18	16	166	144	111	192	23	.219

Johnny Kucks

		W	L	PCT	ERA	G	GS	CG	IP	H	BB	SO	Sh	S
1955	NY A	8	7	.533	3.41	29	13	3	126.2	122	44	49	1	0
1956		18	9	.667	3.85	34	31	12	224.1	223	72	67	3	0
1957		8	10	.444	3.56	37	23	4	179.1	169	59	78	1	2
1958		8	8	.500	3.93	34	15	4	126	132	39	46	1	4
1959	2 teams	NY	A (9G 0-1)		KC	A (33G 8-11)								
	total	8	12	.400	4.34	42	24	6	168	184	51	60	1	1
1960	KC A	4	10	.286	6.00	31	17	1	114	140	43	38	0	0
6 yrs.		54	56	.491	4.10	207	123	30	938.1	970	308	338	7	7

WORLD SERIES

		W	L	PCT	ERA	G	GS	CG	IP	H	BB	SO	Sh	S
1955	NY A	0	0	—	6.00	2	0	0	3	4	1	1	0	0
1956		1	0	1.000	0.82	3	1	1	11	6	3	2	1	0
957		0	0	—	0.00	1	0	0	.2	1	1	1	0	0
1958		0	0	—	2.08	2	0	0	4.1	4	1	0	0	0
4 yrs.		1	0	1.000	1.89	8	1	1	19	15	6	4	1	0

Phil Linz

			G	KB	H	2B	3B	HR	R	RB	BB	SO	SB	BA
1962	NY	A	71	129	37	8	0	1	28	14	6	17	6	.287
1963			72	186	50	9	0	2	22	12	15	18	1	.269
1964			112	368	92	21	3	5	63	25	43	61	3	.250
1965			99	285	59	12	1	2	37	16	30	33	2	.207
1966	PHI	N	40	70	14	3	0	0	4	6	2	14	0	.200
1967	2 teams	PHI	N (23G — .222)			NY	N (24G — .207)							
	total		47	76	16	4	0	1	12	6	6	11	0	.211
1968	NY	N	78	258	54	7	0	0	19	17	10	41	1	.209
7 yrs.			519	1372	322	64	4	11	185	96	112	195	13	.235

WORLD SERIES

			G	KB	H	2B	3B	HR	R	RB	BB	SO	SB	BA
1963	NY	A	3	3	1	0	0	0	0	0	0	1	0	.333
1964			7	31	7	1	0	2	5	2	2	5	0	.226
2 yrs.			10	34	8	1	0	2	5	2	2	6	0	.235

Dale Long

			G	AB	H	2B	3B	HR	R	RBI	BB	SO	SB	BA
1951	2 teams	PIT	N (10G — .167)			STL	A (34G — .238)							
	total		44	117	27	5	1	3	12	12	10	25	0	.231
1955	PIT	N	131	419	122	19	13	16	59	79	48	72	0	.291
1956			148	517	136	20	7	27	64	91	54	85	1	.263
1957	2 teams	PIT	N (7G — .182)			CHI	N (123G — .305)							
	total		130	419	125	20	0	21	55	67	56	73	1	.298
1958	CHI	N	142	480	130	26	4	20	68	75	66	64	2	.271
1959			110	296	70	10	3	14	34	37	31	53	0	.236
1960	2 teams	SF	N (37G — .167)			NY	A (26G — .366)							
	total		63	95	24	3	1	6	10	16	12	13	0	.253
1961	WAS	A	123	377	94	20	4	17	52	49	39	41	0	.249
1962	2 teams	WAS	A (67G — .241)			NY	A (41G — .298)							
	total		108	285	74	12	0	8	29	41	36	31	6	.260
1963	NY	A	14	15	3	0	0	0	1	0	1	3	0	.200
10 yrs.			1013	3020	805	135	33	132	384	467	353	460	10	.267

WORLD SERIES

			G	AB	H	2B	3B	HR	R	RBI	BB	SO	SB	BA
1960	NY	A	3	3	1	0	0	0	0	0	0	0	0	.333
1962			2	5	1	0	0	0	0	1	0	1	0	.200
2 yrs.			5	8	2	0	0	0	0	1	0	1	0	.250

Hector Lopez

		G	AB	H	2B	3B	HR	R	RBI	BB	SO	SB	BA
1955	KC A	128	483	140	15	2	15	50	68	33	58	1	.290
1956		151	561	153	27	3	18	91	69	63	73	4	.273
1957		121	391	115	19	4	11	51	35	41	66	1	.294
1958		151	564	147	28	4	17	84	73	49	61	2	.261
1959	2 teams	KC	A (36G — .281)		NY	A (112G — .283)							
	total	148	541	153	26	5	22	82	93	36	77	4	.283
1960	NY A	131	408	116	14	6	9	66	42	46	64	1	.284
1961		93	243	54	7	2	3	27	22	24	38	1	.222
1962		106	335	92	19	1	6	45	48	33	53	0	.275
1963		130	433	108	13	4	14	54	52	35	71	1	.249
1964		127	285	74	9	3	10	34	34	24	54	1	.260
1965		111	283	74	12	2	7	25	39	26	61	0	.261
1966		54	117	25	4	1	4	14	16	8	20	0	.214
12 yrs.		1451	4644	1251	193	37	136	623	591	418	696	16	.269
WORLD SERIES													
1960	NY A	3	7	3	0	0	0	0	0	0	0	0	.429
1961		4	9	3	0	1	1	3	7	2	3	0	.333
1962		2	2	0	0	0	0	0	0	0	0	0	.000
1963		3	8	2	2	0	0	1	0	0	1	0	.250
1964		3	2	0	0	0	0	0	0	0	2	0	.000
5 yrs.		15	28	8	2	1	1	4	7	2	6	0	.286

Jerry Lumpe

		G	AB	H	2B	3B	HR	R	RBI	BB	SO	SB	BA
1956	NY A	20	62	16	3	0	0	12	4	5	11	1	.258
1957		40	103	35	6	2	0	15	11	9	13	2	.340
1958		81	232	59	8	4	3	34	32	23	21	1	.254
1959	2 teams	NY	A (18G — .222)		KC	A (108G — .243)							
	total	126	448	108	11	5	3	49	30	47	39	2	.241
1960	KC A	146	574	156	19	3	8	69	53	48	49	1	.272
1961		148	569	167	29	9	3	81	54	48	39	1	.293
1962		156	641	193	34	10	10	89	83	44	38	0	.301
1963		157	595	161	26	7	5	75	59	58	44	3	.271
1964	DET A	158	624	160	21	6	6	75	46	50	61	2	.256
1965		145	502	129	15	3	4	72	39	56	34	7	.257
1966		113	385	89	14	3	1	30	26	24	44	0	.231
1967		81	177	41	4	0	4	19	17	16	18	0	.232
12 yrs.		1371	4912	1314	190	52	47	620	454	428	411	20	.268
WORLD SERIES													
1957	NY A	6	14	4	0	0	0	0	2	1	1	0	.286
1958		6	12	2	0	0	0	0	0	1	2	0	.167
2 yrs.		12	26	6	0	0	0	0	2	2	3	0	.231

Mickey Mantle

		G	AB	H	2B	3B	HR	R	RBI	BB	SO	SB	BA
1951	NY A	96	341	91	11	5	13	61	65	43	74	8	.267
1952		142	549	171	37	7	23	94	87	75	111	4	.311
1953		127	461	136	24	3	21	105	92	79	90	8	.295
1954		146	543	163	17	12	27	129	102	102	107	5	.300
1955		147	517	158	25	11	37	121	99	113	97	8	.306
1956		150	533	188	22	5	52	132	130	112	99	10	.353
1957		144	474	173	28	6	34	121	94	146	75	16	.365
1958		150	519	158	21	1	42	127	97	129	120	18	.304
1959		144	541	154	23	4	31	104	75	94	126	21	.285
1960		153	527	145	17	6	40	119	94	111	125	14	.275
1961		153	514	163	16	6	54	132	128	126	112	12	.317
1962		123	377	121	15	1	30	96	89	122	78	9	.321
1963		65	172	54	8	0	15	40	35	40	32	2	.314
1964		143	465	141	25	2	35	92	111	99	102	6	.303
1965		122	361	92	12	1	19	44	46	73	76	4	.255
1966		108	333	96	12	1	23	40	56	57	76	1	.288
1967		144	440	108	17	0	22	63	55	107	113	1	.245
1968		144	435	103	14	1	18	57	54	106	97	6	.237
18 yrs.		2401	8102	2415	344	72	536	1677	1509	1734	1710	153	.298
WORLD SERIES													
1951	NY A	2	5	1	0	0	0	1	0	2	1	0	.200
1952		7	29	10	1	1	2	5	3	3	4	0	.345
1953		6	24	5	0	0	2	3	7	3	8	0	.208
1955		3	10	2	0	0	1	1	1	0	2	0	.200
1956		7	24	6	1	0	3	6	4	6	5	1	.250
1957		6	19	5	0	0	1	3	2	3	1	0	.263
1958		7	24	6	0	1	2	4	3	7	4	0	.250
1960		7	25	10	1	0	3	8	11	8	9	0	.400
1961		2	6	1	0	0	0	0	0	0	2	0	.167
1962		7	25	3	1	0	0	2	0	4	5	2	.120
1963		4	15	2	0	0	1	1	1	1	5	0	.133
1964		7	24	8	2	0	3	8	8	6	8	0	.333
12 yrs.		65	230	59	6	2	18	42	40	43	54	3	.257

Roger Maris

			G	AB	H	2B	3B	HR	R	RBI	BB	SO	SB	BA
1957	CLE	A	116	358	84	9	5	14	61	51	60	79	8	.235
1958	2 teams		CLE	A (51G — .225)			KC	A (99G — .247)						
	total		150	583	140	19	4	28	87	80	45	85	4	.240
1959	KC	A	122	433	118	21	7	16	69	72	58	53	2	.273
1960	NY	A	136	499	141	18	7	39	98	112	70	65	2	.283
1961			161	590	159	16	4	61	132	142	94	67	0	.269
1962			157	590	151	34	1	33	92	100	87	78	1	.256
1963			90	312	84	14	1	23	53	53	35	40	1	.269
1964			141	513	144	12	2	26	86	71	62	78	3	.281
1965			46	155	37	7	0	8	22	27	29	29	0	.239
1966			119	348	81	9	2	13	37	43	36	60	0	.233
1967	STL	N	125	410	107	18	7	9	64	55	52	61	0	.261
1968			100	310	79	18	2	5	25	45	24	38	0	.255
12 yrs.			1463	5101	1325	195	42	275	826	851	652	733	21	.260
WORLD SERIES														
1960	NY	A	7	30	8	1	0	2	6	2	2	4	0	.267
1961			5	19	2	1	0	1	4	2	4	6	0	.105
1962			7	23	4	1	0	1	4	5	5	2	0	.174
1963			2	5	0	0	0	0	0	0	0	1	0	.000
1964			7	30	6	0	0	1	4	1	1	4	0	.200
1967	STL	N	7	26	10	1	0	1	3	7	3	1	0	.385
1968			6	19	3	1	0	0	5	1	3	3	0	.158
7 yrs.			41	152	33	5	0	6	26	18	18	21	0	.217

Pedro Ramos

			W	L	PCT	ERA	G	GS	CG	IP	H	IP	H	ShO	SV
1955	WAS	A	5	11	.313	3.88	45	9	3	130	121	39	34	1	5
1956			12	10	.545	5.27	37	18	4	152	178	76	54	0	0
1957			12	16	.429	4.79	43	30	7	231	251	69	91	1	0
1958			14	18	.438	4.23	43	37	10	259.1	277	77	132	4	3
1959			13	19	.406	4.16	37	35	11	233.2	233	52	95	0	0
1960			11	18	.379	3.45	43	36	14	274	254	99	160	1	2
1961	MIN	A	11	20	.355	3.95	42	34	9	264.1	265	79	174	3	2
1962	CLE	A	10	12	.455	3.71	37	27	7	201.1	189	85	96	2	1
1963			9	8	.529	3.12	36	22	5	184.2	156	41	169	0	0
1964	2 teams		CLE	A (36G 7-10)			NY	A (13G 1-0)							
	total		8	10	.444	4.60	49	19	3	154.2	157	26	119	1	8
1965	NY	A	5	5	.500	2.92	65	0	0	92.1	80	27	68	0	19
1966			3	9	.250	3.61	52	1	0	89.2	98	18	58	0	13
1967	PHI	N	0	0	—	9.00	6	0	0	8	14	8	1	0	0
1969	2 teams		PIT	N (5G 0-1)			CIN	N (38G 4-3)							
	total		4	4	.500	5.23	43	0	0	72.1	81	24	44	0	2
1970	WAS	A	0	0	—	7.88	4	0	0	8	10	4	10	0	0
15 yrs.			117	160	.422	4.08	582	268	73	2355.1	2364	724	1305	13	55

Hal Reniff

		W	L	PCT	ERA	G	GS	CG	IP	H	BB	SO	ShO	SV
1961	NY A	2	0	1.000	2.58	25	0	0	45.1	31	31	21	0	2
1962		0	0	—	7.36	2	0	0	3.2	6	5	1	0	0
1963		4	3	.571	2.62	48	0	0	89.1	63	42	56	0	18
1964		6	4	.600	3.12	41	0	0	69.1	47	30	38	0	9
1965		3	4	.429	3.80	51	0	0	85.1	74	48	74	0	3
1966		3	7	.300	3.21	56	0	0	95.1	80	49	79	0	9
1967	2 teams		NY	A (24G 0-2)		NY	N (29G 3-3)							
	total	3	5	.375	3.80	53	0	0	83	82	37	45	0	4
7 yrs.		21	23	.477	3.27	276	0	0	471.1	383	242	314	0	45

WORLD SERIES														
1963	NY A	0	0	—	0.00	3	0	0	3	0	1	1	0	0
1964		0	0	—	0.00	1	0	0	.1	2	0	0	0	0
2 yrs.		0	0	—	0.00	4	0	0	3.1	2	1	1	0	0

Bobby Richardson

		G	AB	H	2B	3B	HR	R	RBI	BB	SO	SB	BA
1955	NY A	11	26	4	0	0	0	2	3	2	0	1	.154
1956		5	7	1	0	0	0	1	0	0	1	0	.143
1957		97	305	78	11	1	0	36	19	9	26	1	.256
1958		73	182	45	6	2	0	18	14	8	5	1	.247
1959		134	469	141	18	6	2	53	33	26	20	5	.301
1960		150	460	116	12	3	1	45	26	35	19	6	.252
1961		162	662	173	17	5	3	80	49	30	23	9	.261
1962		161	692	209	38	5	8	99	59	37	24	11	.302
1963		151	630	167	20	6	3	72	48	25	22	15	.265
1964		159	679	181	25	4	4	90	50	28	36	11	.267
1965		160	664	164	28	2	6	76	47	37	39	7	.247
1966		149	610	153	21	3	7	71	42	25	28	6	.251
12 yrs.		1412	5386	1432	196	37	34	643	390	262	243	73	.266

WORLD SERIES													
1957	NY A	2	0	0	0	0	0	0	0	0	0	0	—
1958		4	5	0	0	0	0	0	0	0	0	0	.000
1960		7	30	11	2	2	1	8	12	1	1	0	.367
1961		5	23	9	1	0	0	2	0	0	0	1	.391
1962		7	27	4	0	0	0	3	0	3	1	0	.148
1963		4	14	3	1	0	0	0	0	1	3	0	.214
1964		7	32	13	2	0	0	3	3	0	2	1	.406
7 yrs.		36	131	40	6	2	1	16	15	5	7	2	.305

Eddie Robinson

		G	AB	H	2B	3B	HR	R	RBI	BB	SO	SB	BA
1942	CLE A	8	8	1	0	0	0	1	2	1	0	0	.125
1946		7	27	11	0	0	3	5	4	1	4	0	.407
1947		95	318	78	10	1	14	52	52	30	18	1	.245
1948		134	493	125	18	5	16	53	83	36	42	1	.254
1949	WAS A	143	527	155	27	3	18	66	78	67	30	3	.294
1950	2 teams	WAS	A (36G — .240)		CHI	A	(119G — .311)						
	total	155	553	163	15	4	21	83	86	85	32	0	.295
1951	CHI A	151	564	159	23	5	29	85	117	77	54	2	.282
1952		155	594	176	33	1	22	79	104	70	49	2	.296
1953	PHI A	156	615	152	28	4	22	64	102	63	56	1	.247
1954	NY A	85	142	37	9	0	3	11	27	19	21	0	.261
1955		88	173	36	1	0	16	25	42	36	26	0	.208
1956	2 teams	NY	A (26G — .222)		KC	A	(75G — .198)						
	total	101	226	46	6	1	7	20	23	31	23	0	.204
1957	3 teams	DET	A (13G — .000)		CLE	A	19G — .222)		BAL	A	(4G — .000)		
	total	36	39	6	1	0	1	1	3	4	4	0	.154
13 yrs.		1314	4279	1145	171	24	172	545	723	520	359	10	.268

WORLD SERIES

		G	AB	H	2B	3B	HR	R	RBI	BB	SO	SB	BA
1948	CLE A	6	20	6	0	0	0	0	1	1	0	0	.300
1955	NY A	4	3	2	0	0	0	0	1	2	1	0	.667
2 yrs.		10	23	8	0	0	0	0	2	3	1	0	.348

Bobby Shantz

		W	L	PCT	ERA	G	GS	CG	IP	H	BB	SO	ShO	SV
1949	PHI A	6	8	.429	3.40	33	7	4	127	100	74	58	1	2
1950		8	14	.364	4.61	36	23	6	214.2	251	85	93	1	0
1951		18	10	.643	3.94	32	25	13	205.1	213	70	77	4	0
1952		24	7	.774	2.48	33	33	27	279.2	230	63	152	5	0
1953		5	9	.357	4.09	16	16	6	105.2	107	26	58	0	0
1954		1	0	1.000	7.88	2	1	0	8	12	3	3	0	0
1955	KC A	5	10	.333	4.54	23	17	4	125	124	66	58	1	0
1956		2	7	.222	4.35	45	2	1	101.1	95	37	67	0	9
1957	NY A	11	5	.688	2.45	30	21	9	173	157	40	72	1	5
1958		7	6	.538	3.36	33	13	3	126	127	35	80	0	0
1959		7	3	.700	2.38	33	4	2	94.2	64	33	66	2	3
1960		5	4	.556	2.79	42	0	0	67.2	57	24	54	0	11
1961	PIT N	6	3	.667	3.32	43	6	2	89.1	91	26	61	1	2
1962	2 teams	HOU	N (3G 1-1)		STL	N	(28G 5-3)							
	total	6	4	.600	1.95	31	3	1	78.1	60	25	61	0	4
1963	STL N	6	4	.600	2.61	55	0	0	79.1	55	17	70	0	11

1964	3 teams	STL	N	(16G 1-3)		CHI	N	(20G 0-1)	PHI	N	(14G 1-1)			
	total	2	5	.286	3.12	50	0	0	60.2	52	19	42	0	1
16 yrs.		119	99	.546	3.38	537	171	78	1935.2	1795	643	1072	16	48

WORLD SERIES

1957	NY A	0	1	.000	4.05	3	1	0	6.2	8	2	7	0	0
1960		0	0	—	4.26	3	0	0	6.1	4	1	1	0	1
2 yrs.		0	1	.000	4.15	6	1	0	13	12	3	8	0	1

Rollie Sheldon

		W	L	PCT	ERA	G	GS	CG	IP	H	BB	SO	ShO	SV
1961	NY A	11	5	.688	3.60	35	21	6	162.2	149	55	84	2	0
1962		7	8	.467	5.49	34	16	2	118	136	28	54	0	1
1964		5	2	.714	3.61	19	12	3	102.1	92	18	57	0	1
1965	2 teams	NY	A	(3G 0-0)		KC	A	(32G 10-8)						
	total	10	8	.556	3.86	35	29	4	193.1	185	57	112	1	0
1966	2 teams	KC	A	(14G 4-7)		BOS	A	(23G 1-6)						
	total	5	13	.278	4.12	37	23	2	148.2	179	49	64	1	0
5 yrs.		38	36	.514	4.08	160	101	17	725	741	207	371	4	2

WORLD SERIES

1964	NY A	0	0	—	0.00	2	0	0	2.2	0	2	2	0	0

Norm Siebern

		G	AB	H	2B	3B	HR	R	RB	BB	SO	SB	BA
1956	NY A	54	162	33	1	4	4	27	21	19	38	1	.204
1958		136	460	138	19	5	14	79	55	66	87	5	.300
1959		120	380	103	17	0	11	52	53	41	71	3	.271
1960	KC A	144	520	145	31	6	19	69	69	72	68	0	.279
1961		153	560	166	36	5	18	68	98	82	92	2	.296
1962		162	600	185	25	6	25	114	117	110	88	3	.308
1963		152	556	151	25	2	16	80	83	79	82	1	.272
1964	BAL A	150	478	117	24	2	12	92	56	106	87	2	.245
1965		106	297	76	13	4	8	44	32	50	49	1	.256
1966	CAL A	125	336	83	14	1	5	29	41	63	61	0	.247
1967	2 teams	SF	N (46G — .155)		BOS	A	(33G — .205)						
	total	79	102	18	1	3	0	8	11	20	21	0	.176
1968	BOS A	27	30	2	0	0	0	0	0	0	5	0	.067
12 yrs.		1408	4481	1217	206	38	132	662	636	708	749	18	.272

WORLD SERIES

1956	NY A	1	1	0	0	0	0	0	0	0	0	0	.000
1958		3	8	1	0	0	0	1	0	3	2	0	.125
1967	BOS A	3	3	1	0	0	0	0	1	0	0	0	.333
3 yrs.		7	12	2	0	0	0	1	1	3	2	0	.167

Bill Skowron

			G	AB	H	2B	3B	HR	R	RBI	BB	SO	SB	BA
1954	NY	A	87	215	73	12	9	7	37	41	19	18	2	.340
1955			108	288	92	17	3	12	46	61	21	32	1	.319
1956			134	464	143	21	6	23	78	90	50	60	4	.308
1957			122	457	139	15	5	17	54	88	31	60	3	.304
1958			126	465	127	22	3	14	61	73	28	69	1	.273
1959			74	282	84	13	5	15	39	59	20	47	1	.298
1960			146	538	166	34	3	26	63	91	38	95	2	.309
1961			150	561	150	23	4	28	76	89	35	108	0	.267
1962			140	478	129	16	6	23	63	80	36	99	0	.270
1963	LA	N	89	237	48	8	0	4	19	19	13	49	0	.203
1964	2 Teams		WAS	A (73G — .271)		CHI	A	(73G — .293)						
	total		146	535	151	21	3	17	47	79	30	92	0	.282
1965	CHI	A	146	559	153	24	3	18	63	78	32	77	1	.274
1966			120	337	84	15	2	6	27	29	26	45	1	.249
1967	2 teams		CHI	A (8G — .000)		CAL	A	(62G — .220)						
	total		70	131	27	2	1	1	8	11	4	19	0	.206
14 yrs.			1658	5547	1566	243	53	211	681	888	383	870	16	.282

WORLD SERIES

			G	AB	H	2B	3B	HR	R	RBI	BB	SO	SB	BA
1955	NY	A	5	12	4	2	0	1	2	3	0	1	0	.333
1956			3	10	1	0	0	1	1	4	0	3	0	.100
1957			2	4	0	0	0	0	0	0	0	0	0	.000
1958			7	27	7	0	0	2	3	7	1	4	0	.259
1960			7	32	12	2	0	2	7	6	0	6	0	.375
1961			5	17	6	0	0	1	3	5	3	4	0	.353
1962			6	18	4	0	1	0	1	1	1	5	0	.222
1963	LA	N	4	13	5	0	0	1	2	3	1	3	0	.385
8 yrs.			39	133	39	4	1	8	19	29	6	26	0	.293

Enos Slaughter

			G	AB	H	2B	3B	HR	R	RBI	BB	SO	SB	BA
1938	STL	N	112	395	109	20	10	8	59	58	32	38	1	.276
1939			149	604	193	52	5	12	95	86	44	53	2	.320
1940			140	516	158	25	13	17	96	73	50	35	8	.306
1941			113	425	132	22	9	13	71	76	53	28	4	.311
1942			152	591	188	31	17	13	100	98	88	30	9	.318
1946			156	609	183	30	8	18	100	130	69	41	9	.300
1947			147	551	162	31	13	10	100	86	59	27	4	.294
1948			146	549	176	27	11	11	91	90	81	29	4	.321
1949			151	568	191	34	13	13	92	96	79	37	3	.336
1950			148	556	161	26	7	10	82	101	66	33	3	.290
1951			123	409	115	17	8	4	48	64	68	25	7	.281
1952			140	510	153	17	12	11	73	101	70	25	6	.300

Year	Team	Lg	G	AB	H	2B	3B	HR	R	RBI	SO	BB	SB	AVG
1953			143	492	143	34	9	6	64	89	80	28	4	.291
1954	NY	A	69	125	31	4	2	1	19	19	28	8	0	.248
1955	2 teams		NY	A (10G — .111)		KC	A (108G — .322)							
	total		118	276	87	12	4	5	50	35	41	18	2	.315
1956	2 teams		KC	A (91G — .278)		NY	A (24G — .289)							
	total		115	306	86	18	5	2	52	27	34	26	2	.281
1957	NY	A	96	209	53	7	1	5	24	34	40	19	0	.254
1958			77	138	42	4	1	4	21	19	21	16	2	.304
1959	2 teams		NY	A (74G — .172)		MIL	N (11G — .167)							
	total		85	117	20	2	0	6	10	22	16	22	1	.171
19 yrs.			2380	7946	2383	413	148	169	1247	1304	1019	538	71	.300

WORLD SERIES

Year	Team	Lg	G	AB	H	2B	3B	HR	R	RBI	SO	BB	SB	AVG
1942	STL	N	5	19	5	1	0	1	3	2	3	2	0	.263
1946			7	25	8	1	1	1	5	2	4	3	1	.320
1956	NY	A	6	20	7	0	0	1	6	4	4	0	0	.350
1957			5	12	3	1	0	0	2	0	3	2	0	.250
1958			4	3	0	0	0	0	1	0	1	1	0	.000
5 yrs.			27	79	23	3	1	3	17	8	15	8	1	.291

Bill Stafford

Year	Team		W	L	PCT	ERA	G	GS	CG	IP	H	BB	SO	ShO	SV
1960	NY A		3	1	.750	2.25	11	8	2	60	50	18	36	1	0
1961			14	9	.609	2.68	36	25	8	195	168	59	101	3	2
1962			14	9	.609	3.67	35	33	7	213.1	188	77	109	2	0
1963			4	8	.333	6.02	28	14	0	89.2	104	42	52	0	3
1964			5	0	1.000	2.67	31	1	0	60.2	50	22	39	0	4
1965			3	8	.273	3.56	22	15	1	111.1	93	31	71	0	0
1966	KC A		0	4	.000	4.99	9	8	0	39.2	42	12	31	0	0
1967			0	1	.000	1.69	14	0	0	16	12	9	10	0	0
8 yrs.			43	40	.518	3.52	186	104	18	785.2	707	270	449	6	9

WORLD SERIES

Year	Team		W	L	PCT	ERA	G	GS	CG	IP	H	BB	SO	ShO	SV
1960	NY A		0	0	—	1.50	2	0	0	6	5	1	2	0	0
1961			0	0	—	2.70	1	1	0	6.2	7	2	5	0	0
1962			1	0	1.000	2.00	1	1	1	9	4	2	5	0	0
3 yrs.			1	0	1.000	2.08	4	2	1	21.2	16	5	12	0	0

Tom Sturdivant

		W	L	PCT	ERA	G	GS	CG	IP	H	BB	SO	ShO	SV
1955	NY A	1	3	.250	3.16	33	1	0	68.1	48	42	48	0	0
1956		16	8	.667	3.30	32	17	6	158.1	134	52	110	2	5
1957		16	6	.727	2.54	28	28	7	201.2	170	80	118	2	0
1958		3	6	.333	4.20	15	10	0	70.2	77	38	41	0	0
1959	2 teams	NY A (7G 0-2)		KC	A (36G 2-6)									
	total	2	8	.200	4.73	43	6	0	97	90	43	73	0	5
1960	BOS A	3	3	.500	4.97	40	3	0	101.1	106	45	67	0	1
1961	2 teams	WAS A (15G 2-6)		PIT	N (13G 5-2)									
	total	7	8	.467	3.69	28	21	7	165.2	148	57	84	2	1
1962	PIT N	9	5	.643	3.73	49	12	2	125.1	120	39	76	1	2
1963	3 teams	PIT N (3G 0-0)		DET	A (28G 1-2)		KC	A (17G 1-2)						
	total	2	4	.333	3.95	48	3	0	116.1	98	45	68	0	2
1964	2 teams	KC A (3G 0-0)		NY	N (16G 0-0)									
	total	0	0	—	6.40	19	0	0	32.1	38	8	19	0	1
10 yrs.		59	51	.536	3.74	335	101	22	1137	1029	449	704	7	17

WORLD SERIES														
1955	NY A	0	0	—	6.00	2	0	0	3	5	2	0	0	0
1956		1	0	1.000	2.79	2	1	1	9.2	8	8	9	0	0
1957		0	0	—	6.00	2	1	0	6	6	1	2	0	0
3 yrs.		1	0	1.000	4.34	6	2	1	18.2	19	11	11	0	0

Bob Turley

		W	L	PCT	ERA	G	GS	CG	IP	H	BB	SO	ShO	SV
1951	STL A	0	1	.000	7.36	1	1	0	7.1	11	3	5	0	0
1953		2	6	.250	3.28	10	7	3	60.1	39	44	61	1	0
1954	BAL A	14	15	.483	3.46	35	35	14	247.1	178	181	185	0	0
1955	NY A	17	13	.567	3.06	36	34	13	246.2	168	177	210	6	1
1956		8	4	.667	5.05	27	21	5	132	138	103	91	1	1
1957		13	6	.684	2.71	32	23	9	176.1	120	85	152	4	3
1958		21	7	.750	2.97	33	31	19	245.1	178	128	168	6	1
1959		8	11	.421	4.32	33	22	7	154.1	141	83	111	3	0
1960		9	3	.750	3.27	34	24	4	173.1	138	87	87	1	5
1961		3	5	.375	5.75	15	12	1	72	74	51	48	0	0
1962		3	3	.500	4.57	24	8	0	69	68	47	42	0	1
1963	2 teams	LA A (19G 2-7)		BOS	A (11G 1-4)									
	total	3	11	.214	4.20	30	19	3	128.2	113	79	105	2	0
12 yrs.		101	85	.543	3.64	310	237	78	1712.2	1366	1068	1265	24	12

WORLD SERIES

1955	NY	A	0	1	.000	8.44	3	1	0	5.1	7	4	7	0	0
1956			0	1	.000	0.82	3	1	1	11	4	8	14	0	0
1957			1	0	1.000	2.31	3	2	1	11.2	7	6	12	0	0
1958			2	1	.667	2.76	4	2	1	16.1	10	7	13	1	1
1960			1	0	1.000	4.82	2	2	0	9.1	15	4	0	0	0
5 yrs.			4	3	.571	3.19	15	8	3	53.2	43	29	46	1	1

INDEX

Boldface page numbers indicate interviews.

215